THE UN-POLITICS
OF AIR POLLUTION

MATTHEW A. CRENSON holds a doctorate in political science from the University of Chicago and is with the Department of Political Science at The Johns Hopkins University.

MATTHEW A. CRENSON

THE UN-POLITICS OF AIR POLLUTION

A Study of Non-Decisionmaking in the Cities

THE JOHNS HOPKINS PRESS   Baltimore and London

Contents

Preface

TODAY ENVIRONMENTAL POLLUTION has become one of the nation's chief worries. Unfortunately, although pollution itself has been with us for many years, the worrying has begun only recently. This book attempts to discover some of the reasons why the concern was so late in developing, why many cities and towns in the United States failed to make a political issue of their air pollution problems.

Air pollution, of course, is not the only urban problem that has been a victim of political neglect. Poverty and racial discrimination, for example, as well as pollution, have been present in American cities for some time but provoked little in the way of political action. There appear to be many subjects of great moment in contemporary American politics which had the status of "non-issues" in the past. Some observers, in fact, have contended that neglect of this kind is a pervasive feature of American political life. The issues that we ignore sometimes seem to be more important than the ones that receive attention. The decisions that we fail to make often seem to be more critical for the life of the nation than the ones that we do make.

Most empirical political research, like the political system, has overlooked these non-issues and non-decisions, and the oversight is understandable. Where there are no political issues or decisions, there are no political events to investigate—or so it would seem. The analysis of non-decisions and non-issues seems to require that the analyst provide an explanation for things that do not happen, and some political scientists have argued that there is simply no reasoned and reliable way to construct such explanations. The present study attempts to find a way to do so.

Many people and institutions have helped to make this attempt possible, and others have done what they could to keep it from becoming a failure. For his advice and assistance I am especially grateful to J. David Greenstone, who offered his guidance from the very beginning of the enterprise to its completion. Duncan MacRae and David Easton reviewed the entire manuscript, and their comments were most helpful. Some bits of advice offered by Peter Rossi while the project was still in its formative stage later proved to be invaluable, and it was Peter Rossi and Robert Crain who made it possible for me to collect the necessary data. Without their generosity, and the generosity of the National Science Foundation, I would never have been able to undertake this project. Robert Crain's role in data collection was far more important than my own, and I dare not consider the results had things been the other way round. I am also grateful to James Vanecko and others at the National Opinion Research Center who worked on the study.

A research fellowship from The Brookings Institution made it possible for me to give full-time attention to the manuscript for a year, during which Gilbert Steiner provided both scholarly advice and administrative assistance. To my wife, Alene, goes the credit for typing the first draft and for being more patient than I had any right to expect.

THE UN-POLITICS
OF AIR POLLUTION

Introduction

IN MID-NOVEMBER 1953 a warm air mass, on its march to the Atlantic, glided to a noiseless halt over New York City, but New Yorkers enjoyed no immediate respite from their chilly autumn. The newly arrived warm air had come to rest high above the city streets, leaving a "damp chilly gloom" at ground level.[1] Occurrences of this sort are called temperature inversions, and the appearance of this 1953 inversion in New York seems to have meant that about two hundred residents of the city would have less than a week to live.

Had normal weather conditions prevailed, the air temperature would have decreased with altitude. Ordinarily, air that is near the ground is relatively warm. Since warm air rises, this ground-level air is always changing places with the air above it. The result is a continuous vertical circulation of air, a natural ventilation system by which the windborne wastes of man and nature are carried to great heights and dispersed. When a temperature inversion occurs, this ventilation system is shut off. Natural and manmade garbage—soot, dust, smoke, waste gases, and the like—begins to accumulate in the stagnant cool air close to the earth's surface. It was just such a buildup of airborne wastes that enveloped New York in November 1953.

New Yorkers were not entirely oblivious to the abnormally dirty air and its unpleasant consequences. It reduced visibility on the New Jersey Turnpike. It "produced a cheerless atmosphere for Saturday football crowds." It caused headaches, nausea, burning eyes, and loss of appetite. It even prevented a group of local astronomers from observing the transit of Mercury across the sun, a celestial event that

[1] *New York Times*, 15 November 1953.

would not be repeated for another fifty-nine years.[2] But what was most notable about New Yorkers' observations on the "smaze" was that they failed to perceive its most serious result: it had killed people. Not until nine years later, in 1962, did a careful study of mortality statistics reveal that the dramatic buildup of dirty air was accompanied by a fairly sharp increase in deaths. By comparing the mid-November daily death rates for 1953 with those for previous and subsequent years, investigators were able to estimate that there had been about two hundred deaths in excess of the usual number during the week of the pollution incident.[3]

Even in 1953, however, there were observable indications of the damage that dirty air might do to health—the headaches, nausea, and burning eyes, even the "sluggish and distressed" pigeons in the parks[4]—and evidence of the smaze attack's more lethal consequences could have been extracted from the city health records. But at the time there was no sustained demand for such an investigation. City residents and leading municipal officials seem to have lost interest in the air pollution problem soon after the local pollution level returned to "normal." The local Bureau of Air Pollution Control continued to do its work in relative obscurity, with a small staff, small budget, and under existing legislation. This inattention to air pollution problems was not extraordinary—in fact, New York in 1953 was more alert to the dangers of dirty air than were many other cities. Its modest air pollution bureau was a symbol of local apprehension—also modest but present all the same. For at least some New Yorkers, normal air pollution levels, as well as extraordinary buildups of airborne dirt, were cause for alarm,[5] but it would seem that even their concern was inadequate to the seriousness of the problem. A hazard which had probably cost the city two hundred lives in a week—possibly many more in the future—would seem to deserve much more attention. How could there be such a gap between the magnitude of the problem and the magnitude of public concern?

That there actually was a disjunction between the size of the problem and the volume of public alarm is a matter not for scientific determination but for moral judgment. It might be argued that two hundred deaths in a city the size of New York do not constitute a

2 *Ibid.*
3 Leonard Greenburg et al., "Report of an Air Pollution Incident in New York City, November 1953."
4 Editorial, *New York Times*, 21 November 1953.
5 *Ibid.*

grave calamity and that New Yorkers could not be blamed for their lack of interest in the matter. In this view, there was no gap between the level of public concern and the severity of the air pollution problem. New York was not inattentive or neglectful, and its lack of interest in atmospheric pollution requires no explanation. The matter was simply not important enough to deserve much attention. But people with different opinions concerning the value of human life might arrive at different conclusions. The gap between the "real" importance of the air pollution issue and the importance actually accorded it increases, decreases, or disappears entirely according to the opinion of the observer concerning the value of human life. The magnitude, even the existence, of such a disjunction cannot be determined solely on the basis of empirical evidence. It is therefore not surprising that some political scientists have consciously avoided the investigation of these elusive "gaps." Students of urban and community politics recognize them as creations of moral judgment, not observable features of empirical reality, and, apparently for this reason, some have concluded that an unbiased, scientific investigation of such "gaps" is impossible.[6]

The present study attempts to show that an unbiased explanation of municipal neglect in the field of air pollution *is* possible and, further, that it is worth the trouble. In the first place, a bias results from the failure to take it into account. A scholar who makes it his policy to ignore instances of municipal inaction, as most political scientists do, would conduct his investigation of air pollution policy-making in New York as though he had made the moral judgment that there is nothing questionable about municipal neglect of dirty air. He would proceed on the implicit assumption that a town can never pay too much or too little attention to its dirty air, or to any other problem which it faces. When a city ignores some issue, it is simply because the issue in question is not an important one. It is not important because the city, by ignoring it, has said that it is not important.

This is one way to dispose of the troublesome notion that there may be some mismatch between the amount of attention that a town devotes to a local problem and the amount of attention that it actually deserves, but the solution adds nothing to scientific objectivity.

---

[6] For an argument along these lines (and others), see Nelson W. Polsby, *Community Power and Political Theory*, pp. 96–97; Aaron Wildavsky, *Leadership in a Small Town*, p. 11.

Though it successfully divests the research enterprise of certain personal biases, it replaces them with the political biases of the town whose affairs happen to be under scrutiny. The investigator and the community that he is investigating both look at the world through the same lens, with the same blind spots and distortions. Matters which are ignored by the community are ignored by the investigator as well. No attempt is made to account for seemingly important decisions that are never made, significant policies that are never formulated, and issues that never arise. In short, there is no attempt to account for possible blind spots in community political institutions.

It is hardly more objective and scientific to ignore non-decisions and non-issues than to account for these phenomena. Admittedly, the attempt to explain non-decisions encounters some grave methodological difficulties, which will be considered shortly. Of greater importance, however, is the reason why anyone should regard non-issues and non-decisions as items of general political significance not just for our respiratory well-being but for the understanding of political systems in general. Non-issues have seldom been regarded as politically revealing phenomena. Actions, decisions, and issues have almost always seemed more fruitful objects of investigation. Political scientists have only infrequently asked why certain seemingly important topics never get to be issues.

Perhaps their lack of interest in this question may be attributed not only to a misguided concern for objectivity but to the prevailing view that its answer lies beyond the scope of political science—that there is no *political* explanation for the existence of non-issues in American cities. In the United States, it is thought, no political inhibitions prevent citizens from converting their private discontents into subjects of public debate: "The independence, penetrability, and heterogeneity of the various segments of the political stratum," writes Robert Dahl, "all but guarantee that any dissatisfied group will find spokesmen in the political stratum."[7] It follows that if people remain mute on some topic, or if some potential issue is never raised, the silence cannot be attributed to political constraints upon the expression of discontent. The failure of an issue to emerge into the "political stratum" may indicate that there is simply no discontent about the subject or it may signify that, although dissatisfaction exists, countless private distrac-

[7] Robert A. Dahl, *Who Governs? Democracy and Power in an American City*, p. 93.

tions have diverted the citizens from registering their complaints with their political leaders.[8] In any case, the political institutions of American cities do not produce non-issues. As a rule, the political stratum is open to any sizable group of citizens who are interested and energetic enough to voice their demands. The "penetrability" of the political system thus assures that almost any "important" problem can be converted into a political issue.

It is precisely this penetrability which is called into question when the effort is made to provide a political explanation for non-issues and non-decisions, and this is a second reason why it is worth the trouble to look into these things. At stake in this investigation is the allegation of democratic openness in American local politics. There is the possibility that instances of municipal inaction and neglect are not politically random but politically enforced occurrences. It is this possibility that the present study will examine, in an attempt to construct an unbiased, verifiable political explanation for the fact that many cities and towns in the United States have ignored their dirty air.

Such an examination is especially pertinent to the politics of air pollution. Municipal inaction has been a regular response to the air pollution problem in communities throughout the nation. The political immobility of American cities in this matter has become a major consideration for would-be air pollution policymakers. In 1966 a leading federal air pollution official testified before a House subcommittee that "one of the impediments to more rapid progress in pollution abatement relates to the existence and scope of state and local government regulatory and control activities. I would like to point out to the committee that not more than half of the urban areas which are in need of regulatory and control programs for air pollution control now have them and of these . . . the majority are operated at an inadequate level." The pollution expert added that he regarded the cities' slowness to act as primarily the result of political and social obstacles, not technological difficulties.[9] If this assessment is accurate, then the explanation for local inattention to the air pollution issue lies squarely within the province of political science.

---

8 *Ibid.*, p. 224.
9 U.S., Congress, House, Committee on Science and Astronautics, Subcommittee on Science, Research, and Development, *The Adequacy of Technology for Pollution Abatement*, p. 57.

THE THREAT OF DIRTY AIR

Today almost every citydweller is aware that there are some good reasons why public authorities ought not to overlook the air pollution problem. Growing interest in the air pollution problem has been accompanied by a growing body of evidence concerning the damage that dirty air does to human beings. The most dramatic examples arise from pollution crises like the one that struck New York in 1953. By comparison with the experience of other cities, New York's dirty air disaster was only a minor catastrophe. One heavy "fog" that blanketed the city of London for five days in December 1952 is thought to have resulted in about four thousand deaths. Many of the victims dropped dead on London streets; about fifty bodies were removed from one small park in the South End of the city.[10] A subsequent investigation of similar "fog" episodes in the winter months of 1873, 1880, 1882, 1891, and 1892 showed that there were suspicious increases in the London death rate in each of these foggy periods.[11]

Of all the recorded pollution incidents, the most remarkable was one that began in the eastern United States late in November 1962, and, like the monster in a classic science fiction movie, swept halfway around the world, bringing disease and sometimes death to the residents of one city after another. In New York respiratory complaints among the elderly increased. In London, where heavy pollution set in about a week later than it did in New York, approximately seven hundred excess deaths were recorded. In Rotterdam at about the same time the pollution rate rose sharply, followed by a slight increase in mortality and in hospital admissions, especially among people over fifty years of age suffering from heart and lung conditions. In Hamburg, where the wave of pollution crested next, it was thought to have brought an increase in deaths from heart disease. A week later the pollution rate in Osaka increased sharply, and about sixty excess deaths were recorded. Other cities may have suffered in the episode, but the lack of mortality and morbidity statistics makes it impossible to determine whether those populations were noticeably affected by the wave of dirty air.[12]

Investigations of pollution incidents in this country and abroad

---

10 Donald E. Carr, *The Breath of Life*, p. 47.
11 Lewis Herber, *Crisis in Our Cities*, p. 33.
12 Arthur Stern, ed., *Air Pollution*, 1: 560–61.

demonstrate that air pollution can be a killer, but they do not disclose the full range of damage that dirty air may do. Exposure to extraordinarily heavy pollution for short periods of time is clearly harmful, but there is some evidence that prolonged exposure to "normal" levels of air pollution may also be dangerous. The evidence for this danger is much more uncertain than that for the damage done by dramatic accumulations of dirty air, but it is reasonably clear that prolonged, "normal" exposure to dirty air can be a causal factor in some lung and heart diseases. Atmospheric pollution is strongly implicated as a cause of sickness and death from emphysema and chronic bronchitis. It may also cause or aggravate some cases of asthma and heart disease. The evidence for a connection between pollution and lung cancer remains inconclusive, but synthetically generated air pollution can produce lung cancer in laboratory animals. Clinical and statistical studies have not yet demonstrated that dirty air can produce lung cancer in human beings.[13]

Different kinds of pollution naturally present different kinds of health hazards. A combination of sulfur dioxide and suspended particulates is thought to have been responsible for the deaths that occurred in London and for the increase in mortality that accompanied New York's "smaze" incident. Sulfur dioxide is a gaseous by-product of fuel combustion. Its major sources are coal and fuel oil. The gas is colorless and odorless in small amounts. Laboratory tests have shown that only relatively high concentrations of sulfur dioxide are capable of interfering noticeably with respiration, and city air seldom contains such large amounts of the gas, but in city air sulfur dioxide coexists with particles of floating dirt, and these suspended particulates seem to heighten the harmful properties of SO_2. In the presence of metal oxides, molecules of the gas may react with water vapor to form a fine mist of sulfuric acid. SO_2 is also absorbed by solid particles in the air, which, when inhaled, can penetrate more deeply into the crevasses of the lungs than sulfur dioxide alone. These sulfate particles can also remain in the lungs longer than can free-floating sulfur dioxide. A relatively low concentration of sulfur dioxide in combination with suspended particulates can therefore produce more serious lung irritation than can sulfur dioxide alone.[14]

[13] *Ibid.*, pp. 568–74.
[14] For some interesting evidence on this point, see U.S., Congress, Senate, Public Works Committee, Subcommittee on Air and Water Pollution, *Air Pollution—1967*, pp. 2103–18.

There are several possible methods for limiting the damage done by SO₂. Some cities have chosen to attack the problem by prohibiting the use of fuels containing more than a fixed amount of sulfur, but control efforts of this kind have been hampered by the fact that low-sulfur fuels are not readily available, or by the fact that they are generally more expensive than the high-sulfur variety. Devices that extract sulfur dioxide from flue gases have been developed, but they remain costly. British officials claim to have achieved some success in reducing the lethal potential of SO₂ by reducing the amount of floating dirt in city air. There are a number of feasible techniques for reducing the emission of solid and semisolid particles into the air, and by controlling these particles, the British hope to deprive SO₂ of the vehicles that carry it deep into the lungs.[15]

Sulfur dioxide and suspended particulates are major constituents of air pollution in the eastern United States, but they are not the only ones. The atmosphere above many American cities is also tinged with a chemically complex product of automobile exhausts. Nitrogen oxides and unburned hydrocarbons—both constituents of automobile exhaust—react with each other in the presence of sunlight to produce a brownish haze called "photochemical smog." The known health effects of photochemical pollution are not especially serious: eye, nose, and throat irritation are common, but on no occasion have pollution experts been able to establish a connection between heavy concentrations of photochemical smog and increases in mortality rates. It has been pointed out, however, that the sensory irritation produced by smog may reduce the resistance of the body to more serious disorders. Experiments conducted in Los Angeles show that when patients with chronic respiratory conditions are exposed to unfiltered Los Angeles air, their symptoms grow noticeably worse. Experimental animals exposed to concentrations of ozone, one component of photochemical smog, develop symptoms of bronchitis and emphysema, and the exposure seems to lower their resistance to some pulmonary infections, pneumonia, for example. The ozone concentrations which produced these effects in the laboratory animals were about two or three times as great as the ones that are usually present in Los Angeles air. Given present levels of automotive pollution, therefore, ozone and the other toxic substances in photochemical smog do not constitute an immediate danger to human health.

[15] Stern, *Air Pollution*, pp. 568–74.

Photochemical smog remains more an irritating nuisance than a serious threat to the survival of urbanites.[16] The nuisance has been irritating enough to provoke widespread complaints, however, especially in southern California. California officials have played an important part in inducing the automobile industry to do something about the smog problem.

Automobile manufacturers began to install pollution control devices on new cars in 1963. The first of these devices was designed to reduce the emission of pollutants from automobile crankcases. In 1966 the industry agreed to install an additional piece of equipment which would cut down the emissions of carbon monoxide and unburned hydrocarbons, and early in 1967 a petroleum products company announced that it had developed and patented a simple, inexpensive device that would remove up to 85 per cent of the nitrogen oxides from automobile exhaust. The invention was submitted to the automobile manufacturers for testing. None of the devices for controlling automotive pollution is completely effective, and their effectiveness declines sharply if automobile owners fail to have them checked and adjusted regularly. They cannot be expected, therefore, to cleanse the urban atmosphere of every trace of smog, and even the limited gains that are achieved by these devices may be wiped out by future increases in the stock of automobiles. Should the severity of automotive pollution increase substantially, it is quite conceivable that photochemical smog may yet endanger human life. The damage done by pollution is, of course, not confined to human beings. Photochemical smog, for example, can cause serious damage to crops and to vegetation in general. Economic studies have shown that severe pollution can lower the value of real estate in affected areas, and other costs of dirty air show up in laundry bills and in expenses for building maintenance.[17] The possible justifications for making an issue of dirty air are therefore numerous.

There are numerous techniques for coping with pollution problems. Precipitators, scrubbers, afterburners, and other devices can trap many undesirable products of combustion before they are released into the air, and in many cases it is possible to achieve substantial reductions in pollution emissions without the use of any special apparatus. Relatively simple (though sometimes expensive) measures like restricting the kinds of fuel that may be burned, adjusting the

16 *Ibid.*, pp. 604–8.
17 Ronald Ridker, *The Economic Costs of Air Pollution.*

equipment that burns it, and regulating the time and place of burning can all contribute to a reduction of air pollution. Neglect of dirty air cannot be attributed to the absence of a technical capacity for dealing with it.

There also exists a legal capacity for coping with dirty air. The federal courts have declared that local regulation of air pollution "clearly falls within the exercise of even the most traditional concept of what is compendiously known as the police power,"[18] and municipalities have devised a number of legislative instruments for bringing this power to bear upon polluters. Some have done no more than to include air pollution among the common-law nuisances that are susceptible to local regulation. Other localities have proceeded more systematically, establishing maximum permissible emission standards for the various species of pollutants. Still others have attempted to curb pollution by regulating the installation and use of fuel-burning equipment or the fuel itself. Registration, licensing, and inspection of fuel-burning installations are popular variants on this regulatory technique.[19] American cities and towns have at hand a wide variety of legal methods for dealing with locally produced air pollution.

Some pollution, however, drifts across municipal boundaries from neighboring jurisdictions or is emitted by mobile sources like automobiles, whose very mobility enables them to elude effective local regulation. For the solution of these pollution problems, municipalities have relied increasingly on state and federal authorities. Control of automobile emissions, for example, is almost entirely a matter of state and federal, rather than municipal, policy. State and federal governments have also had a hand in the creation of metropolitan area or regional authorities for the regulation of interlocality pollution.

The political center of gravity for pollution policymaking has moved steadily higher within the federal system, but this upward movement has not been produced by pressure from below. The federal government has taken on new responsibilities in the field of pollution abatement, not so much because state and local officials demand it, but because these lower levels of government have often failed to take action themselves. Even when the federal government has provided financial incentives for state and local initiative in the field of pollution control, as it did under the Clean Air Act of 1963, the

---

[18] *Huron Portland Cement Co.* v. *City of Detroit*, 362 U.S. 440 (1960).
[19] Health Law Center, University of Pittsburgh, *Digest of Municipal Air Pollution Ordinances*, pp. iv–v.

response has been feeble.[20] Though there is a technical capacity to reduce air pollution substantially, a legal ability to take significant action, and considerable financial and technical assistance to support that action, many local governments have remained inactive in the face of a demonstrably serious problem and despite an apparent intensification of public concern about the perils of dirty air.

PUBLIC OPINION AND THE POLLUTION PROBLEM

Before World War II Americans seldom worried about their dirty air, and it is often suggested that their prewar complacency in this matter was largely justified. The air was simply not dirty enough to be worrisome. Today's dirty air is regarded as a symbol of postwar economic prosperity and technological prowess. It is a pervasive sign that population and consumption have been growing, that industries have been booming, that automobile ownership has been expanding, and that Americans have more garbage to incinerate than ever before. The recent increase in national concern about air pollution reflects the fact that pollution itself has increased.[21]

There is undoubtedly some truth to this explanation. Two or three decades ago, for example, automobiles certainly constituted a less potent source of pollution than they do today, and industrial processes which have come into use only during the last generation have unquestionably added something new to the nation's air burden. Nevertheless, the available evidence indicates that, in spite of these new and expanding sources of pollution, the nation's dirty air problem is in some ways less serious now than it was twenty, thirty, or forty years ago. As new sources of pollution have arisen, older sources have declined, and with them has gone a considerable amount of the airborne contamination that once hovered over American cities. For example, in the days when furnaces and railroad locomotives all burned coal, the air above some of the nation's major cities seems to have contained substantially more sulfur dioxide than it does today. In Pittsburgh, Chicago, Salt Lake City, and St. Louis, prewar measures of sulfur dioxide were several times as high as today's measures

---

[20] House, *Adequacy of Technology for Pollution Abatement*, p. 58; Senate, *Air Pollution—1967*, p. 764. The 1963 legislation also provided for federal technical assistance to states and localities and for a mechanism that would enable states and municipalities to proceed against interstate and interlocality pollution problems.

[21] Marshall Goldman, ed., *Controlling Pollution*, pp. 5–6.

for these cities.[22] And recent research conducted by the U.S. Public Health Service indicates that where sulfur dioxide levels are high, the amount of airborne dirt (suspended particulates) is also likely to be high.[23] It is certainly possible that this relationship between SO_2 and suspended dirt came into being only within the past decade or so. But if it did not, as is more likely, then it is possible that urban air of the 1920's and 1930's contained not only a heavier burden of sulfur dioxide but also much more dirt than the city air of the 1950's and 1960's.

The recent intensification of national interest in dirty air, then, cannot be attributed entirely to a sudden increase in air pollution rates during the period after World War II. It is far from certain that the air really is dirtier now than it was before the war. Of course, the nature of pollution has very likely changed, and this difference may help to account for the shift in public attitudes about pollution, but not all the relevant changes have been confined to the physical composition of urban air. People have changed as well, and these human changes are probably partly responsible for the recent increase in public concern about dirty air. Today's citydwellers are probably more fastidious about the air that they breathe than were previous generations of urbanites. Although there is no conclusive evidence, the analysis of some existing data suggests that the contention is a highly plausible one. In 1963 the Department of Health, Education, and Welfare sponsored a study of public attitudes toward dirty air in the St. Louis metropolitan area. At the same time, the Department sponsored a survey of pollution rates in St. Louis and its suburbs. The results of the pollution survey were compared with the results of the attitude survey in order to see how closely citizen opinion about dirty air is tied to actual pollution levels. The findings permit some tentative inferences about the extent to which the physical quality of the air, on the one hand, and the qualities of human beings, on the other, are responsible for variations in people's concern about dirty air.

The St. Louis pollution data come from seventeen suspended particulate sampling stations scattered around the St. Louis area and from eleven sulfur dioxide stations. The HEW pollution study identi-

22 L. R. Burdick and J. F. Barkley, *Concentration of Sulfur Compounds in City Air.*

23 Thomas B. McMullen et al., "Air Quality and Characteristic Community Parameters" (Paper delivered at the Annual Meeting of the Air Pollution Control Association, Cleveland, Ohio, 1967), Appendix.

fies each of these stations by its location on a grid-square map of the St. Louis region. The locations of the residences of the respondents in the opinion survey are also identified by their grid-square co-ordinates. Using the grid-square map, squares three miles on each side were drawn around each of the seventeen particulate sampling stations and each of the eleven SO_2 stations. Respondents whose homes fell within one of the seventeen particulate sampling blocks were selected for membership in one subsample of attitude survey respondents. Those who lived within one of the SO_2 sampling squares were chosen for another, overlapping subsample of opinion survey respondents. The selection procedure guaranteed that no resident of a square lived more than about two miles from the air sampling station at the center of his square.

If citizen concern about dirty air is tied to actual pollution rates, residents of high-pollution squares (defined as areas that scored above the median particulate rate for all sampling areas in the St. Louis metropolitan area) should be more likely to be bothered by air pollution than residents of low-pollution squares. The findings reported in Table I–1 show that this was the case for at least one type of pollution—suspended particulates. Geographic variation in the level of suspended particulates was accompanied by some variation in the probability that citizens would say that they have been bothered by air pollution. However, variation in sulfur dioxide levels seems to produce relatively little variation in citizen opinion, as indicated in Table I–2. It is probable that the relative insensitivity of the public to sulfur dioxide has something to do with the fact that it is colorless and usually odorless, while airborne dirt is a much more tangible form of pollution.

Actual air pollution conditions do have some effect on people's

TABLE I–1: REACTIONS OF RESIDENTS TO SUSPENDED PARTICULATE RATES, ST. LOUIS METROPOLITAN AREA, 1963

Particulate Level	Respondents Bothered	No. of Cases
High	62.7%	134
Low	46.7%	182
		(320)*

* Four responses n.a.
Note: Throughout the tables numbers in parentheses represent numbers of respondents.

TABLE I–2: REACTIONS OF RESIDENTS TO SULFUR
DIOXIDE LEVELS, ST. LOUIS METROPOLITAN AREA,
1963

Sulfur Dioxide Level	Respondents Bothered	No. of Cases
High	53.5%	200
Low	48.3%	145
		(347)*

* Two responses n.a.

attitudes about air pollution. But the survey results reported in
Table I–3 show that there are other factors that seem to have an even
more substantial impact upon a person's sentiments concerning the
air he breathes, the most important of which is his own age. Table I–3
shows that people over forty are much less likely to be bothered by
air pollution than are people under forty who live in similarly polluted
neighborhoods. The finding is a notable one. Studies of the health
effects of air pollution have consistently shown that dirty air is a
greater threat to older people than to younger people. We might
therefore anticipate that people over forty would show more concern
about air pollution than people under forty, but the St. Louis survey
data yield just the opposite result, which tends to substantiate the
contention above that today's citydwellers are more fastidious about
the air they breathe than were their predecessors. The findings reflect
an increase, from one generation to the next, in aggravation about the
air pollution problem. Pollution levels that were acceptable in the past
are intolerable to many younger urbanites.

There are several promising explanations for this generation gap,
the most promising of which is that younger people in the United
States tend to be better educated than their elders, and better-educated
people, as Table I–3 indicates, are much more likely to be bothered
by air pollution than their less well-educated neighbors. Increased
years of schooling may have made Americans more sensitive to their
surroundings, and this increased sensitivity, evident in the well-
educated younger generation, may account for the rising chorus of
complaint about dirty air. Perhaps more important, rising standards
of education have gone hand in hand with rising standards of living.
As young Americans have become more accustomed to comfort,
convenience, and cleanliness, dirty air may have become a more
noticeable flaw in their environment.

Because younger people tend to be better educated than older
people, and because education seems to heighten people's concern

TABLE I–3: CHARACTERISTICS OF RESPONDENTS BOTH-
ERED BY AIR POLLUTION, BY PARTICULATE LEVEL,
ST. LOUIS METROPOLITAN AREA, 1963

Respondent Characteristic	Particulate Level High	Low
	%	%
Age		
40 and over	51.8	41.7
	(83)	(108)
Under 40	82.0	52.2
	(50)	(69)
		n.a. = 10
Education		
High school or more	74.2	48.4
	(41)	(102)
Less than high school	48.6	40.4
	(92)	(74)
		n.a. = 11
Annual income		
$5,000 and over	76.9	46.9
	(39)	(96)
Under $5,000	51.2	45.2
	(82)	(62)
		n.a. = 41
Race		
White	70.3	48.8
	(64)	(153)
Non-white	55.1	38.5
	(70)	(26)
		n.a. = 7

Note: Numbers in parentheses represent total respondents in each category.

about air pollution, it seems reasonable to surmise that it is increased
education which has made young people more concerned about
dirty air than their elders. Younger and older people who are
similarly educated should differ little or not at all in their opinions
about dirty air. The recent intensification of public interest in air
pollution may thus be attributed to the fact that the public is better
educated and more prosperous than ever before. The findings reported
in Table I–4 cast considerable doubt upon this line of explanation.

TABLE I–4: RESPONDENTS BOTHERED BY AIR POLLUTION, BY AGE, EDUCATION, AND
PARTICULATE LEVEL, ST. LOUIS METROPOLITAN AREA, 1963

Education Age	High Particulate Levels Under 40	40 and over	Low Particulate Levels Under 40	40 and over
High school or more	81.0%	*	60.0%	36.6%
	(29)	(12)	(50)	(52)
Less than high school	82.8	47.9	*	45.5
	(21)	(71)	(19)	(55)

* Insufficient cases to compute a percentage.

Educational differences between younger and older people do not seem to account for the generation gap in public attitudes about dirty air. Even when we control for the effects of educational differences, younger St. Louis residents are much more likely to be bothered by air pollution than are older St. Louisans of similar educational attainments. Furthermore, the generation gap could not be explained away by controlling for other variables that have a substantial impact on attitudes about air pollution—income and race.

One remaining explanation for the generational difference is that young urbanites have experienced a different sampling of American history than their elders. They have been exposed to a different set of events and institutions. They may react differently to the conditions of city life than do their elders because they have come to adulthood in different kinds of cities. It may be that they are inclined to make an issue of dirty air because the urban institutions which have shaped their experience encourage them to do so. In order to explain why younger urbanites are different from older urbanites, therefore, it may be useful to ask what is different about the recent history of American cities.

One recent urban development to which political scientists have paid particular attention is the decline and disappearance of the political machine. The ward politician, who dispensed patronage, favors, and friendship in bits and pieces to individuals, has given way to the reform politician, who dispenses his favors in wholesale lots to the entire community or to large segments of it. The possible significance of this political change for the dirty air issue consists in the fact that clean air is a "favor" which can be dispensed only in wholesale lots. It is an individual benefit which does not lend itself to the machine politician's way of doing business, and for that reason it is probable that machine politicians were less likely to make an issue of clean air than reform politicians.

It is also probable that the machine politician's way of doing business had some impact upon the attitudes and perspectives of the people with whom he dealt. The kinds of demands and complaints generated by his clientele came to reflect the kinds of favors and benefits that he had to offer—not general benefits like clean air but more specific and individualized favors like jobs or street repairs or building permits. The machine shaped the attitudes of people who were exposed to it, and older people have been exposed to the influence of the machine for larger portions of their lives than younger people. Older citydwellers, then, who came to adulthood while the machine was still in working order, exhibit attitudes that may reflect the particularistic practices of the machine. Younger urbanites, who have spent all or most of their adult lives in the presence of reform politicians and reform politics, hold different kinds of attitudes. They are more likely than their elders to frame demands for general benefits (like clean air) and to make complaints about general nuisances (like dirty air). The generational difference in attitudes about air pollution may therefore reflect a change in the nature of urban political institutions.

Just such a trend is evident in the recent political history of St. Louis, where "good government" forces took control of the city administration in 1949,[24] and it may be that this political shift helps to explain the notable shift in opinion between older and younger St. Louisans. There is nothing in the St. Louis survey results to prove that this explanation is correct, but the data do indicate that such a shift has occurred. The generational difference in attitudes about air pollution suggests that people have become more concerned about the air that they breathe; the evidence indicates that this increase in concern probably reflects something other than an increase in actual pollution rates; and the findings suggest that the generational opinion shift cannot be attributed entirely (or even substantially) to changes in the individual characteristics of urbanites—their educational attainments, for example.

Urban social and political institutions constitute the most likely remaining sources of change. Alterations in these institutions may produce shifts in the kinds of urban problems that citydwellers choose to complain about. Recent public concern about air pollution may therefore have been generated in part by institutional change. This tentative conclusion has some especially important implications for the nature of urban political institutions. Perhaps these institutions need not simply mirror the concerns of urbanites; they may also help to shape these concerns. The kinds of demands that rise to prominence within a political system—its key political issues—are determined in part by the polity itself. Likewise, issues that fail to become prominent may have been consigned to political oblivion by the operations of local political institutions. In other words, community political systems may be "impenetrable" where certain issues are

24 Edward C. Banfield, *Big City Politics*, pp. 125–27.

concerned, and those issues, like the dirty air issue prior to World War II, consequently became non-issues.

In many cities and towns the dirty air problem has remained a non-issue until quite recently. The immediate object of the chapters that follow is to account for the fact that many communities have ignored their dirty air, but it is also hoped that the investigation of local non-issues and non-decisions will illuminate the character of local political systems—particularly with respect to their "penetrability"—in a way that the study of issues and decisions cannot.

PLURALISM AND POLITICAL PENETRABILITY

The belief in the penetrability of community political systems is one component in a more comprehensive view of the structure and operations of local politics. The proponents of this view are adherents of the "pluralist alternative."[25] Theirs is an alternative, in both method and conclusions, to the "reputational" or "elitist" approach which has attracted a sizable following among sociologists.

The reputational analysts have tended to see the political system as a reflection of the stratification system. Political power accrues to those who hold high social status within their communities, and especially to men who control great wealth. The local economic elite therefore becomes the local political elite and local government, an executive committee of the capitalist class. Political power tends to be concentrated within a small, cohesive plutocracy which rules in its own interests. This elitist conclusion is supported by reputational studies of community politics, which have attempted to uncover the organization and distribution of political power in communities by identifying those leaders whom knowledgeable local residents regard as influential. In other words, the reputational method relies upon a sampling of informed community opinion to disclose the location of political power.

The pluralists, on the other hand, insist that an accurate description of community political organization can be achieved only by examining a sample of political actions, not opinions. According to the pluralist view, power can be said to exist only when it has been exercised. It cannot be exercised unless the supposed power-holder

25 Polsby, *Community Power and Political Theory*, p. 113.

takes some observable action, and this action must be followed by an appropriate and observable response on the part of his "victim."[26] The pluralists suggest that we should look for these acts of power and subservience wherever there are "key political issues," subjects that residents of a community regard as important enough to fight about.[27] These important and visible struggles to influence the course of local policy reveal the distribution of community power more surely than any sounding of local opinion.

From studies of decisionmaking activities in key issues, the pluralists have assembled the evidence to support their pluralistic conception of community politics. Against the reputational view, the pluralists argue for the independence of local political systems. The polity, they contend, is no mere annex of the economy but an autonomous sphere of activity. The distribution of political power and the course of political events are not determined by the distribution of wealth and status.[28] In insisting that the political system is something more than the reflex of the class system, the pluralists seem to suggest that political institutions are not entirely at the mercy of their environments and that they may in fact be capable of exerting some independent influence upon their surroundings. This proposition is implicit in our earlier interpretation of the St. Louis survey findings, which holds that political institutions may help to shape public opinion and perceptions. But having granted such causal autonomy to the political system, the pluralists seem reluctant to recognize it. They insist instead that local political systems are highly "penetrable," that is, political institutions and leaders are highly vulnerable to the aspirations and concerns of the citizenry and are, for the most part, unable to influence or ignore those popular sentiments.[29] The pluralists reject the subordination of the political system to the class system, but only to subordinate the polity even more thoroughly to its environment.

Obviously, there is more involved here than the causal efficacy of political institutions. To affirm the independence of the political system from its non-political environment is to deny, to some degree, the responsiveness and penetrability of local politics. That denial would undermine what may be the most significant pluralist contention, namely, that political pluralism helps to assure political democ-

---

26 Robert A. Dahl, "The Concept of Power," pp. 202–3.
27 Robert A. Dahl, "A Critique of the Ruling Elite Model," pp. 466–69.
28 Dahl, *Who Governs?*, pp. 11–86.
29 *Ibid.*, pp. 164–65.

racy. The pluralists support this contention with their evidence concerning the distribution of political power in communities. They concede that only a minority of local citizens actively exercise influence in community decisions. Nevertheless, this power-holding minority will tend to be responsive to the sentiments of the majority. Their responsiveness is a result of division and competition among themselves, which renders them vulnerable to popular sentiment.

Power, according to the pluralist view, is not concentrated within a unified political elite. It tends to be fractionated and fleeting. This is so because power is issue-based. It passes from one set of hands to another as different local issues rise and subside. Because it is issue-based, it cannot be centralized within some small ruling class which oversees the handling of all local issues from its position at the peak of a unified political hierarchy. Instead, community power will be scattered across a spectrum of local leaders and groups, each capable of exercising influence in only one or a few issue-areas. Within each of these policymaking areas, there is likely to be a further fragmentation of influence, so that the resolution of a local dispute will often involve a laborious effort to assemble the many bits and pieces of power held by a multiplicity of leaders.

In the eyes of the pluralists the decentralized and heterogeneous character of local politics is proof of the penetrability of the political stratum. It signifies that the entry of new leadership and new issues into community politics is not regulated by some small clique of all-powerful insiders who can exclude from the political stratum all men and issues uncongenial to their own temperaments. Heterogeneity helps to guarantee political penetrability and stands as evidence of past penetrations. The diversity and disjointedness of community political systems are signs of the openness of local politics.[30]

But this community political portrait may be more ordered and inhibited than the pluralist interpretation would lead us to believe. The mere fact that a diversity of independent political groups has been able to introduce a diversity of issues into the political statum does not mean that "any dissatisfied group will be able to find spokesmen in the political stratum," as Dahl says, or that any issue can penetrate the political stratum. The pluralists' reasoning on those points resembles the logic of the argument that there is no racial discrimina-

---

[30] Polsby, *Community Power and Political Theory*, p. 131; Herbert Kaufman and Nelson W. Polsby, "American Political Science and the Study of Urbanization," pp. 134–35.

tion in the United States because Jackie Robinson, Joe Louis, and Lena Horne are all to be found in socially or economically prominent positions. Visible diversity does not necessarily imply openness. The undeniable pluralism of observable political activity may in reality be pluralism of a highly restricted sort.

One might argue that if such restrictions do exist, we would certainly find traces of them in the pluralists' own studies of political action and decisionmaking—cases in which local powerholders act to suppress the political activities of some rising new leader or to block the emergence of some embryonic political issue. We need not depart from pluralist methods, therefore, to examine instances of political impenetrability,[31] and these methods have produced little, if any, evidence that such instances actually do occur. It has been pointed out, however, that the pluralist approach suffers from a serious short-coming which could diminish its sensitivity to the signs of political impenetrability. Specifically, the pluralist emphasis upon political activists and their actions may lead investigators to overlook the power of obstruction—of enforcing inaction and thereby maintaining the impenetrability of the political process. Local political influence need not lie wholly with decisionmakers in key issue-areas. Researchers may also have to reckon with "non-decisionmakers," people whose political power consists in their ability to prevent the consideration of some kinds of issues. Peter Bachrach and Morton Baratz have observed that

power is exercised when A participates in the making of decisions that affect B. But power is also exercised when A devotes his energies to creating or enforcing social and political values and institutional practices that limit the scope of the political process to public consideration of only those issues which are comparatively innocuous to A. To the extent that A succeeds in doing this, B is prevented, for all practical purposes, from bringing to the fore any issues that might in their resolution be seriously detrimental to A's set of preferences.[32]

This power to restrict the scope of the political process—to make it impenetrable in certain respects—is not revealed by the investigation of political activities in key issue-areas because the issues in which this kind of power is likely to be significant are precisely the ones that never become "key."

31 Polsby, Community Power and Political Theory, p. 97.
32 Peter Bachrach and Morton Baratz, "The Two Faces of Power," p. 948.

It is not unreasonable to suppose that this power really does exist. Any community, after all, must find some way to restrict its political attentions and energies to a handful of issues if it is not to be overwhelmed by demands upon its attention. It must be able to select just a sample of political concerns from an infinity of possible political interests.[33] The pluralists contend, in effect, that the sample chosen for attention is likely to approximate a random one, or, at least, that it cannot be biased in any significant way by local political institutions or leaders. Yet there is reason to believe that the sampling process *is* biased and that political leaders and institutions, by their ability to enforce inaction in some issue-areas, play an important role in introducing that bias.

The existence of such a bias is lent some credibility by the uncertain impression of many amateur and professional political observers that there is something called "local political climate" or "political atmosphere" or "political culture," which varies in some consistent fashion from one town to another. One important aspect of this "climate" seems to be the substantive content of local political debate—the kinds of issues that have preempted the attentions of the local political stratum. What this notion suggests is that local political issues can all be integrated in some coherent cultural configuration, which expresses the "spirit," or perhaps the "cultural motivation," of a community.[34] More precisely, any city tends to exhibit a general and consistent bias in favor of some kinds of political issues and in opposition to others. Systematic empirical studies of community politics tend to support the casual impression that different cities develop different arrays of political concerns, which reflect underlying variations in local political predispositions. Furthermore, there is some evidence to suggest that community political institutions may be influential in determining the strength and character of these local biases.[35]

E. E. Schattschneider has suggested a reason why political institutions should promote bias in the selection of political issues. "The crucial problem in politics," he says, "is the management of conflict. No regime could endure which did not cope with this problem. All politics, all leadership, all organization involves the management of conflict. All conflict allocates space within the political universe. The consequences of conflict are so important that it is inconceivable that

[33] David Easton, *A Systems Analysis of Political Life*, pp. 58–59.
[34] For a more elaborate treatment of these concepts, see Ruth Benedict, *Patterns of Culture*, chap. 3.
[35] Oliver Williams and Charles Adrian, *Four Cities*, chaps. 9–13.

any regime could survive without making an attempt to shape the system." In the interest of their own political survival, therefore, leaders and organizations must make sure that issues which threaten their existence, their own allocations of political space, are not admitted to the political arena. Toward some species of conflict they must remain impenetrable. The nature of their resistance will depend, of course, upon what kinds of leaders or organizations they are, but all of them, according to Schattschneider, will exhibit an insensitivity to some issues. "All forms of political organization," he writes, "have a bias in favor of the exploitation of some kinds of conflicts and the suppression of others because *organization is the mobilization of bias.* Some issues are organized into politics while others are organized out."[36]

Schattschneider's observations suggest a view of community politics which is different in certain fundamental respects from the one that has been advanced by the pluralists. Implicit in the latter position is the assumption that pluralistic political systems can do very little to insulate themselves from their non-political environments. They are vulnerable to almost all the demands, discontents, and issues that private citizens choose to thrust upon them. The present study, relying primarily upon the insights of Schattschneider and of Bachrach and Baratz, proceeds on a contrary hypothesis. It suggests that pluralistic polities, for all their apparent penetrability and heterogeneity, may in reality restrict the scope of the political process to a limited range of "acceptable" issues and political demands. Much of this restrictive influence is likely to be exerted indirectly. For example, the citizens of a community will probably tend to frame their demands in such a way as to achieve a good political reception. They will often adapt their requests to the presumed inclinations of local political institutions and political leaders, perhaps omit some requests altogether. Local political forms and practices may even inhibit citizens' ability to transform some diffuse discontent into an explicit demand. In short, there is something like an inarticulate ideology in political institutions, even in those that appear to be most open-minded, flexible, and disjointed—an ideology in the sense that it promotes the selective perception and articulation of social problems and conflicts, and so a town develops its own unique "political climate."

The nature and sources of this unstated bias must elude research

36 E. E. Schattschneider, *The Semisovereign People*, p. 71.

efforts like those of the pluralists, which mirror the movements of political systems, making inquiries only where there have been observable actions and institutionally recognized issues. Such an investigation incorporates institutional biases in the design of its research. If these biases are the presuppositions of research, they cannot be its objects. It is not difficult to imagine the kinds of phenomena that may be overlooked in this way. By virtue of their preoccupation with observable political actions and key political issues, pluralist investigators would naturally overlook the sort of political influence whose medium is not observable political action. For example, in order to avoid the anger and active participation of some potentially powerful group, political activists might avoid all issues that could adversely affect its interests. The actual distribution of community influence in such a situation would not be disclosed in the usual pluralist inventory of political participants and their actions. Nonparticipants would also have exerted influence to enforce inaction. Moreover, by comparison with the potential issues which this offstage influence has suppressed, the visible and supposedly important issues of local politics may turn out to be relatively trivial. There is no reason to assume that the only important issues are the visible ones. Visible issues may be distinguished only by the fact that they are relatively "safe."

The existence of an offstage power to enforce political inaction would suggest that there are some types of local policy issues and decisions (the non-issues and non-decisions) in which community power may assume a unitary or monolithic configuration: on such matters there is neither bargaining nor visible disagreement. This observation, though it appears to require a modification of the pluralists' disjointed view of community politics, is not really inconsistent with their line of analysis. We can extend the pluralist proposition that power is tied to issues: just as the identities of power-holders vary from one policymaking region to the next, so the organization of power varies from one issue-area to another. In some matters this power will be highly decentralized; in others, decentralization, compromise, and negotiation all disappear. The local political system becomes unified and impenetrable, and political activists all bow to the presumed interests of an offstage power-holder.

The power to enforce inaction need not always lie outside the orbit of visible political actions and issues, of course. Political activists could be the wielders, as well as the victims, of this power. By monopolizing their town's civic energies for their own favorite issues, the activists could deprive other issue-areas of the political resources necessary for decisionmaking. What is more likely is that the political projects which engage their attention may simply discourage other kinds of pursuits. For example, a vigorous effort by local decision-makers to enact an air pollution ordinance could deter other, would-be decisionmakers from launching a program to attract heavy industry to the community. In this instance, the power of enforcing inaction is in the hands of active participants in local policymaking; its effects are felt by those who remain offstage and outside the spotlight of pluralist research.

Occurrences like this one have inconvenient implications for the pluralist view of community politics. They suggest that the influence of political activists may extend well beyond the boundaries of the issue-area in which they are observed to be active. A leader who participates in decisionmaking only in matters of downtown com-mercial development may also be helping to enforce immobility in the field of public housing. If this were the case, the very pluralism of pluralist theory might have to be re-evaluated. Activists in a single issue-area could influence a number of other issue-areas—some actual, some only potential—raising the possibility that a community may be governed not by an amorphous collection of independent political sovereignties but by a hierarchy of sovereignties and semi-sovereignties. The prominence of some issue-areas may be related to the subordination of others.

This finding would not, of course, call in question the basic empirical results of pluralist research, only the pluralists' interpreta-tion of those results. The discovery of a power to enforce inaction does not invalidate the finding that local political activists tend to specialize in one or a few issue-areas, nor does it necessarily imply that communities are governed by small, cohesive, and hidden elites whose members manage to have their way in every local decision. What it does suggest is that the pluralism of observable political activity may actually be a rather stunted kind of diversity, hedged about by concentrations of political influence which prevent the further growth of local political heterogeneity. It also suggests that in some matters, local political activists may behave as though they did constitute a cohesive elite or as though they were all responding to the directives of an elite. The effect of this behavior is to restrict the range of community political concerns, to fix local political horizons, and to relegate some potential issues to political oblivion. These processes of non-decisionmaking will not be brought to light by scrutinizing decisionmaking activities in key issue-areas. The proper object of investigation is not political activity but political inactivity.

RESEARCH METHODS

Anyone who hopes to construct an explanation for political inaction immediately faces difficulties. The task, after all, is a peculiar one. We must account for things that do not happen, and it might be argued that such a curious enterprise must inevitably stray far from the hard facts about politics—the observable actions, conflicts, and events that are the raw materials for any reliable piece of social science research. This objection is not, however, a crippling one. Inaction is just as much a fact, just as susceptible to empirical verification, as is action. There is no obvious reason why a study of non-events cannot be factual.

Some scholars have indicated a few not so obvious reasons for regarding such a study as impossible: "For every event that occurs, there must be an infinity of alternatives. Then which non-events are to be regarded as significant?"[37] From the infinity of non-events available, why should we pick those related to air pollution instead of those related to the prevention of elephant stampedes or the persecution of witches? In many modern American communities we could easily verify the presence of all three types of inaction, each just as "factual" as the others. It is the necessity of choosing among these and an infinity of other alternatives that, in the opinion of some scholars, "presents truly insuperable obstacles to research." These obstacles cannot be evaded by stipulating that we are interested in some non-events—the neglect of the air pollution issue—rather than others. "It is obviously inappropriate for outsiders to pick among all the possible outcomes that did not take place a set which they regard as important but which community residents do not." The fundamental difficulty here is one already mentioned. The assertion that some local problem deserves more attention than community residents have given it, it is charged, is "likely to prejudice the outcomes of research."[38]

[37] Polsby, *Community Power and Political Theory*, p. 97.
[38] *Ibid.*

This study has already exhibited the prejudice alleged by suggest-
ing that there is a political explanation for instances of political
inaction and neglect. The implication which has been pursued here
is that inaction results from the operations of political influence and
political institutions, but it may also be the case that a community
neglects certain subjects simply because local residents regard the
topics as trivial ones. For example, it would obviously be preposter-
ous to maintain that the citizens' failure to make an issue of the
witch menace results from the repressive power of the local sorcery
interests. Most people simply do not believe in witches, and it takes
no exercise of power to deter them from witch hunting. If we insist
on seeing a concentration of influence behind every such instance of
political inaction, we will inevitably arrive at a bizarre view of community politics. The result would be only slightly less unrealistic if
we were to confine our attention to "important" kinds of inaction—
inaction on the air pollution issue, for example, instead of the witch
menace. Though the issue may seem terribly important to an outsider, we cannot assert that there is something "unnatural" in the
citizens' neglect of it, nor can we argue that they must have been
deceived concerning their true interests or that some entrenched
power-holders have frustrated the desires of the people by enforcing
silence on the matter of dirty air. The public may be genuinely uninterested in air pollution.

It is clear that an investigator cannot impose his own political
priorities upon a community and then arbitrarily attribute all lapses
from these standards to the obstructive operations of political influence, but it is also arbitrary to assume, as does the pluralist
approach, that when a community neglects some topic, it is simply
because no one cares about it. Local political institutions and political
leaders may, as we have already suggested, exercise considerable control over what people choose to care about and how forcefully they
articulate their cares. We can assume neither that the neglect of an
important issue is "unnatural" nor that it is "natural."

The method which we shall use to examine and explain non-issues
makes neither of these assumptions. It recognizes that standards of
political importance vary from one community to another, producing
various patterns of political neglect and attentiveness, and it seeks to
relate certain aspects of this variation to observed differences in the
political characteristics of communities. If there is a political explanation for ignoring dirty air, then we should find some relationship

between the neglect of the air pollution issue and characteristics of local political leaders or institutions. If we do not find this relationship, the pluralist contentions will have been substantiated.

The proposed research strategy will require, first, a measure of the extent to which air pollution has become a political issue in each of a number of cities. Second, where we find differences between cities in the prominence of the dirty air issue, we will look for accompanying inter-city political differences. In this way we should be able to ascertain whether or not there is a political explanation for local inattention to the air pollution problem. It will become apparent that certain kinds of local political systems tend to be "impenetrable" with respect to the dirty air issue—at least that is one conclusion that might be drawn from the discovery of an association between neglect of the issue and the political characteristics of local leaders and institutions. But we might also conclude that towns with certain kinds of leaders and institutions tend to have relatively mild pollution problems, and that it is the mildness of the problem—not the impenetrability of the institutions—which prevents dirty air from becoming a major political issue. This ambiguity can be eliminated rather easily by controlling for the actual level of local air pollution.

A second ambiguity, however, is not so easily overcome. It might be argued that towns with certain kinds of political leaders and institutions also happen to have citizens who are relatively unconcerned about the air that they breathe, and that it is the indifference of the citizens, not the unresponsiveness of the leaders and institutions, that prevents the inclusion of the issue on local political agendas. Ideally, we might solve the problem by conducting a public opinion survey in each of a number of cities in order to find out just how indifferent to the air pollution problem various local populations are. That, however, would be an excessively expensive solution. Instead, we can use the survey findings from St. Louis, which show that citizen concern about dirty air is related to age, education, income, and race. We will therefore control for those variables in trying to determine whether or not political leaders and institutions are responsible for local inattention to the pollution issue. In this way, it should be possible to distinguish the effects of political factors from those of non-political factors like the private perceptions and sentiments of the citizens.

It should be noted that those problems which proceed from the assumption that air pollution deserves more attention than American cities have given it have not been solved. The statement remains value-laden, but the bias implicit in it no longer threatens to undermine the validity of the research enterprise. It has been replaced by an alternative presupposition. Instead of asserting that some cities have given insufficient attention to their air pollution problems, we need only recognize that some cities have been less concerned with dirty air than others. Our job is to explain those variations in local concern.

It is true that this explanation may itself reflect a moral judgment. Though we are dealing only with inter-city variations in the political importance of the air pollution issue, we have chosen to focus on those cities which have accorded comparatively little importance to dirty air and to account for their neglect of the issue. We might just as easily have concentrated on towns which have assigned it a relatively high priority. Special interest in the inattentive towns is prompted by the judgment that the air pollution problem is important and deserves extensive consideration, that cities should pay a great deal of attention to their dirty air, and that when they do not, the oversight is worthy of an explanation. This explanatory effort is clearly not value-free, but its presuppositions do not diminish its empirical validity. Anyone who regards air pollution as a trivial issue and chooses to make contrary evaluative assumptions can use the evidence presented in the pages that follow to construct his own explanation for the fact that some cities have devoted an inordinate amount of attention to this insignificant urban problem.

There remain some other possible weaknesses in the proposed method of investigation, however. Perhaps the most uncertain step in the research procedure is the one that calls for an assessment of the extent to which dirty air has become a political issue. Though "issues" and "non-issues" have been mentioned repeatedly, "issue-ness" has not yet been defined, nor have we suggested how it might be measured. When politicians talk about an "issue," they are usually referring to a subject of controversy, but they may also be speaking about an unsettled matter which is ready for a decision.[39] The definition used here is closer to the latter meaning. An issue is any unresolved matter, controversial or non-controversial, which awaits an authoritative decision. It is a topic which has been included on a community's political agenda. The problem is to decide at just what point a topic becomes an agenda item and is therefore ripe for authoritative resolution.

It is unlikely that anyone can identify with certainty the moment

[39] *Webster's New Collegiate Dictionary*, 7th ed., s.v. "issue."

in which a subject of discussion is "ready" for a decision. We can expect to find that there are subtle gradations of "readiness" between subjects that are completely ignored and those that command leading priorities for attention. One axis of variation follows the stages of the decisionmaking process from the recognition of a problem to its consideration by local authorities. The more advanced an item is in this process, the more clearly it is a component of a community's political agenda. Recognized community problems are closer to being agenda items than unrecognized ones; discussed problems, closer than undiscussed ones.[40]

But the passing recognition of a problem and the idle discussion of it by a few citizens do not seem sufficient to transform a matter previously ignored into a political issue. The conventional definitions of "issue-ness" appear to require more than this. It is also necessary that there be serious consideration of "possible authoritative action" in the matter,[41] and the possibility of authoritative action is likely to increase with the authority of the people who take the matter under consideration. A topic which attracts the attention of civic leaders is therefore more nearly an agenda item than one that has only captured the concern of ordinary citizens.

It is also important to take account of the manner in which civic leaders address themselves to a prospective issue—whether they merely discuss it without committing themselves to any policy recommendations or whether they take public positions with respect to possible authoritative action. Only when advocacy or opposition has made an appearance among community leaders will we say that a topic has taken its place on the local political agenda. Both advocacy and opposition are signs that at least a few local leaders seriously desire some authoritative action on a given issue. There is a relatively high probability that the publicly stated policy preferences of these prominent men and women will provoke the governing authorities to make some decision about the topic under discussion. The subject has therefore become an issue, an unresolved matter which is ripe for authoritative action. If the leaders disagree among themselves about the action to be taken, we will say that the subject has become controversial. If there is no disagreement, it is non-controversial.

Each of the issues on a local political agenda represents a decision-

---

[40] For a more detailed enumeration of the stages in decisionmaking, see Robert E. Agger, Daniel Goldrich, and Bert Swanson, *The Rulers and the Ruled*, pp. 40–51.

[41] Easton, *Systems Analysis of Political Life*, p. 140.

making process which has reached a particular stage of maturation. Some of these processes will have cut through broad channels of the political stratum: a large proportion of the civic leadership will have been swept into these policymaking episodes. Other decisions will be brought about with only small trickles of activity and involving just a handful of political actors. In other words, some issues are bigger than others. The greater the proportion of civic leaders who take positions, the bigger the issue.

How can we determine whether and to what extent a subject of political concern has met the criteria of "issue-ness"? By what kinds of actions does a member of the political stratum signify that he has taken a position on a subject, and how do we distinguish civic leaders from ordinary citizens? If we were conducting a study in a single town, an investigation of local decisionmaking episodes would probably supply the information necessary to identify its active leaders. Inspection of their political activities would probably yield an extensive catalogue of the ways in which civic leaders can take positions on matters of public concern. It might even be possible to distinguish different degrees of leadership and subtle variations in the strength of conviction that political activists display when they take sides on an issue. Unfortunately, in order to identify with any precision the determinants of political inaction, we must be able to make comparisons among many cities, and an extensive study of this kind must settle for something less than the rich detail that is possible in an investigation whose financial and intellectual resources are focussed upon the affairs of a single town. It will, therefore, be impractical to gauge the "issue-ness" of air pollution or of any other local problem by a direct, intensive examination of local decisionmaking activities. The method of inquiry must be more economical than those used in conventional case studies of community policymaking.

The information about urban political issues and activities contained in this study comes from a survey, conducted by the National Opinion Research Center during late 1966 and early 1967, of formal leaders in fifty-one American cities, ranging in population from 50,000 to 750,000.[42] The leaders (ten from each city) are the heads of organizations and institutions which are likely to be found in almost any urban area: mayors, Chamber of Commerce presidents, presidents of local bar associations, chairmen of local Democratic and

[42] For a description of this survey, see Peter Rossi and Robert Crain, "The NORC Permanent Community Sample."

Republican Party organizations, city or county health commissioners, municipal planning or urban renewal directors, local labor council presidents, editors of leading community newspapers, and the president of the largest bank in each of the cities surveyed. These formal leaders provide most of the testimony on which "issue-ness" of air pollution is gauged and the political characteristics of the fifty-one towns determined.

The reliability of the leaders' testimony obviously depends in part upon the kinds of information that they have been asked to supply. Past community research has shown, not surprisingly, that respondents are most accurate as informants when they are answering questions about their own activities or about occurrences in which they have been directly involved.[43] Questions of this kind were relied upon in order to gather the information necessary for measuring the "issue-ness" of air pollution. The respondents were asked, for example, whether their organizations had ever taken positions on the matter of air pollution. They were also asked to describe any organizational activities related to air pollution or pollution control—special meetings on the subject, studies conducted, publicity campaigns, and so on. Their answers to these questions were used to construct an index of the "issue-ness" of air pollution.[44]

In effect, the assumption was made that the local panels of organizational leaders could serve as human yardsticks for estimating the level and nature of decisionmaking activity in each of the cities under study. They serve in this capacity not because they themselves are sure to be influential decisionmakers but because they are almost sure to stand in the path of influence and decisionmaking. Their formal authority is likely to make them essential in the formulation and execution of local policy decisions. From the strategic vantage points which they occupy, we can scan various policymaking regions for signs of activity. They themselves are likely to reflect the policymaking concerns of their communities in their own organizational activities. These activities will almost never tell the whole story about any decisionmaking episode, but they will indicate what kinds of issues have engaged the attention of the local political stratum. The bigger the issue, the more activity we can expect to find among the members of our panel.

[43] Raymond Wolfinger, "A Plea for a Decent Burial," p. 842.
[44] See below, pp. 94–102.

SUMMARY

The analysis of the information collected must, of course, be quite rough. In order to assure the reliability of the local informants, it was necessary to ask them only simple questions, and simple questions, as everyone knows, can be expected to elicit only simple answers. The kinds of information which the respondents have been able to supply, therefore, do not justify the testing of very subtle propositions about local politics, nor are they likely to afford an intimate view of local political activity.

It is important, therefore, not to demand too much of the evidence that has been assembled. The data supply a crude measure of variation, from one town to another, in the political prominence of the air pollution issue. In addition, they provide some indicators of the general characteristics of local political leaders and institutions. After taking into account the level of local air pollution and certain relevant attributes of local populations, statistical relationships will be sought between the neglect of the air pollution issue and the political characteristics of local leaders and institutions. These statistical associations are useful in explaining why some cities have failed to cope with their dirty air. They suggest that local political strata with certain characteristics tend to be "impenetrable" where the air pollution issue is concerned, and they stand as evidence of a local "non-decision-making process" in which certain people and institutions have the power to enforce inaction.

The rationale for this conclusion is quite similar to the one that underlies the pluralists' conclusions about the existence and distribution of community power. The pluralists identify a power relationship as one in which A can get B to do things that B would not otherwise do.[45] The critical step in the analysis of power is therefore to find out what B *would* ordinarily do. One way to make this determination is to observe people who are similar to B and who face similar circumstances, save for the circumstance of A's presence. If A has power over B, B's behavior will differ from the behavior of other, similar people who are not exposed to the influence of A. In our case B is the entire population of a particular town. The town's political actions on the air pollution issue will be compared with the actions of other towns whose populations are similar in age, education, income, and race. These comparisons will be further adjusted to assure that the

45 Dahl, "The Concept of Power," pp. 202–3.

populations in question face similar conditions—in this case, similar levels of air pollution. After determining how the actions of similar B's vary from one town to another, these variations are related to differences in the characteristics of various A's—local political institutions and leaders. In this way, it will be possible to find out how different kinds of A's affect the activities of similar B's and, specifically, whether certain kinds of A's are able to deter B's from making an issue of dirty air.

For the purposes of this study, as for the pluralists, the indicator of a power relationship is a statistical association between the actions or characteristics of A and the actions or inaction of B. Where such associations exist, the inference is drawn that A has somehow induced a response in B. Some question has been raised concerning the legitimacy of this inference, as well as its relevance to the concept of power. It has been objected that there must be more in a power relationship than the mere association of stimulus and response. If we insist simply that "he who stimulates has power over the respondent," then we must "do violence to the conception of power which one has by *Verstehen*." We must concede, for example, that "the victim who incautiously displays a well-filled wallet has power over the thief who robs him."[46] Clearly, something is missing from any notion of power founded simply upon the association of stimulus and response. In the case of the thief and his victim, the victim does not want to be robbed. As for the thief, he is probably aware of his victim's aversion to robbery but not deterred by it. In short, the stimulus-response conception of power fails to account for the way in which men define their own interests and the way in which others perceive and respond to those interests.

These subjective aspects of power relationships are beyond the scope of a comparative, extensive study such as the present one, but an attempt has been made to recapture some of the subjective complexities of power relations by conducting detailed political case studies in a pair of cities with similar populations and similar air pollution problems but substantial differences in their handling of the air pollution issue. By examining these differences, I hope to illustrate how political power can produce political inaction and impenetrability and to give an example, at least, of the subjective context in which this kind of power operates.

---

[46] Francis J. Wormuth, "Matched-Dependent Behavioralism: The Cargo Cult in Political Science," p. 817.

11 | Two Case Studies: Gary and East Chicago

When the city of Gary, Indiana, was being put together just after the turn of the century, its low skyline was already streaked with industrial smoke. Before Gary had a city hall, or a public school, or paved streets, it had a steel mill. Before the steel mill, there was an uninhabited stretch of sand dunes and boggy meadow where the city of Gary now stands. Engineers employed by U.S. Steel found only an unoccupied hunting lodge on the site of the future city when they arrived in 1906, but they rapidly added a complex of blast furnaces, open hearths, and coke ovens to the local landscape, and the southern shore of Lake Michigan soon bristled with industrial smokestacks. A few hundred yards from the new mill, U.S. Steel started to build the town that would house its employees. Company engineers moved inland to lay out city streets. A U.S. Steel subsidiary, the Gary Land Company, divided the emergent town into lots, put up the first of thousands of steelworkers' bungalows, made home loans to U.S. Steel employees, and exercised a veto over architectural plans for all buildings erected in Gary. Even the name of the new metropolis came from the company: Judge Elbert Gary had been the corporation's president and it was the Judge who selected the site for his company's new midwestern mill.[1]

Today, thanks largely to Judge Gary and his corporation, there is a city of more than 180,000 on a site that late nineteenth-century entrepreneurs considered one of the "most desolate available in the United States."[2] The town has the second largest steel mill in the

[1] Works Progress Administration Indiana Writers' Project, *The Calumet Region Historical Guide*, pp. 149–61.
[2] *Ibid.*, p. 24.

35

world, an impressive domed city hall, about twenty public schools, many miles of paved streets, and it often lies under a heavy blanket of dirty air. Shoppers on Gary's main street can frequently see a ponderous plume of pink or rust-colored smoke rising behind the city hall dome, and motorists on the Indiana Toll Road often encounter the same rusty haze when they near the city limits. In 1962 a more systematic observer of air pollution, the U.S. Public Health Service, ranked sixty American cities according to the dirtiness of their air. Gary stood at the head of the list.[3]

Gary has not ignored its atmospheric pollution. Today a special division of the city Health Department is charged with the responsibility for cleaning up the air, but municipal activity in the field of air pollution is a relatively recent development in Gary. Though local residents testify to a long history of smoky skies and gritty window sills, it was not until the mid-1950's that air pollution became a public issue in the city, and only in 1962 did the City Council finally see fit to pass an air pollution ordinance.

Some Gary residents maintain that their city's slowness to confront its dirty air calls for no special explanation, that a "natural" and self-evident inertia in political affairs and public sentiment accounts for the neglect of new and highly technical issues like air pollution. Where such novel topics are concerned, they argue, it is simply axiomatic that the public and the political system will tend to remain at rest. But while Gary remained at rest, other cities were growing restive. East Chicago, Indiana, a town of sixty thousand that shares Gary's western boundary, began serious deliberations on an air pollution law early in 1948 and passed an ordinance in the following year. The city thus got around to the matter of dirty air about seven years before Gary did. Moreover, once it had addressed itself to the air pollution problem, East Chicago produced legislative results in about a year, less than one-fifth the time that it took Gary to draft and enact an ordinance.

When measured against East Chicago's speedy performance, Gary's lethargic handling of the air pollution problem appears somewhat less than natural and axiomatic. The political inertia that some prominent citizens of Gary seem to have taken for granted merits an explanation. The pronounced difference in inertia between the two towns must reflect some other differences between them—differences visible in their respective modes of air pollution policymaking.

[3] Gary *Post-Tribune*, 15 December 1962.

Outwardly, Gary and East Chicago are kindred cities, the homes of massive manufacturing installations. In both towns, factory properties form a solid margin along the Lake Michigan shore, and there are sizable industrial outcroppings in the territory to the south. East Chicago, the less populous and spacious of the two cities, is more cluttered with industrial sites than Gary. It is not uncommon for an East Chicago resident to see factory smokestacks from his back yard or live on a street which comes to a dead end at the fenced boundary of some industrial domain. In Gary the factories and mills more frequently keep their distance from residential neighborhoods, but that distance, though great by East Chicago standards, is not sufficient to put factories out of sight and smell. There are some homes even in the town's upper-income "executive" neighborhood where it is possible to take in the lake, the patio, and U.S. Steel's new oxygen-electric furnace at a single glance.

Gary and East Chicago have arrived at their present similar appearances through slightly different courses of development. Unlike Gary, East Chicago did not spring into existence under the auspices of a single large corporation. Its origins were modest and its growth largely unsupervised. In the late 1880's and early 1890's the town emerged as the haphazard product of a few small industrial settlements. By 1901, when the Inland Steel Company bought land in East Chicago, a small town and several factories were already standing in the neighborhood of its property. Unlike U.S. Steel in Gary, therefore, Inland did not have the opportunity to build its own industrial city from the ground up, nor was the company large enough at the time to undertake such an enterprise. East Chicago therefore matured without the benefit of an initial plan of development. Its appearance has been shaped by the uncoordinated site selection decisions of a variety of industrial corporations, but the physical results are quite similar to those in Gary.[4]

The visible pre-eminence of heavy industry in East Chicago is accompanied by visibly dirty air. Like Gary, East Chicago suffers from a relatively severe pollution problem; in fact, because the two towns are adjacent to one another, they often share the same problem. Dirty air, as pollution officials of both cities readily point out, is no respecter of municipal boundaries, and there are no sharp differences in air quality between the two. In both towns, for example, monitoring stations of the National Air Sampling Network report

4 WPA Indiana Writers' Project, *The Calumet Region Historical Guide*, pp. 217–19.

comparable amounts of airborne dirt, as Table II–1 indicates. Those differences that exist between the two towns show that East Chicago's air is somewhat cleaner than Gary's, a fact which makes Gary's relative insensitivity to the air pollution issue all the more curious. Of course, the available data do not tell us what East Chicago's air was

TABLE II–1: ANNUAL GEOMETRIC MEANS FOR SUSPENDED PARTICULATES*

Year	Gary	East Chicago	National Urban Average
1958	262	214	108
1960	190	152	99
1962	192	173	89

SOURCE: U.S. Public Health Service, *Air Pollution Measurements of the National Air Sampling Network, 1957–1961*; U.S. Public Health Service, *A Summary of National Air Sampling Network Data, 1957–1965*.

* Micrograms of particulates per cubic meter of air.

like before the town enacted its pollution ordinance in 1949. At that time, well before the establishment of the Air Sampling Network, the town's air may have been just as polluted as Gary's. Given the proximity of the two cities and their common industrial character, it is quite unlikely that they would ever differ sharply in air quality.

A look at national air pollution averages underlines the resemblance between dirty air in Gary and dirty air in East Chicago. In 1962, for example, when Gary's mean particulate count stood at 192 micrograms and East Chicago's at 173, the geometric mean for suspended particulates at all urban monitoring stations of the National Air Sampling Network was 89 micrograms per cubic meter of air. Where dirty air is concerned, Gary and East Chicago clearly are more similar to each other than is either to the "average" American city.

Sulfur dioxide measurements for Gary and East Chicago are available, but most of the annual SO_2 averages for Gary are based on air samples which were not numerous enough to meet the standards of the National Air Sampling Network. There are, however, adequate measures of airborne sulfates for both towns. The NASN sulfate measurements are based upon chemical analyses of suspended particulates. The sulfate content of the particulates can serve as an index of the amount of airborne sulfur compounds, both gaseous and solid. Unfortunately, even these measurements do not provide a completely satisfactory basis for making comparisons between Gary and East Chicago. The sulfate data for East Chicago were collected in 1958, for Gary, in 1960. The measurements show that East Chicago's mean sulfate count was 19.0 micrograms per cubic meter of air. The mean for Gary was 16.9 micrograms. The national urban average for the years 1957 through 1960 was 11.8 micrograms. Again, though sulfate pollution seems to be somewhat higher in East Chicago than in Gary, the cities are closer to each other than either is to the national average.

Local industries appear to be responsible for most of the pollutants that burden the air in Gary and East Chicago. A 1966 study of pollution emissions in northwest Indiana indicated that industrial sources accounted for about 90 per cent of particulate emissions and about 60 per cent of hydrocarbon emissions in the region.[5] The industrial contribution to air pollution in Gary and East Chicago is probably even larger than it is in other cities in the area because most of the major industrial installations in northwest Indiana are located in one or the other of the two towns. The predominant industries, steel production and petroleum refining, account for a substantial part of the area's air pollution and for most of its jobs. All three steel mills in northwest Indiana in 1966 were located in either Gary or East Chicago. They accounted for almost 70 per cent of the particulate pollutants, about 56 per cent of the nitrogen oxide emissions, and about 20 per cent of sulfur oxide emissions. Three of the region's four oil refineries were located in East Chicago. Their most notable contributions to local pollution were hydrocarbons. Emissions from East Chicago refineries accounted for about 44 per cent of all hydrocarbons released in northwest Indiana.

The industrial character of Gary and East Chicago is also reflected in their populations. Both communities are steelworkers' towns. In 1960 the three steel companies in the area—Inland, Youngstown and Sheet and Tube, and U.S. Steel—employed 43 per cent of East Chicago's work force and 36 per cent of Gary's.[6] Citizens of the two towns were similar in most respects which the survey found to affect people's attitudes toward dirty air. The median age of Gary residents was almost identical to that of East Chicagoans. Median education

[5] Guntis Ozolins and C. Rehmenn, "Air Pollutant Emission Inventory of Northwest Indiana."

[6] U.S., Bureau of the Census, Census of Population: 1960. Detailed Characteristics, Indiana.

was about the same for both towns, though Gary's citizens appear to be somewhat better educated, on the average, than residents of East Chicago. The median income of Gary residents was also slightly higher than that of residents of East Chicago, but here again the difference was not large. A more substantial difference existed in racial composition: in 1960 about 39 per cent of Gary's residents were non-white, while the figure for East Chicago was only 24 per cent.

There is an additional dissimilarity between the two towns which overshadows all the others. While East Chicago's population grew by only 6 per cent between 1950 and 1960, Gary's increased by one-third. A similar difference is recorded for the decade 1940 to 1950, when Gary's population grew by almost 20 per cent while East Chicago suffered a slight decline. East Chicagoans have a simple explanation for the fact that their city has virtually stopped growing: there is simply no more space available in the town. Land for new housing and new factories is almost impossible to find, and its scarcity has all but halted population growth in East Chicago.

Because of Gary's growth and East Chicago's stability, their populations have come to differ slightly. In 1950 they were more nearly alike than they were in 1960. In 1950 there was almost no difference between the cities in median income or median education, and the proportion of the local work force employed in the steel industry was 45 per cent in East Chicago and 42 per cent in Gary. Even in 1950 there was a noticeable difference between the proportion of non-whites in Gary and in East Chicago, but the difference was smaller than it had become by 1960. In the late 1940's, when East Chicago began to consider the enactment of an air pollution ordinance, the populations of the two cities were, in a number of respects, more nearly similar than they are today.

EAST CHICAGO TRIES TO CLEAR THE AIR

Political Background

In the late 1940's the stability of East Chicago's population seems to have been accompanied by a kind of tranquility in local politics. It was not that East Chicago politicians had stopped disagreeing with one another—bickering was frequent, and sometimes quite intense—but subjects for disagreement seem to have been rather scarce because politicians were seldom called upon to resolve questions of public policy. Only a few identifiable policy issues disturbed the local political routine. Zoning squabbles, generated by the scarcity of land, sometimes supplied the substance for political debate, and there were always taxes to argue about. In addition, a few special projects aroused the interest of East Chicago civic activists. One of these was the passage of an ordinance that would require the installation of crossing gates on all railroad lines that ran through the city. Another was the consolidation of all previously enacted city ordinances into a simple, rationally organized municipal code. Such statutory stock-taking was a fitting enterprise for a community that had reached a plateau in its development.

City patronage provided another focus for the attentions of East Chicago politicians. No civil service regulations restricted the partisan attachments of city employees, and proved loyalty to the Democratic Party was usually a prerequisite for officeholding. The Democratic Party, however, could not be said to constitute a single object of loyalty. It was a loose collection of as many as half a dozen independent groups, each headed by a different Democratic chieftain. Members of these intraparty factions were seldom bound to their respective leaders by ideology. Ethnic and neighborhood ties seem to have been more important than shared political beliefs, and the hope for municipal employment may also have helped to maintain factional loyalties. The mayor of East Chicago, who doubled as the local party chairman, recruited most of his city officials from those intraparty groups which had provided him with electoral support. Not all party factions were willing to meet this requirement, however. The mayor presided over, but did not completely control, the various sub-chiefs within his party. This, at least, is the way East Chicago's Democratic Party organization is described by people who were active in it during the late 1940's, and the election returns of the period tend to bear them out. In 1947, when the incumbent mayor ran successfully for re-election, he was able to command only a little more than 40 per cent of the Democratic primary vote. His electoral showing was hardly what would be expected from the autocratic boss of a smoothly run political machine. The mayor's political success depended upon an uncertain coalition of factions and leaders which he managed to hold together by a judicious distribution of municipal jobs.

One leading municipal jobholder was Loyd Cohen, East Chicago's city attorney since 1939. He had been a moving spirit in the local crossing gate campaign and again in the movement for consolidation of city ordinances. While he worked on these two projects, Cohen was also taking the first steps toward the enactment of a local ordinance that would effectively reduce the emission of smoke and fumes from the city's factories. As a public official Cohen was unusual in East Chicago. Though he was an influential member of the city administration, he was only a peripheral figure in the Democratic Party organization. He was not identified with any of the ethnic or neighborhood factions that supplied the mayor with votes or political manpower, and he could not deliver any bloc of electoral support to his political chief. Had he been interested in gathering votes, he would probably have been handicapped by his inability to claim ethnic kinship with the Greeks, Serbians, Poles, Italians, and Hungarians who figured prominently among local party adherents. Moreover, Cohen does not seem to have been temperamentally suited to partisan operations. He was, according to a local Democrat of long standing, "a fine boy," but one who "wasn't liking politics."

For East Chicagoans "politics" has a somewhat different meaning than it does for political scientists. The community definition is probably best illustrated by the comment of a local newspaper editor asked to explain a disagreement that had arisen during the discussion of a local political issue: "In this town, people don't disagree about *issues*. It's just politics." "Politics" in East Chicago is distinct from the public process by which matters of community concern are debated and resolved. In the eyes of many local residents, the political system is a complex network of private feuds which often have nothing to do with the public issues under consideration. One retired municipal official, for example, was asked about a dispute between a local doctor and a local undertaker which arose during an evaluation of the town's air pollution control program. He explained that it had little to do with dirty air. The undertaker had been interested in enlarging his profits by using his hearse, when it was idle, as an ambulance. The doctor, for reasons of professional dignity, refused to refer his ambulance cases to an undertaker. The undertaker retaliated by publicly attacking the physician's stand on the air pollution program. In another case, it was explained that a local tavern owner, coal merchant, and former City Council member had testified before the Council on behalf of the local air pollution ordinance not only because the fumes from a neighborhood factory irritated the patrons of his bar, but because the owners of the factory had ordered him to remove his coal yard from land which they had leased to him in the past. His support of the air pollution ordinance was his way of getting even with the company.

These explanations can only be regarded as bits of political gossip. It was impossible to check their veracity against newspaper reports, and most respondents, though they frequently referred to the existence of private feuds, were understandably reluctant to talk about details. Nevertheless, although local gossip may not accurately portray the motives that lie behind political events—or even the events themselves—it does reveal something about the way in which politically active East Chicagoans regard local politics. For them, political activity appears primarily as a means for private advancement and private revenge. This view is shared even by those citizens who are not active in partisan affairs. Representatives of the local business community seem to have regarded some especially vigorous attempts to enforce the local air pollution ordinance not as efforts to clean the air but as attempted "shakedowns." It was even alleged that certain local politicians on one occasion explicitly demanded a bribe in return for assuring a favorable decision concerning air pollution regulations. Again, these charges are only rumors, but they reveal the attitudes of East Chicagoans toward the nature and purposes of the political process.

In the minds of East Chicago political activists, Loyd Cohen was set apart from the private funding and the alleged venality of the local political system. To some he was a puzzling figure. They found it difficult to understand why a man should choose to remain city attorney for thirteen years when he could profit so much more by entering private legal practice. No one was able to suggest any "private" reasons for Cohen's choice, nor could anyone perceive a devious scheme for private advancement in his campaign against dirty air. Others might use the air pollution issue for personal revenge. But even the most suspicious local Democrats believed that Cohen supported the cause of clean air simply because he opposed dirty air. He was a politician who "wasn't liking politics."

Raising the Issue

As city attorney, Cohen was an ex officio member of the East Chicago Board of Public Works and Safety. By local tradition, citizens with grievances were welcome to appear before the Board and state their complaints. Officially, the Board was authorized neither to hear complaints nor to do much about them, but East Chicagoans seem to have valued the chance to make the Board aware of their opinions, and, in the late 1940's at least, scarcely a Board meeting passed at which some irate citizen did not appear to register his demand or complaint. Frequently, the complaints were about dirty air, and it was Cohen's repeated exposure to them that, by his own account, prompted him to draft a clean air ordinance.

Blast furnace "slips" at the two local steel mills regularly provoked a heavy turnout of angry citizens at the weekly meeting of the Board. Slips occur when there is a sudden shift in the load of limestone, coke, and iron ore which is being roasted in a blast furnace. The resulting increase in pressure opens the furnace's safety valves, which then release billows of heavy black smoke into the air. When slips occurred in East Chicago, the Board could look forward to an uncomfortable confrontation with local housewives at its next scheduled meeting. Occasionally the protesters also appeared at City Council sessions. The Council, perhaps to avoid these confrontations or to draw attention away from public officials, made it a practice to invite representatives of smoke-producing industries to appear at meetings of the Board of Public Works and Safety. When the executives attended, they became the primary targets for complaints about smoke and soot.

A typical confrontation between local housewives and corporate management occurred in September 1948, just a few weeks before Loyd Cohen was to submit his draft air pollution ordinance to the City Council. Mrs. Steve Serdel, a local newspaper reported, arrived at the Board meeting accompanied by two other housewives. She was carrying a soiled dress belonging to her daughter. The trainmaster for the Indiana Harbor Belt Railroad was also present at the meeting, and Mrs. Serdel explained that his company's locomotives had been responsible for soiling her daughter's clothing. "She was on the porch," said Mrs. Serdel as she brandished the dress, "on her way to church, and in just a matter of a few seconds the dress was dirty." The railroad representative apologized and explained that responsibility for the dirty dress lay with company employees who were not acquainted with "proper procedure." He promised that disciplinary action would be taken to prevent similar accidents in the future. At least one of the housewives was not satisfied. "Maybe we should call up the railroad," she said, "to find out when it's safe to put our wash out." Loyd Cohen now entered the discussion in an attempt to pacify the housewives. He announced in public for the first time that he intended to submit a draft air pollution ordinance to the City Council, and he asked the complaining ladies to appear before the Council in support of his ordinance.[7]

Cohen had begun to work on the air pollution law in 1945, three years before he made his appeal for public support. His progress was slow largely because he began his efforts at ordinance drafting with almost no knowledge of the technical aspects of pollution control. At the outset, his only guide was an ineffective smoke ordinance which has been enacted in 1941 by the East Chicago City Council without much public notice. Cohen soon came to regard the 1941 law as a legal expression of industrial management's view that home furnaces and backyard burning, not factory operations, were responsible for the town's extraordinarily dirty air and was determined that his own ordinance would allocate responsibility for air pollution more realistically. Cohen turned instead to the laws which other cities had enacted in order to cope with the pollution problem. The dirty air ordinances of St. Louis, Pittsburgh, and Los Angeles County seemed suitable models for an East Chicago law. He also contacted officials of the National Institute of Municipal Law Officers, of which he was a member, and requested the Institute's drafting service to provide him with a model air pollution ordinance. While he waited, he consulted with the corporation counsels of Pittsburgh, St. Louis, and Los Angeles County at the annual conventions of the Institute. During the first two years of preparation, Cohen never sought the advice of the numerous industrial engineers who were employed by firms in East Chicago; in fact, he made no effort to inform any East Chicagoans of his work on the air pollution law. It was not until late 1947 that Cohen finally notified Mayor Frank Migas of his intention to submit a dirty air ordinance to the City Council. The Mayor, according to Cohen, was mildly favorable to the proposal but hardly enthusiastic. Cohen continued to polish up his ordinance.

By early 1948 Cohen had completed a satisfactory first draft. The legislation provided for two kinds of regulation. One type specified maximum permissible emission standards for smoke and suspended

[7] Hammond, Indiana, *Times*, 23 September 1948. There are two weekly newspapers in East Chicago but no daily. The newspaper of a neighboring town, Hammond, provides daily coverage of East Chicago affairs. The Hammond paper was used as a source of information about East Chicago's dirty air debate because its coverage was somewhat more extensive than that of East Chicago papers and because copies of it were more easily obtained.

particulates,[8] and anyone whose furnace or factory exceeded these limits could be fined as much as $300 and sentenced to 180 days in jail. A second set of regulations had to do not with pollution emissions but with the apparatus that generated them. These provisions were intended to regulate the design, installation, and upkeep of all fuel-burning equipment as well as "any article, machine, equipment, structure, or other contrivance, the use of which may cause the issuance of air contaminants within the city." Enforcement of equipment and emission standards was to be entrusted to a chief air pollution control inspector. Any citizen who intended to install a piece of equipment that was likely to "cause the issuance of air contaminants" would be required to submit two sets of plans to the pollution inspector. If the blueprints met all pollution control requirements, the inspector would issue a construction permit, for which there would be a small charge. In addition to reviewing blueprints, the inspector would be authorized to conduct a yearly inspection of every pollution-producing installation in East Chicago. Owners of equipment that met the local pollution control standards would be issued an annual certificate of operation. Any installation that failed to pass the yearly inspection would be "sealed" until necessary corrections had been made.[9] The costs of blueprint approval and annual inspection programs were to be covered entirely by fees that the inspector collected for licenses and certificates. Under Cohen's plan, any East Chicagoan who had reason to be dissatisfied with a decision of the pollution inspector might appeal the ruling to an Air Pollution Control Advisory and Appeals Board. The draft ordinance required that members of this body must "have no other interests which may conflict with the air pollution control program";[10] in other words, representatives of local industry were not eligible for appointments to the Board.

But it was to the representatives of local industry that Cohen first turned in order to secure approval of his pollution control proposal. In February 1948 he called a private meeting at City Hall, to which he invited the officers of the East Chicago Chamber of Commerce. George Applegate, the Chamber's newly appointed assistant secretary-manager, represented the organization. At the Chamber's next board

[8] *Municipal Code of East Chicago Indiana*, Title 1, secs. 2401–8; Title 5, secs. 709–99.
[9] *Ibid.*
[10] *Ibid.*

of directors meeting, Applegate reported that "it was his opinion that the City Administration is definitely determined to adopt an [air pollution] ordinance," and he noted that the City Attorney had requested Chamber cooperation in framing the law. After deliberation, the board of directors decided that it was advisable for the organization to take an "active interest" in the drafting of the pollution control legislation. A five-member Smoke Abatement Committee was set up to act as the Chamber's delegation at drafting sessions with Loyd Cohen. The chairman was to be Dr. Edward Cotter, a local physician whose clinic served many East Chicago industrial workers under company health plans.[11]

Negotiations

During the next eight months, representatives of the Chamber Smoke Abatement Committee met with Cohen at least twenty times. Dr. Cotter was present at none of these sessions, and it was George Applegate who led the Chamber delegation. At most of the meetings, the organization's contingent included one or more engineers employed by East Chicago industrial firms; Charles Molnar, the assistant city engineer, also attended some of the sessions. With the exception of these technical specialists, no East Chicagoans but Loyd Cohen and the Chamber committeemen took part in the air pollution negotiations at City Hall. Nor were any other East Chicagoans invited to participate, and in the hope that no one else would ask to do so, Cohen took care to avoid publicizing the meetings.

The City Attorney's effort to maintain secrecy was part of his attempt to win the confidence of local industrial managers. Cohen anticipated that the businessmen would be unfriendly to his air pollution proposal, and he believed that the success of his ordinance depended upon his ability to overcome this business animosity. The City Hall negotiating sessions were therefore intended to disarm potential opponents before their opposition had a chance to crystallize. Cohen was convinced that if East Chicago corporations believed that they had a hand in the writing of the air pollution ordinance, they would take a more lively and benevolent interest in the legislation than if the city administration snubbed them. He limited participation in the drafting sessions to Chamber of Commerce representatives

[11] East Chicago Chamber of Commerce, Minutes of the Board of Directors meeting, 5 August 1948.

because he was afraid that if he opened the meetings to other East Chicagoans, the result would be public pressure for a quick conclusion to the negotiations and rapid enactment of a strong air pollution law. The City Attorney was particularly concerned lest some city councilmen demand that the dirty air ordinance be submitted immediately to the Council, before it was "ready"—that is, before it had been modified to meet the major objections of local industries. An effort to snatch the legislation from the hands of the Chamber delegation, he thought, would frighten local businessmen and "cause industrial opposition to jell prematurely." The corporations would then transfer their battle against the pollution ordinance to the state courts, where the program might be tied up in litigation for years. By avoiding publicity, Cohen also hoped to induce the businessmen to take his proposal seriously. If he were to advertise his efforts on behalf of pollution control, he thought, the Chamber members might dismiss him as an upstart public official out to achieve public notoriety. Secrecy would help him to secure the Chamber's cooperation.

Cohen found an unexpected ally in George Applegate. Though he did not endorse every provision of Cohen's draft ordinance, he was convinced that some air pollution legislation ought to be enacted for East Chicago. Applegate seems to have acted as chief intermediary between the Chamber and the City Attorney. During the course of the negotiations with Cohen at City Hall, he also participated in a parallel set of meetings which were held at Chamber of Commerce headquarters. The purpose of these special meetings was to work out a unified organizational position on each section of the air pollution legislation. Applegate and other members of the Smoke Abatement Committee reported to the Chamber on the modifications in the draft ordinance to which Cohen had agreed. Further modifications could be suggested by the engineers and industrial executives who were present at these meetings, and recommendations were made concerning those provisions of the law which were yet to be discussed with Cohen. After disagreements among the Chamber members had been settled, Applegate and the Smoke Abatement delegation conveyed their organization's views to Cohen.

At the City Hall bargaining sessions there were seldom more than half a dozen participants, but the Chamber meetings frequently attracted as many as twenty or thirty representatives of corporate management. Dr. Cotter usually presided at these gatherings, but Applegate and Oliver Campbell, a combustion engineer for a large oil refining company, seem to have done most of the talking. Within the Chamber there was less than complete agreement concerning the proposed air pollution legislation. According to the reports of people who participated in the conferences, internal differences were greatest at the outset of the negotiations with Cohen and eight months later, when the deliberations were drawing to a close. At the start of the discussions, the representative of a small tar products company stood alone in his opposition to any kind of air pollution legislation whatsoever. The range of business opinion ran from this extreme view through a series of subtle gradations to the positions of Applegate and Campbell.

Campbell, a member of the Smoke Abatement Committee, was largely responsible for rewriting Cohen's draft ordinance so that it would meet Chamber specifications. He also seems to have been influential in modifying those specifications so as to minimize the inconsistencies between the Chamber position and Cohen's original proposal. At the Chamber's smoke abatement meetings, he attempted to persuade local industrial executives that the costs of many pollution control measures required by the proposed ordinance would be more than covered by savings in industrial expenditures for fuel. Air pollution, he argued, was often a sign of inefficient fuel combustion; by increasing the efficiency of combustion, therefore, some East Chicago industries might save money.

Campbell's frequent appeals to the principles of economy and efficiency were not the only arguments raised in support of the proposed legislation. It was also pointed out that if municipalities failed to take action against air pollution, the federal government might eventually decide to do so. Most of the businessmen seem to have preferred dealing with local rather than federal officials, and some of them saw the approval of a municipal pollution ordinance as one way to forestall federal regulation of their pollution-producing industries.

Apprehension about federal intervention and considerations of efficiency seem to have convinced many Chamber members that an air pollution control program was desirable. One month after the initiation of talks with the City Attorney, the Chamber was willing to go on record as a supporter of an air pollution ordinance, but the law would have to be "reasonable, practical, and sufficiently flexible to meet changing conditions." In the Chamber's view, Cohen's original proposal did not meet these requirements. The Chamber further insisted that "the smoke problem be recognized as one subject to solution only on a long range basis." In other words, East Chicagoans could not expect local industries to comply immediately with any new restrictions on the emission of contaminants. In some cases, large expenditures and extensive research might be required before effective methods of pollution control could be put into effect. Finally, the Chamber recommended that the pollution ordinance ought to be modeled after one that had been enacted in Chicago some years earlier.[12] The Chicago ordinance was apparently regarded as more reasonable, practical, and flexible than Cohen's proposal.

Cohen refused to scrap his own ordinance and draw up another draft based on the Chicago law. The Chicago ordinance, he believed, failed to assign sufficient responsibility to industry as a source of air contaminants. To adopt the Chicago legislation as a model would mean surrendering the essential purpose of his own proposal, the regulation of factory pollution. The Chamber representatives seem not to have pressed Cohen on this point. They agreed to use his original proposal as the basis for further negotiations, but they made it clear that his ordinance would have to be modified in several important respects to win Chamber approval.

The discussion of these modifications occupied all subsequent meetings. Most of the changes demanded by the Chamber representatives and their technical advisers would have exempted certain kinds of industrial equipment, under certain conditions, from the pollution standards that Cohen had written into his ordinance. The general argument of the members of the Chamber delegation was that it was technologically impossible, in some circumstances, for certain kinds of industrial apparatus to meet Cohen's emission standards, and that it would therefore be unreasonable to apply the standards to those pieces of machinery. Cohen was ill-equipped to resist these demands and disinclined to ignore them. He was naturally reluctant to dispute the professional judgments of the technical specialists who accompanied the Chamber's negotiating team. Cohen's only technical adviser was the Assistant City Engineer, who was not really an engineer at all but a music teacher who had earned a place in the municipal bureaucracy. Moreover, the charge that certain provisions of the proposed ordinance were "unreasonable" made Cohen particularly cautious. An allegation of unreasonableness might provide the grounds for a successful legal challenge of the pollution law in the state courts. It was just such a legal battle that he had hoped to

12 *Ibid.*, 4 March 1948.

avoid by negotiating with the Chamber representatives. He therefore agreed to most of the Chamber's revisions in the draft ordinance,[13] and by August 1948 George Applegate could report to the Chamber's board of directors that the City Attorney and the Chamber negotiating team had been able to achieve "95 per cent agreement" on the proposed legislation.[14]

A few points remained, however, on which Cohen declined to make concessions. The Chamber representatives had requested that open hearth furnaces and Bessemer converters[15] be exempted from the provisions of the dirty air ordinance. There was, they said, no feasible method for controlling the emission of air pollutants from this equipment. Cohen refused to grant these exemptions. His refusal was not based upon any independent judgment of the steel industry's technological capability to curb pollution from these sources; he simply felt that the steel industry was the largest single contributor to air pollution in East Chicago and that open hearths and Bessemer converters accounted for a major part of its emissions. To exempt these pieces of equipment from the regulations, Cohen believed, would cut the heart from his program.[16]

A final point of contention between the City Attorney and the Chamber had to do with the administration of the proposed air pollution control program. Specifically, the Chamber objected to the provision in Cohen's ordinance that excluded representatives of local industry from membership on the Air Pollution Control Advisory and Appeals Board. On this matter, too, Cohen stood firm. His reasons

[13] Among the concessions was one that exempted the infamous blast furnace slips from anti-pollution regulations.

[14] East Chicago Chamber of Commerce, Minutes of the Board of Directors meeting, 5 August 1948.

[15] Both of these devices are designed to convert pig iron, the product of blast furnace operations, into steel ingots. Open hearths account for about 90 per cent of steel production in the United States. Bessemer converters are obsolete pieces of equipment which today account for only about 2 per cent of national output. See Jean J. Schuenemann et al., *Air Pollution Aspects of the Iron and Steel Industry*, p. 78.

[16] Through he had no way of knowing it at the time, Cohen probably overestimated the contribution of Bessemer converters to East Chicago air pollution. By comparison with other sorts of steelmaking equipment, Bessemer converters cannot have been a very significant source of dirty air. There were only a few converters still in operation in East Chicago. Moreover, even today there are no known techniques for controlling pollutant emissions from Bessemer converters. As for the open hearth exemption, the Chamber's argument seems to have been somewhat less sound. Recent studies indicate that open hearths account for a substantial portion of the steel industry's contribution to community air pollution, and as early as 1950 pollution control devices were installed and successfully used on open hearth furnaces in California. One cannot be certain, of course, that the control apparatus used on the newer California models would have worked equally well for steel mills in East Chicago.

for refusing to compromise are reminiscent of the rhetoric of Jack-sonian democracy: "I've always been a little wary of complete domi-nation of local officialdom by local industry. [I wanted to] exclude industry from the Board. It would spread involvement to put private citizens on the Board—promote more citizen participation in govern-ment."

It was to private citizens that Cohen next appealed in order to gain support for his ordinance. In September, with the exemptions for Bessemer converters and open hearths still in dispute and the com-position of the Advisory and Appeals Board also a matter for disagreement, Cohen closed the City Hall negotiations. He announced to the Chamber representatives that he intended to submit a draft air pollution ordinance to the East Chicago City Council on Septem-ber 27. Five days before the target date, on September 22, Mrs. Serdel had appeared at the Board of Public Works and Safety meeting with her daughter's soiled dress, as mentioned earlier, and Cohen had been prompted to make an advance announcement of his ordinance and a plea for public support. He also announced that he had been persuaded to delay the introduction of his ordinance for two weeks, until October 11.

George Applegate and the Chamber of Commerce were responsible for the postponement. Applegate explained to a newspaper reporter that the Chamber Smoke Abatement Committee had "worked closely with the city government on this important measure, so we asked for this last chance to go over the final draft before it goes before the Council."[17] Chamber negotiators met with Cohen once during the first week in October in a last attempt to settle differences. Cohen stood firm on the major points of contention but accepted a few minor revisions in the draft ordinance.

When Cohen appeared at the City Council meeting on October 11, it was only to report that there would be another two-week delay before his ordinance could be presented. After questioning by Council members, he explained that the postponement had been ordered by a "higher authority." The councilmen were not pleased. After attacking several local corporations for their failure to control industrial pollu-tion, one of them "bellowed that he had expected the smoke ordinance at the meeting and was deeply disappointed by the delay."[18]

Mayor Migas was the "higher authority" who had ordered the

17 Hammond *Times*, 23 September 1948.
18 *Ibid.*, 12 October 1948.

second postponement. Representatives of a large industrial corporation with a plant in East Chicago had approached him to ask for the delay, and Migas had granted their request. The Mayor assured Cohen that the new postponement did not mean that East Chicago's air pollution legislation was in danger, and he promised that there would be no further delays in introducing the ordinance. According to Cohen, the Mayor did not explain why the postponement had been requested or what corporation had requested it. Some East Chicago informants, though they decline to name the firm involved, suggest that local executives of the company asked for the postponement in order to settle a difference of opinion between the corporation's East Chicago branch and its central office. The headquarters officials believed that the East Chicago Chamber of Commerce—and their own East Chicago executives—had conceded too much to Loyd Cohen on the matter of air pollution control. The local managers sought to gain time to placate their superiors. No industrial representatives approached Cohen to ask for further changes in the draft legislation.

On October 25 Cohen finally submitted his ordinance to the Council. He thanked George Applegate and the Chamber committee for their assistance in drafting the law, but he acknowledged that the Chamber negotiators were not completely satisfied with his own version. To the Council members, Cohen explained that the uneasy agreement which existed between the city administration and local industry might be disrupted by incautious amendment of the air pollution legislation.[19] East Chicago's city councilmen seem to have heeded Cohen's warning. During the three months in which they considered the proposal, they made only one change in the draft that Cohen had submitted to them. The change had to do with installation specifications for coal-burning furnaces—not a matter of any great importance to local industries, but one that seems to have aroused the concern of apartment house owners, who had not been parties to the negotiations between Cohen and the Chamber. In general, the councilmen seem to have been more interested in understanding the provisions of the air pollution bill than in changing them. In public hearings before the Council's Health and Morals Committee, Cohen and representatives of local industry attempted to explain the pollution control regulations to the Committee members and to East Chicago residents who raised questions concerning the ordinance.

[19] *Ibid.*, 26 October 1948.

By February 1949 the Health and Morals Committee had completed its consideration of the dirty air bill, and the ordinance reached the Council floor. Discussion was brief and did not touch at all on the substance of the law. The councilmen were concerned about the kinds of qualifications that would be required of appointees to the post of air pollution control inspector—whether or not the inspector would have to be a graduate engineer. Having expressed themselves on this point, they unanimously approved the air pollution control ordinance.

Epilogue

East Chicago's city administration almost immediately began to prepare for the enforcement of the dirty air law. Charles Molnar, the assistant city engineer, was appointed air pollution inspector, and within a few months he initiated the first annual round of inspections and fee collections. But Molnar never completed the certification program. Local industries refused to pay their fees for certificates of operation and notified the city administration that they would continue to withhold the fees so long as the Pollution Inspector continued to "misinterpret" the air pollution law. Molnar, they argued, had insisted on charging inspection fees for pieces of industrial equipment that were clearly not within the scope of the inspection program authorized by the new ordinance. Under public pressure to deal sternly with the local industrial corporations, he had attempted to apply the pollution regulations to refrigeration equipment, air conditioners, exhaust fans, septic tanks, and other items on the grounds that each of these installations was likely to "cause the issuance of air contaminants."

Once again, the Chamber of Commerce Smoke Abatement Committee entered into negotiations with representatives of the city administration—the Mayor, the Pollution Inspector, and the Air Pollution Control Advisory and Appeals Board—and by the next October an agreement was finally reached concerning the enforcement of the dirty air ordinance. Under the terms of the compromise, Molnar was to exempt thirty-two items of equipment from the annual air pollution inspections. For their part, the industrial managers agreed to pay their inspection fees in full for 1950, but not for 1949.[20]

[20] East Chicago Chamber of Commerce, memorandum to membership, 27 October 1950.

Once under way, East Chicago's pollution control program turned out to be somewhat different from the one that Loyd Cohen had envisioned. Under Mayor Migas' successor, a new pollution control inspector established more peaceful relations with local industry than Charles Molnar had been able to achieve. One consequence of this amity was to deprive the Air Pollution Control Advisory and Appeals Board of its chief function. Under the new regime, few East Chicago businessmen felt the need to appeal to the Board, and the Pollution Control Inspector almost never asked for its advice. There was also a change in the scope of the pollution control program. An informal agreement between the Inspector and local businessmen exempted from the pollution standards, but not from the certification fees, all pieces of equipment installed prior to the enactment of the dirty air ordinance.

In spite of this important restriction, it appears that East Chicago's efforts at cleaning the air achieved a partial, if temporary, success. Pollution data show a steady and substantial decline in suspended particulates in the city from 1957 through 1961. In 1962, however, the downward trend was reversed. The turning point coincided with the adoption of a new steelmaking technique at one of the East Chicago mills, a method known to generate relatively heavy particulate emissions.[21] By 1965, the latest year for which pollution data are available, East Chicago particulate rates were approaching their 1957 level.

GARY HOLDS ITS BREATH

Political Background

The city of Gary was not roused to action by its neighbor's anti-pollution efforts. It was not until late 1955—almost seven years after East Chicago enacted its dirty air ordinance—that the matter of air pollution finally surfaced as a political issue in Gary. Having made its entry into the city's political life, it became snared in a political situation less congenial to its growth than the one that existed in East Chicago during the late 1940's.

In Gary, as in East Chicago, the city administration was intimately connected with the machinery of the Democratic Party. No legal barriers separated the municipal from the partisan bureaucracy, but,

[21] Schuenemann, *Air Pollution Aspects of the Iron and Steel Industry*, pp. 49–50.

unlike East Chicago, the Democratic Party was not a precarious coalition of independent ethnic groups. By 1955 it was well on its way to becoming a tightly organized political instrument. At the heart of the Party was an organization called the Club Sar, an inter-ethnic coalition of eastern and southern Europeans which began to function in local politics during the 1930's. In 1951 the Club took custody of both the Democratic organization and the city administration. Club Sar's mayoral candidate, Peter Mandich, drew about 35 per cent of the vote in that year's Democratic primary, more than any of the other seven mayoral candidates, and went on to win the general election. Four years later, when Mandich ran for re-election, he received a substantially larger share of the primary vote—about 53 per cent. In 1959 he traded offices with George Chacharis, the founder of Club Sar, who was then serving as county sheriff. Chacharis carried the Democratic primary with more than 80 per cent of the vote, demonstrating that Club Sar had the Democratic organization well in hand.

Between 1951 and 1959 Gary's Democratic Party was undergoing an important transformation whose end product would be a unified political organization. During the same period, other changes were also disturbing the stability of local public affairs. Rapid population growth imposed an expanding burden upon local public facilities. Existing streets and parking spaces were no longer sufficient to the transportation needs of Gary's residents, and existing public housing units could not meet the needs of low-income residents. Changes in the composition of the town's population, however, seem to have raised problems that were even more serious than those produced by population growth alone. During the 1950's an increase in the proportion of Negro residents in Gary coincided with the gradual emergence of racial conflicts in local politics. The race issue, when it could not be avoided, was handled gingerly, sometimes without mentioning race at all. Departures from this discreet practice were generally unacceptable to Gary's civic leaders. Undisguised debate about racial problems was apparently not considered a legitimate form of political discussion. On one occasion, for example, a debate between white and Negro members of the City Council concerning "inefficiency" in the distribution of occupants among public housing projects was disrupted by a newly elected white councilman who asserted that racial segregation, not administrative "efficiency," was actually the subject of the discussion. He went on to accuse the Gary

Housing Authority of practicing racial discrimination, and the chairman of the Authority promptly filed a slander suit against him. The prospective defendant was Milton Roth, a young Gary attorney who became a member of the City Council in 1955. During his career as an elected official, which was brief, Roth regularly assumed the political role of an issue-raiser. He was seldom able to contribute much to the resolution of these issues: his time in office was too short, his influence too small, and, moreover, the issues that attracted him were not easily resolved, at least not in Gary. They were almost all politically delicate or risky topics—racial discrimination, alleged abuses in the distribution of municipal patronage, water fluoridation (a controversial matter almost everywhere), and air pollution (a subject of particular delicacy in Gary).

Roth's attempts to place these matters on Gary's political agenda were not calculated to increase his popularity among the town's Democratic leaders. In fact, very few of his political activities were likely to win him friends within the Democratic organization. He ran for the City Council in 1955 without party endorsement. In order to win his at-large seat, he had to displace one of the regulars from the Democratic ticket, and he accomplished this in the party primary. Once elected, he joined with two other likeminded councilmen in an unsuccessful effort to win control of committee assignments from representatives of the Club Sar faction, who were than a majority within the Council.

Perhaps even more than Loyd Cohen, Roth was a political figure set apart from his town's major partisan organization. While Cohen merely refrained from participation in most Democratic Party activities, Roth actively opposed the Democratic organization on a number of occasions. It was because of his unfriendliness to the Party, says Roth, that he lost his City Council seat in the 1959 primary—the same election in which Club Sar's mayoral candidate captured more than 80 per cent of the Democratic vote. Roth's electoral support in both of his campaigns came, not from the network of regular Democratic precinct captains but from a group of about thirty people whom he describes as Gary's "liberal wing" and from the League of Women Voters. His sources of support distinguished him from most of Gary's Democratic politicians, as did his organizational affiliations. He was the president of the Gary chapter of the United World Federalists, a member of the ACLU, and a member of the NAACP, from which he received an award in 1957 for his work in race relations.

Raising the Issue

The air pollution problem was an issue in Milton Roth's first campaign for a City Council seat but not in the campaigns of the other candidates for municipal office. The subject was suggested to him by a friend of his parents as one likely to attract the attention of the electorate. Roth followed this advice and mentioned the air pollution problem in several campaign speeches. He advanced no specific remedies but merely cited the obvious severity of the problem and promised that, if elected, he would try to do something about it.

Whether his discussion of dirty air actually won any support among the voters Roth could not be certain. In fact, it was difficult for him to determine whether his own expression of concern about dirty air corresponded to any widespread citizen interest in the problem. The city administration had provided no special forum for the expression of residents' complaints. Like East Chicago, Gary had a Board of Public Works and Safety, but its members did not see it as one of their regular responsibilities to hear citizen grievances. If Gary residents did wish to complain about dirty air prior to 1959, therefore, it would have been relatively difficult for them to make their complaints public. Their dissatisfaction with local air quality would not have been easily detected by many of Gary's civic leaders and public officials. Unlike Loyd Cohen, therefore, Roth launched his antipollution campaign without visible and repeated assurances that local residents were seriously concerned about dirty air.

In 1956 Roth took the first step toward fulfilling his campaign promise to do something about air pollution. He wrote a letter to U.S. Steel. In it, he noted that he was concerned about Gary's dirty air problem, and he inquired what the company planned to do about air pollution. A prompt and polite reply came back in which a company representative told him that U.S. Steel recognized the need to do something about air pollution and was trying to devise methods and equipment for reducing the emission of pollutants from steel mills. A U.S. Steel official soon paid a personal visit to Roth's law office. He was Granville Howell, an assistant to the company's executive vice-president for operations. Howell was in charge of U.S. Steel's activities in matters of air and water pollution control. A former resident of Gary, he already knew the Roth family, and members of his own family still lived in the city. Howell's sister, in fact, was the friend who originally suggested that Roth should make a campaign issue of the air pollution problem.

Howell's visit was both a social and an official call. As a representative of his company, he reaffirmed its recognition that the air pollution problem merited serious attention. U.S. Steel, he said, would be willing to cooperate in any "reasonable" program of pollution control that the city of Gary might choose to adopt. The alternative to cooperation with local authorities, he said, might be strict federal regulation, something that the company would like to avoid. Roth need not be concerned, therefore; that U.S. Steel would actively oppose his pollution control proposals. Of course, the company's cooperation would not bring an immediate solution to local dirty air problems. Pollution control would be an expensive and technically difficult enterprise, and the company's contribution to any pollution abatement drive would therefore have to be "programmed"—spread out over a number of years. Just how many years Howell did not say, but in a public statement made some time after his conversation with Roth, he indicated that about twenty-five years would be sufficient for achieving full pollution control at his company's Gary mill.[22] Finally, Howell told Roth that U.S. Steel could not be expected to take the initiative in Gary's pollution control campaign. The company would have to be prodded into activity. Once Gary had its pollution control ordinance, U.S. Steel would willingly cooperate with city officials, but until then Roth could expect no active assistance from the corporation.

In several respects, Howell's remarks were a remarkably faithful restatement of the policies that had guided U.S. Steel during the regime of Judge Elbert Gary. The Judge, hoping to avoid federal antitrust proceedings against his corporation, had consistently attempted to convince both the public and the government that U.S. Steel was one of the "good trusts." It was good, said Gary, because its managers had good intentions. They had no disposition to behave like monopolists. Though they had plentiful opportunities for corporate expansion and the resources to exploit them, they would, the Judge promised, exercise self-restraint. If federal authorities nevertheless saw fit to impose restrictions upon the corporation's activities, U.S. Steel's managers would make no attempt to resist the will of the government. The company was a potential tyrant which had chosen

[22] Gary *Post-Tribune*, 28 September 1962.

not to exercise its capacity for domination. By Gary's account, it was a benign, pliable, and passive giant.[23] This was the gist of the message that Granville Howell later brought to Milton Roth.

The policy of corporate quietism was not new to Gary. Even as U.S. Steel executives were giving the city its name, its streets, and its first buildings, they were determined not to become the barons of a company town. The unpleasant experiences of the Pullman Company at its community in Illinois had convinced U.S. Steel that it was inadvisable to take an active role in the direction of local affairs. An attempt to manage the public business of Gary might bring trouble to a corporation that was doing its best to avoid both trouble and the public attention that was sure to follow it.[24] Long after the era of Judge Gary, U.S. Steel remained faithful to the principle of noninterference in local politics. In 1963, when the civil rights issue boiled up in Birmingham, Alabama, U.S. Steel, the city's largest employer, was urged to use its enormous economic power to achieve a rapprochement between the races. Roger Blough, the corporation president, announced that U.S. Steel would not intervene in the affairs of Birmingham. The notion that a company should "attempt to have its own ideas of what is right for the community enforced upon that community by some sort of economic means" was, he said, "repugnant" to him and to the other officers of the corporation.[25] Once again, U.S. Steel elected to take a passive role in community politics.

Assured that the company would adhere to a similar policy in matters of air pollution control, Milton Roth proceeded with his attempt to launch an anti-pollution campaign in Gary. In late March 1956 he announced publicly that he would soon be taking preliminary steps to promote municipal action on the dirty air problem. On the same day that Roth issued his statement, Roger Blough happened to be paying a routine visit to the Gary mill. At a press conference a local reporter asked him what U.S. Steel planned to do about the city's air pollution problem. Blough answered that the company intended to apply the lessons that had been learned from Pittsburgh's successful smoke abatement program to the solution of Gary's pollution problem. The Pittsburgh findings, he said, showed that the

[23] Ida Tarbell, *The Life of Elbert H. Gary*, pp. 124, 137, 212; Gertrude Schroeder, *The Growth of Major Steel Companies*, pp. 44–45.

[24] Charles N. Glaab and A. Theodore Brown, *History of Urban America*, pp. 275–77.

[25] *U.S. News and World Report*, 11 November 1963.

city's "main troubles stemmed, not from the mills, but from coal-fired home furnaces."[26]

Blough's comments underlined those of Granville Howell. If home furnaces, and not steel industry operations, were the chief sources of air pollution, then there was no need for the steel industry to take the initiative in cleaning the atmosphere. Responsibility for battling air pollution lay primarily with local homeowners. The "Pittsburgh findings" appeared to justify the steel industry's unwillingness to take the lead in anti-pollution efforts. In short, U.S. Steel seemed to be conducting itself much as Granville Howell had said it would.

The effect of Blough's statement was to raise some doubts concerning the nature of Gary's air pollution problem. Roth's original inquiry to U.S. Steel had assumed that the major source of local pollution was the company mill. Blough suggested that the problem originated elsewhere. Roth's first proposal concerning the dirty air problem was therefore designed to resolve this difference of opinion. He recommended that the city of Gary should commission a study of local pollution in order to determine its sources and severity. Before formally submitting his proposal, Roth discussed it with Mayor Mandich. The Mayor, Roth recalls, was not opposed to an air pollution study, but he was not enthusiastic about it. He observed that pollution control might be a "nice idea," but he added that as long as he saw smoke issuing from the stacks at the steel mill, he knew that Gary was prosperous. Roth left the conference with the impression that, like U.S. Steel, the city administration would not obstruct his activities on behalf of pollution control.

Roth had already selected a research organization to conduct the pollution survey. From a friend he learned that the Armour Research Institute, an affiliate of the Illinois Institute of Technology, was experienced in such studies and might be willing to undertake the investigation. After his conversation with Mayor Mandich, Roth contacted the Armour Institute in Chicago, explained to Institute officials what it was that he wanted, and received a promise of cooperation. The cost of a Gary survey, he was told, would be about ten thousand dollars, and it would take from nine to eighteen months. The Institute would submit a formal research proposal to Mayor Mandich as soon as possible. Once the Mayor approved the prospectus and the City Council appropriated funds for the survey, work would begin. It was

26 Gary *Post-Tribune*, 25 March 1956.

agreed that during the course of the study a special committee of Gary citizens would represent the city in dealings with the Institute. Roth informed Mayor Mandich of his progress, and in midsummer the Institute sent its proposal to Gary. By mid-October the Mayor had still not responded. Roth wrote to the Armour officials explaining that the Mayor had been preoccupied with the enactment of legislation creating municipal parking lots but would soon be free to make his decision. A month later Mandich announced the proposal and informed citizens of the forthcoming study. He claimed no part in arranging for the survey: all the credit, he said, belonged to Milton Roth.[27] Perhaps the Mayor's statement was simply an act of political generosity to a sometime enemy, but one possible consequence of his magnanimity, unnoticed at the time, was to disassociate himself and his administration from the study and from the anti-pollution effort that it represented. By giving all credit for the pollution study to Milton Roth, the Mayor avoided taking a public position on the air pollution issue.

Less than a week after securing the Mayor's acquiescence, Roth attempted to extract the ten thousand dollars for the study from the City Council. When he introduced a resolution that would provide the necessary money, it was defeated. The rejection of the resolution, the Council president explained, did not signify that the Council was opposed to the conduct of an air pollution study. The problem, he said, was that Roth had submitted his resolution verbally, and "in a matter of such import" the Council felt that legislation ought to be introduced in writing.[28] But Roth has a different explanation for his initial defeat: "Whatever originated with me had a good chance of not winning." He came to the next Council meeting armed with a written version of his resolution. It was approved without a dissenting vote, but almost two months passed before work began on the pollution survey. Mayor Mandich, said the Gary *Post-Tribune*, was responsible for this interval of inactivity. He had been slow appointing a committee to act on the city's behalf in dealing with the Armour Institute.[29] Once the town's representatives had been selected, the Armour investigators began their work almost immediately. Dustfall collectors were installed at six locations around the city. From the roof of the Hotel Gary, an Armour staff member made smoke sightings and measurements of wind velocity and direction. Together with

27 *Ibid.*, 15 November 1956.
28 *Ibid.*, 21 November 1956.
29 *Ibid.*, 5 February 1957.

the smoke, wind, and dustfall findings, information from a land use survey of the town helped the investigators to determine the sources of local air pollution. After eighteen months of study, the necessary data had been collected, and the Institute submitted its final report to the Mayor.

The survey's most notable finding was that "only about half" of the airborne dust and smoke in Gary originated at U.S. Steel's mill. The estimate was founded upon four pieces of evidence: (1) only northerly winds carried mill smoke over the city, and northerly winds blew only about half the time; (2) at low wind velocities, mill smoke did not reach groundlevel—it rose above the city and dispersed; (3) even with high-velocity, northerly winds, mill smoke seldom covered more than a quarter of the city; and (4) non-industrial polluters—home furnaces, automobiles, and incinerators—had been observed to produce a lasting haze over parts of the city. The report did not reveal the reasoning which led the investigators from these items of evidence to their conclusions about U.S. Steel's contribution to local dirty air, but it spared no detail in its recommendations for the solution of that problem. It even suggested how much the city ought to pay a pollution control officer and what should be spent to equip him.[30]

The pollution control program outlined for Gary was, in some respects, quite similar to the one already adopted in East Chicago. The maximum emission standards suggested were almost identical to the ones in East Chicago's pollution ordinance. But there were also some notable differences. The Armour proposal suggested special exemptions from the pollution standards for certain kinds of industrial equipment. The exemptions included some which Loyd Cohen had been unwilling to grant and others that East Chicago industrialists had not even requested. Almost all of the exceptions recommended in the Armour report were intended to ease the impact of pollution restrictions upon "metallurgical processes." The investigators noted that it might be difficult or impossible for some of these processes to meet the recommended standards, though future technological developments might improve their performance. To demand immediate compliance with all pollution requirements

can cause more harm than benefit. On the other hand, to lower all standards to the level attainable by this industry is also unrealistic. It would waste the capacity for improvement of a considerable sector of Gary industry and citizens. Thus, it is suggested that for a period

[30] Armour Research Institute, "Air Pollution Survey of Gary, Indiana."

of about 10 years the following existing metallurgical processes be exempted from the suggested provisions: open hearth furnaces, blast furnaces, Bessemer furnaces, ferrous foundries, driers, kilns, and roasters.[31]

In other words, U.S. Steel was to be virtually immune from regulation for a decade, but Gary's smaller industries and homeowners were to abide by the dirty air regulations. Like Cohen's program, the Armour proposal provided for an advisory committee to oversee the activities of the local pollution control officer, but while Cohen had taken care to exclude industry representatives from the advisory board, the Armour Institute wanted to assure that the members of the board were people who might "enjoy the confidence" of both "the public and industry."[32]

Some Gary residents, among them a few members of the special committee appointed by Mayor Mandich, were not entirely convinced by the Armour report or satisfied with its recommendations. Some found it difficult to believe that U.S. Steel contributed "only about half" of the pollutants in Gary's air. The unscientific evidence of sight and smell seemed to support a higher estimate. An examination of the Armour recommendations convinced at least one observer that the Institute "had the interests of U.S. Steel closer to its heart than the interests of Gary." Such skepticism toward the Institute's work was expressed in other cities as well. While the Armour investigators were completing their survey in Gary, the Institute and its parent institution, the Illinois Institute of Technology, were helping to draft an air pollution ordinance for Chicago. Critics of the Chicago law subsequently charged that the investigators were excessively concerned about the welfare of local industries:

The city's pollution control ordinance was drafted by scientists at the Illinois Institute of Technology. IIT is a school that is supported heavily by major industries with research grants—the steel, oil and chemical industries in particular.

It is not surprising, therefore, that IIT produced a document that was not only friendly to industry but left loopholes that permitted industries to delay air pollution control expenditures for many years.[33]

In Gary, as in Chicago, a few citizens believed that their town had

[31] *Ibid.*, p. 27.
[32] Gary *Post-Tribune*, 5 October 1958.
[33] Jay McMullen, "We Get the Big Runaround on Air Pollution Control," Chicago *Sun-Times*, 1 January 1968.

been made the victim of an academic-industrial complex. But other less sinister explanations might account for the Armour Institute's solicitous handling of possible industrial objections to air pollution control. Its responsiveness to the presumed interests of industry need not have been prompted by its own interest in lucrative grants and research contracts. The Institute investigators may have perceived that no pollution control program could be enacted in Gary without the acquiescence of local manufacturers, particularly U.S. Steel, and may have drawn up their recommendations with an eye to securing this acquiescence.

Whatever the explanation, it is clear that the Institute was far less firm with local industries than Loyd Cohen had been, and it is fairly certain that the Armour investigators underestimated U.S. Steel's share in the dirty air problem. More recent studies indicate that the steel industry's contribution to community air pollution is enormous relative to the contributions of home furnaces, automobiles, and refuse disposal. On an average winter day in a northern city, 35,500 coal-burning home furnaces—certainly many more than Gary had in 1958—release only about as much particulate matter as a battery of thirteen open hearth furnaces. (At its plant in Gary U.S. Steel had fifty-five open hearth furnaces). A quarter of a million homeowners burning rubbish in open fires would generate only slightly more particulate matter than four blast furnaces with rudimentary pollution control equipment. (U.S. Steel had twelve blast furnaces at its Gary works.)[34]

In spite of local reservations about the Armour report, Roth solicited the Institute's assistance during the next stage of his anti-pollution campaign. In February 1959, about three months after the completion of the pollution survey, he announced that he was attempting to draft a pollution control ordinance for Gary. The law was "highly technical and difficult to write," and it might be some time before he would have a final draft ready for submission to the City Council.[35] Roth relied on Pittsburgh's pollution ordinance as a legislative model and on the experts at the Armour Institute for technical advice. For political and moral support, there was the League of Women Voters, which had formed an air pollution study

[34] Schuenemann, *Air Pollution Aspects of the Iron and Steel Industry*, pp. 80–81; American Iron and Steel Institute, *Directory of Iron and Steel Works in the United States and Canada*, pp. 169–70.
[35] Quoted in Gary *Post-Tribune*, 5 February 1959.

committee not long after the completion of the Armour survey. By letter and telephone, the ladies of the League urged Mayor Mandich and members of the City Council to take action against the local dirty air problem, but their efforts had no noticeable effect. When Roth finally submitted his ordinance to the Council shortly before the 1959 elections, it was referred to a committee from which it never again emerged. Roth himself fared no better at the hands of the voters, and the elections ended his career as a member of the City Council.

Raising the Issue: A Second Attempt

For more than a year Gary's air seems to have been the object of no action save that of inhaling and exhaling, but early in 1961 one local resident attempted to take up the job that Roth had left unfinished. Albert Gavit, Jr., chairman of the Civic Improvement Committee of the Junior Chamber of Commerce, suggested to his fellow Jaycees that their organization ought to select the dirty air problem as the target for one of its community service projects. The suggestion was accepted, and Gavit himself led the subsequent effort to organize public support for dirty air legislation.

Gavit was a young attorney newly launched on his career and, like Roth, was a man in search of an issue. Roth had been looking for something that would enliven his campaign for public office and perhaps improve his chances for success. Gavit was a candidate for no office, but he needed a political issue in order to gain recognition from Gary's established civic activists. Because he was young and had been educated away from home at a military school, Gavit was not well known to the business and professional men who had grown up in Gary, men who now presided over the town's civic and fraternal organizations and sat on its citizens' committees. Like Roth, he was a political outsider. By "sponsoring" an issue, Gavit believed that he might establish a reputation as a willing and capable participant in civic affairs. He selected air pollution as the vehicle for his entry into public life because he had a serious personal interest in it. He and other members of his family had suffered from severe respiratory disorders, and he thought that polluted air might have been responsible for producing these illnesses.

Gavit began his anti-pollution campaign quietly. He wrote to the Armour Institute and asked whether any effort had been made to incorporate the recommendations of the Gary pollution study in a draft air pollution ordinance. The Institute answered that it was not permitted to release such information to private citizens and suggested that he direct his inquiry to the city administration. Gavit also wrote to U.S. Steel, inquiring whether the company intended to take any action on the local pollution problem. Once again, Granville Howell was dispatched to Gary. His conversation with Gavit was nearly identical to his talk five years earlier with Milton Roth. He assured Gavit that his corporation was concerned about dirty air and would welcome any "reasonable" attempt by the city to cope with the pollution problem, but no U.S. Steel assistance would be forthcoming in setting up or putting into force a pollution program.

Having made no progress with U.S. Steel or the Armour Institute, Gavit next sought to confront the city administration with some evidence of widespread public support for the enactment of an air pollution ordinance. With the assistance of the League of Women Voters, he circulated a petition among civic organizations and service clubs. It asked the Mayor to justify the expenditure of public funds on the Armour study by sponsoring municipal legislation that would embody some of the Armour recommendations. Organizational endorsements of the petition were plentiful, but there were some significant omissions from the list of signers, the most notable of which was the Gary Chamber of Commerce, whose officers declined to endorse the petition.

Supported by this uncertain mandate, Gavit demanded that Mayor George Chacharis take at least some steps toward the drafting of an air pollution ordinance. The Mayor responded by announcing that he had just requested the Armour Institute to draw up a dirty air law for Gary. The legislation, he said, would be ready in just two weeks.[36] Six months later there was still no word on the ordinance, and Gavit inquired what had become of the Armour Institute's recommendations. Mayor Chacharis replied that he was "pressing" the Institute for a piece of legislation and added that he expected to have a draft ordinance in about a week. City Hall observers remained pessimistic. According to the Gary *Post-Tribune*, they were convinced that Gavit's anti-pollution effort had exposed a lack of public interest in the problem.[37]

[36] *Ibid.*, 3 March 1961.
[37] *Ibid.*, 22 September 1961.

It was more than a year before Mayor Chacharis had another public statement to make concerning Gary's forthcoming pollution ordinance. This mayoral announcement was prompted not by Gavit but by the Indiana state legislature. In 1961 the legislature enacted a bill which empowered state officials to initiate legal proceedings against any municipality that failed to take appropriate action against a local air pollution problem. The law was to become effective on January 1, 1963. In September 1962 a conference was held at Purdue University at which local officials and pollution experts discussed the new state program. Granville Howell was the keynote speaker. His company's major reservation concerning the Indiana law, he said, was that "it does not wish to install the vastly expensive pollution control machinery in its sprawling Gary complex all at the same time." Howell estimated that about twenty-five years would be sufficient time for his corporation to solve its pollution problems. He added that "community air pollution problems are individual in nature— each differing from another. He said that local interests should be given a chance to reach a solution without outside interference."[38]

A few weeks later Mayor Chacharis appeared to endorse Howell's statement when he noted, in a newspaper interview, that pollution conditions in Gary were complex and required long study. He did not feel that "the city should be rushed into action that might prove unwise." Gary's pollution problem presented difficulties that other cities did not face. To the Mayor, the most important of these difficulties was one that "revolves around the fact that U.S. Steel plants here, which are major contributors to the city's economy, are also major contributors to its air pollution." Chacharis said that he "would not want to damage the steel company by imposing a too-stringent pollution ordinance." According to the Mayor, the city administration would shortly produce a pollution law that was appropriate to Gary's special circumstances.[39]

It is difficult to determine exactly what actions city officials had been taking with respect to the air pollution problem. People who would presumably have been involved in Chacharis' announced efforts to draft a dirty air ordinance—staff members at the Armour Institute and some city employees—were either not available for interviews or could not recall any attempt made by the Chacharis administration to draw up an air pollution law. A few suggested that there really

[38] Quoted in *ibid.*, 28 September 1962.
[39] *Ibid.*, 17 October 1962.

had been no such attempt. Mayor Chacharis did not have the chance to substantiate his assertion by producing a draft ordinance. In the fall of 1962 he was indicted for failing to pay federal income taxes on $250,000 in kickbacks from contractors doing business with the city. He resigned from office, and before the winter was over, the founder of the Club Sar was on his way to a federal penitentiary in Michigan.

Raising the Issue: A Successful Attempt

The Mayor's departure left the city government and the local Democratic organization in temporary disarray. A new mayor, John Visclosky, moved up from his post as city comptroller. He was soon approached by Chris Angelidis, a sanitary engineer employed in the city Health Department, who asked permission to write an air pollution ordinance for Gary. Visclosky gave his blessing to the project, and Angelidis rapidly put together the draft. He was well prepared for the job. Before joining the Health Department, Angelidis had been employed by the Inland Steel Company at its East Chicago mill, where he specialized in the management of waste control and disposal processes, including air pollution control. He drew on this experience and on the pollution ordinances of Pittsburgh and Chicago[40] in preparing his legislation. The recommendations of the Armour study played only a small part in the draft ordinance, the advice of U.S. Steel officials almost none at all. Angelidis did not reject the recommendations of industry representatives; they did not have any recommendations to make. On those few occasions when he discussed the air pollution legislation with U.S. Steel officials, Angelidis found them "lethargic," disinclined to advance any suggestions for the revision of his draft. According to Angelidis, they seemed content to let him write the ordinance as he saw fit.

The ordinance that he saw fit to write, however, was in large measure tailored to the interests of U.S. Steel. The reticence of the industrial executives concerning their company's policy preferences did not prevent Angelidis from estimating what those preferences might be and taking them into account. U.S. Steel therefore influenced the content of the pollution ordinance without taking any action on it, and thus defied the pluralist dictum that political power belongs to

---

[40] The Chicago ordinance on which Angelidis relied was not the one that the East Chicago Chamber of Commerce had urged Loyd Cohen to adopt.

political actors. Though the company did not act, Angelidis consciously adapted his anti-pollution proposal so that it would not
offend the interests of U.S. Steel. Perhaps the "lethargy" of the
corporation managers was an indication that Angelidis had correctly
anticipated their objections and had managed to sidestep potential
areas of conflict. The draft ordinance that resulted from Angelidis'
cautious strategy was weaker, he says, than the one he would have
liked to write, but he believed that, faced with stringent pollution
regulations, U.S. Steel's passive acquiescence might change to stub-
born resistance or even active opposition. The dangers of corporate
intractability, he believed, would be greatest when the time came for
enforcement. After the law had been approved and had passed into
the hands of municipal administrators, he thought, the company's
ability to resist regulation would increase, while the interest of the
citizens, momentarily aroused by events surrounding the enactment
of the ordinance, would die down. Gary's pollution control officer
would then find himself virtually alone in his attempt to influence
the actions of a giant corporation.[41] If U.S. Steel chose to ignore his
directives, he would not be likely to subdue the corporation with
threats and punishments. The most serious sanction at his disposal,
shutting down industrial installations that refused to comply with
anti-pollution directives, could hardly be used against Gary's largest
employer. If his attempts to reduce steel industry pollution were thus
frustrated, it would also be difficult to make progress against pollutants from home furnaces and incinerators. Residents would not
readily comply with dirty air regulations if they knew that U.S. Steel
continued to foul the air uninhibited by them. The dirty air program,
thought Angelidis, would then be worthless. Once Gary had an anti-
pollution program, he hoped, it might be possible to strengthen the
dirty air regulations. Several provisions of his ordinance allowed for
a gradual stiffening of pollution restrictions, and there was always
the possibility that, after enactment, the regulations might be made
more rigorous by amendments. Subsequent events showed that
Angelidis' hope for a strengthened pollution program was well
founded, but he perceived no hope for initiating such a program in
1962. The choice, as he saw it, was between timid regulation and no
regulation at all.

[41] Angelidis' fears are confirmed by several studies of government regulation of
business: see, for example, Marver Bernstein, *Regulating Business by Independent
Commission.*

The ordinance that Angelidis drafted was, therefore, less ambitious, in certain important respects, than the one that had been enacted in East Chicago almost thirteen years carliei. Much existing industrial equipment was, for all practical purposes, excluded from the scope of the regulatory program. Open hearth furnaces, Bessemer converters, sintering plants,[42] and electric furnaces currently in operating condition were all immune from the maximum emission limits. The ordinance required only that the operation of these existing pieces of equipment be "consistent with normal good operating practice." Bessemer converters and sintering plants that were installed after the enactment of the law were to continue to operate under this lenient standard.

The ordinance was not so lenient where other sorts of steelmaking equipment were concerned, however. Special restrictions upon the emission of particulates from blast furnaces and newly constructed open hearths were more demanding than the emission standards that East Chicago had adopted, and Angelidis recommended a smoke restriction for coke ovens that was somewhat more rigorous than the East Chicago smoke regulation. The general smoke and particulate standards that Angelidis wrote into his ordinance were also a bit more restrictive than the East Chicago regulations.[43]

Angelidis felt that he could afford to tax the agreeability of the steel industry with these special demands because they had been made before—and accepted. In 1960 Allegheny County, Pennsylvania, passed a pollution law that covered the Pittsburgh area, where U.S. Steel maintained a number of industrial installations, and it was the company's acquiescence in this legislation that now emboldened Angelidis. The provisions of his ordinance that would impose restrictions upon blast furnaces and new open hearths were copied almost word for word from the Allegheny County law. What the company had agreed to accept in Pittsburgh, it could hardly reject in Gary. Perhaps it was Angelidis' reliance upon the Allegheny County pollution law that disarmed the steel company. This, at least, would be one way to account for the fact that U.S. Steel registered no audible objection to any of the pollution restrictions while the Gary ordinance

[42] Sintering plants are enclosed conveyor belts on which iron ore is heated before it goes to a blast furnace. The purpose of sintering is to fuse small pieces of ore and ore dust into larger chunks that are suitable for heating in blast furnaces.

[43] The East Chicago ordinance prohibited particulate emissions greater than 0.85 pounds per thousand pounds of gas released into the atmosphere. The Gary standard was 0.65 pounds.

was being drafted or afterward, when it was before the City Council. Other factors may also have helped to restrain the company, however. There was the new Indiana state pollution law scheduled to go into effect at the beginning of 1963, with its provision for state intervention in the handling of local pollution problems. U.S. Steel may have seen the Angelidis ordinance as a welcome instrument for fending off state officials. There was also a U.S. Public Health Service study, released just a little more than two weeks before the draft ordinance was presented to the City Council, which reported that Gary's air was more heavily burdened with suspended particulates than any of the other fifty-nine urban atmospheres tested. The finding provoked a mild outburst of journalistic consternation on the editorial page of the Gary *Post-Tribune*,[44] and perhaps this manifestation of public concern about dirty air helped to convince U.S. Steel that, for the present, it ought to remain silent on the matter of air pollution, so as to avoid adding to the political salience of the issue.

The appearance of the Public Health Service report may also have sharpened the steel executives' apprehension concerning the possibility of federal participation in the attack on local air pollution. Even as Gary's political leaders were deliberating over the Angelidis ordinance, other political leaders at the National Air Pollution Conference in Washington and within the Kennedy administration were discussing the possibility of a significant federal role in the enforcement of pollution regulations.[45] Here again was a threat of "outside interference" that could deprive "local interests" of the chance to achieve a solution to local air pollution problems. Outside interference could also deprive some local interests of much of their influence. It is likely, for example, that the power of U.S. Steel would be somewhat diluted if the local air pollution issue were to become a state political issue, and it would be diluted still further if the debate were transferred to the national political arena. U.S. Steel preferred to settle the matter at the local level, as Granville Howell made clear. An officer of the local Chamber of Commerce stated the preference for local decisionmaking more bluntly than Howell. Industry wanted the pollution control program to be housed within the Gary city government, he said, "because that's where we can get at it." It was therefore important for U.S. Steel to control the scope of the dirty air

[44] Gary *Post-Tribune*, 15 December 1962.
[45] See James L. Sundquist, *Politics and Policy: The Eisenhower, Kennedy, and Johnson Years*, pp. 351–55.

debate, to keep it within the limits of the local political system.[46] The company's reticence on this subject may have been one way to minimize conflict over air pollution and so keep the issue within bounds.

Gary adopted its own local solution to the dirty air problem with uncharacteristic haste. Late in December 1962 the Angelidis ordinance came before the City Council. Its arrival produced no debate. No amendments were offered. It was approved almost immediately— just three days before the Indiana state pollution law was to become effective. Because of the Council's quick work, Gary's pollution problem remained a local issue, at least for the time being.

The Aftermath: Negotiations

Gary's pollution law did not become effective until more than a year after its passage. The ordinance itself did not require this delay, but Gary's municipal administrators believed that some period of grace was needed in which local homeowners and businessmen might prepare for the enforcement of the pollution law. Chris Angelidis, who had been appointed chief of the new Air Pollution Division within the city Health Department, spent the interval conducting an air sampling program, organizing and staffing his agency, and helping to negotiate agreements between the city government and some of Gary's leading polluters.

These agreements established time schedules for "programmed" obedience to the pollution law. The ordinance authorized Angelidis to permit piecemeal compliance with the pollution requirements in cases where special control equipment had to be installed or where extensive modification of machinery was required to bring a pollution-producing installation up to the standards. For their own part, the polluters were required to give Angelidis satisfactory guarantees that they would take the necessary steps to obey the law within a "reasonable" period of time. The details of these guarantees were the subjects of the negotiations between representatives of the city administration and the operators of pollution-producing installations. Almost all of the polluters who were involved in these discussions were industrial firms, and the most important of these was, naturally, U.S. Steel.

U.S. Steel was among the first of the manufacturing concerns to

[46] On the importance of controlling the scope of conflict, see Schattschneider, *The Semisovereign People*, pp. 2–3.

enter into negotiations with the members of Gary's Air Pollution Control Advisory Board, who were serving as representatives of the city administration, but the company was one of the last local industries to conclude a compliance agreement with the municipal government. The prolonged confrontation between the city and the company was the occasion for the first open breach between U.S. Steel and Gary residents on the matter of dirty air.

Long before the negotiations began, some prominent Gary residents seem to have been impatient for a showdown with the steel company. In August 1963 a columnist for the *Post-Tribune* urged U.S. Steel to "stop killing time" in the matter of pollution control, and a month later the newspaper took up the same cry again in one of its regular editorials. In November 1963, when steel company executives held a preliminary meeting with the Pollution Advisory Board, they were exposed to somewhat more subtle pressures. Chris Angelidis chose the day of the conference to release some results of his air sampling survey, which showed that U.S. Steel was responsible for at least 70 per cent of the particulate matter that floated above the town. On the same day Martin Katz, the new mayor, warned that if Gary's pollution problems could not be solved locally, they might have to be turned over to state or federal authorities. U.S. Steel agreed to submit a detailed compliance schedule by March 1, 1965.[47]

As the deadline approached, public impatience seems to have increased. In editorials the Gary *Post-Tribune* repeated the Mayor's warning that state or federal action might result from the city's failure to deal effectively with the dirty air problem. A city councilman complained that the town's dirty air program was pointless so long as U.S. Steel remained beyond the reach of municipal pollution control efforts. A local branch of the Steelworkers' Union announced that it would "marshal its full resources against the U.S. Steel Corporation" in the struggle to clean Gary's air, and its pledge was soon seconded by another union local.[48]

U.S. Steel presented its compliance proposal two weeks early, and local criticism of the company subsided, but only until mid-March, when the Pollution Advisory Board announced that it was not satisfied with the proposal. The reason for the decision was not the substance of the U.S. Steel compliance program. The Board was content with the eight-year schedule presented by the company. But

[47] Gary *Post-Tribune*, 26 August, 22 September, 6 November 1963.
[48] *Ibid.*, 12 November 1964, 20, 24, 27 January 1965.

the U.S. Steel proposal included a provision that some Board members regarded as an "escape clause." It allowed the mill to halt its pollution control program if the Board of Directors of the company refused to appropriate funds for carrying out the control measures. Bargaining continued for another six weeks, but the negotiations finally broke down early in May. Later in the month, Mayor Katz formally announced the city's rejection of the U.S. Steel compliance plan. He attacked the company's Board of Directors, whom he held responsible for the escape clause, for their "callous, indifferent attitude for people living and working in this area." He threatened grand jury action against the steel company and once again raised the possibility of federal intervention. Katz reserved his expressions of animosity for the headquarters officials of U.S. Steel. The local executives of the company, he said, were "sympathetic and understanding of the problem, but their hands have been tied by the distant attitudes . . . displayed by the directors." Two weeks later, the company—both directors and local officials—agreed to accept a modified escape clause that would permit a moratorium in the pollution control efforts in the event of natural catastrophe, national emergence, strikes, or economic depression.[49]

Epilogue

By the end of 1966, Chris Angelidis could report that the average suspended particulate level in Gary had declined by about 16 per cent since the initiation of local pollution control efforts almost three years earlier. The program which had presumably achieved this partial success was about to be abandoned. Angelidis had already begun to seek the strong pollution control policy that he had not been bold enough to request when he drafted the dirty air law in 1962. The new anti-pollution drive was distinguished from the previous effort by the addition of federal authorities to the ranks of Gary's air pollution policymakers. The federal government had been engaged in anti-pollution activities since 1955, when Congress authorized the U.S. Public Health Service to distribute grants for air pollution research. The agency's clean air program did not bring it into contact with Gary officials until the end of 1964. By that time Congress had widened the scope of Public Health Service air pollution activities in the Clean Air Act of 1963, empowering the agency to distribute

49 *Ibid.*, 20 May, 4 June 1965.

grants-in-aid to state and local governments to support the development and enforcement of pollution control regulations. It was under the authority granted to it by this law that the Public Health Service negotiated an agreement with officials of Gary and three other northwest Indiana cities (East Chicago, Hammond, and Whiting) providing financial support and technical assistance to a proposed Northwest Indiana Air Resources Management program. The regional program was to come into being when each of the four towns enacted an identical pollution ordinance. The ordinance was to be drafted jointly by officials of the four municipalities, and representatives of the Public Health Service would be on hand to assist in its preparation.

The new anti-pollution effort was also distinguished by the behavior of Gary's Chamber of Commerce. This time it was roused to action by the call for pollution restrictions. Together with the Chambers of the other three cities involved, the Gary Chamber drafted a detailed critique of the newly proposed pollution control program and entered into negotiations with municipal and federal pollution officials. In April 1967, after a number of the Chamber recommendations had been incorporated into the draft ordinance, Gary and East Chicago, along with the other two cities, enacted the same dirty air law.

CONCLUSION

Not only did air pollution legislation come slowly to Gary, but the air pollution issue was slow to develop as well. Political and industrial leaders in the town seem to have been reluctant to take positions on the matter of air pollution control, even positions in opposition to control. Mayor Mandich and Mayor Chacharis both exhibited this reluctance, and so, in their own ways, did the Gary City Council and the Chamber of Commerce. Most important, Gary's anti-pollution activists were long unable to get U.S. Steel to take a clear stand. One of them, looking back on the bleak days of the dirty air debate, cited the evasiveness of the town's largest industrial corporation as a decisive factor in frustrating early efforts to enact a pollution control ordinance. The company executives, he said, would just nod sympathetically "and agree that air pollution was terrible, and pat you on the head. But they never *did* anything one way or the other. If only there had been a fight, then something might have been accomplished." What U.S. Steel did not do was probably more important to the career of Gary's air pollution issue than what it did do. Before the passage of the town's first air pollution law, the company never brought its weight to bear on the dirty air debate. Its representatives were seldom visible among Gary's air pollution activists, and when they did appear, it was not to argue or exert pressure. They announced, in effect, that the corporation would not interfere with Gary's effort to initiate an anti-pollution program. It would not resist the enforcement of pollution regulations, nor would it take a hand in the drafting of them. The company's position was that it would take no position. In East Chicago, industrialists reacted quite differently. The local Chamber of Commerce quickly resolved to take an "active interest" in the drafting of anti-pollution regulations. Industrial representatives were responsible for most of the revisions made in Loyd Cohen's proposed ordinance, and industrial pressure forced a modification in the enforcement of the ordinance once it had been passed. In East Chicago, it would appear, industry made an active effort to influence the resolution of the air pollution issue, and the results of that attempt were easily visible in the political outcome.

If successful political action is the measure of political influence, then it is obvious that East Chicago's industrialists were more influential in the air pollution field than were Gary's. But it is also obvious that there is something inappropriate in this conclusion. It suggests that corporations which succumbed quickly to pollution regulations were in fact more powerful in the matter of pollution control than those which succumbed more slowly. A different and more sensible assessment might result if we were willing to recognize that political action is not the only medium through which political influence may operate. In fact, it is absolutely essential to take account of the "inactive" varieties of influence if we are to explain Gary's uneven movement toward an air pollution ordinance, and to understand U.S. Steel's part in that movement.

Though steel company executives were rarely active participants in Gary's dirty air deliberations, the corporation was never really unrepresented in those discussions. While Chris Angelidis was writing his air pollution law, the interests and influence of U.S. Steel were never far from his mind. As a result, the ordinance that he wrote was weaker than he would have liked. The company was on the mind of Mayor Chacharis too, when he counseled unhurried action in the pollution field. He knew that pollution restrictions could impose significant costs upon the corporation, and he sensed that what was costly for U.S. Steel might eventually be costly for Gary. Perhaps apprehensions of this kind also lay behind the Mayor's own hesitancy to do anything about dirty air. A similar concern for U.S. Steel was evident in the Armour Institute's recommendations, with their generous concessions to the special needs of "metallurgical processes." And the actions of both Albert Gavit and Milton Roth were, by their own accounts, influenced by the anticipated reaction of the company to pollution control proposals. Though U.S. Steel never really threw its weight against the anti-pollution forces, its weight was felt all the same. It seems to have put a brake on the progress of the air pollution debate in Gary. Hesitation, timidity, and delay were the results, and it is apparent that these results were not unattractive to U.S. Steel. Granville Howell made the company's inclinations clear when he predicted that it would probably take twenty-five years to achieve effective pollution control at the Gary mill.

In spite of its political passivity, U.S. Steel seems to have had the ability to enforce inaction on the dirty air issue. Apprehension about the company's reaction to pollution control proposals may even have been responsible for Gary's late start in the pollution field. Not surprisingly, the apprehensions of Gary's air pollution activists almost always centered around U.S. Steel's use of its massive economic power. The company, as Mayor Chacharis pointed out, was the mainstay of Gary's prosperity. If it chose, it might do considerable harm to the city's economy. Of course, even U.S. Steel could not afford to do anything it pleased: no one believed that the company would respond to the costs of a local pollution control program by closing down its Gary plant. There were other less drastic actions, however, that could still bring substantial hardship to Gary. It was feared that the corporation might seek to minimize the costs of pollution regulation by diverting production increases or plant expansion from its Gary mill to other installations subject to more lenient pollution control regulations. Or, when the company faced the need for production cutbacks, it might concentrate those reductions at the Gary works rather than at other mills where dirty air restrictions were less stringent. It should be noted that one consequence of federally enforced nationwide pollution standards would be to deprive U.S. Steel and other corporations of the power derived from their ability to exercise options of this kind.

Apprehension about industry reaction to pollution control seems to have been less acute in East Chicago than in Gary. In Gary it was thought that U.S. Steel participation was an essential prerequisite for the enactment of an effective pollution program. Early efforts to promote the pollution issue were almost all intended to involve the company in a discussion of the dirty air problem, and the early frustrations were largely the result of failure to effect its participation. In East Chicago the anti-pollution forces seemed willing, if necessary, to proceed without the benefit of industrial consultation. The difference was apparent from the very beginning of the pollution debate. When George Applegate returned from his first meeting with Loyd Cohen, he reported to his Chamber of Commerce associates that the East Chicago city administration was determined to pass a pollution ordinance. In his opinion, at least, a dirty air law would be enacted whether or not local industry chose to participate in the effort. Applegate's impression of the situation is confirmed by Loyd Cohen, who claims that he would have continued with his anti-pollution campaign even if the Chamber of Commerce had refused his invitation to discuss the provisions of the proposed pollution ordinance. The job, he acknowledges, would have been more difficult, and he would probably have written a weaker and more cautious ordinance, but in the end, East Chicago would still have had its dirty air law.

There were several other signs of a willingness to forego industrial cooperation in the anti-pollution effort. East Chicago's impatient City Council members, for instance, seem to have been anxious to curtail the city-industry negotiations so that they could pass a pollution ordinance. Loyd Cohen was even fearful that the Council members, if given the chance, might ignore industrial wishes entirely. Disregard for industrial goodwill was also evident in the overzealous enforcement of East Chicago's pollution ordinance once it had passed. In general, East Chicagoans seem to have perceived industrial participation as important but not essential to the anti-pollution effort.

There were many reasons for East Chicago residents to be less apprehensive about the power of local industry than were Gary residents. The town, unlike Gary, was not the creation of a single giant corporation. Its emergence was the unplanned result of plant location decisions made by a number of small and medium-sized companies. East Chicago owed its existence to industry, but not to any particular industrial corporation. Its indebtedness was therefore unfocused, as was the attention that local decisionmakers gave to industrial firms. In Gary, one corporation was undeniably the predominant member of the local industrial community—for all practical purposes, it *was* the industrial community. In East Chicago there was no similar focus of attention. The resolution of the dirty air issue, it was thought, might be affected by any one of five or six firms. What is more, it was widely recognized that these companies did not always act as one. The apparent fractionation of industrial power and opinion may have emboldened the partisans of pollution control. East Chicago's economic stability may also have helped. It was clear that the city had reached an economic saturation point. It could absorb little, if any, new industrial enterprise. Though the town might still be vulnerable to production cutbacks, there was little need for East Chicagoans to fret about lost opportunities for industrial growth.

It is not necessary to enumerate all the factors that may have diminished the reputation for power of East Chicago industry. The essential fact, for our purposes, is that pollution activists there seem to have been less apprehensive about industrial power than were decisionmakers in Gary. The difference may help to explain why Gary moved so late and so slowly against its dirty air problem. U.S. Steel, though it usually remained outside the circle of visible political activity, was nevertheless able to affect the course of that activity. In Gary the reputation for power may have been more effective than its exercise. It could have enabled U.S. Steel to prevent political action without taking action itself, and it may have been responsible for the political retardation of Gary's air pollution issue. To the extent that it has an identifiable effect on local politics, the reputation for power is itself a form of power. When adherents of the pluralist alternative dismiss the mere reputation for power as a scientifically worthless datum, they may be dismissing an important part of political reality.

There are other factors that may account for the variation in political behavior between Gary and East Chicago. Even two towns as similar and as close geographically as Gary and East Chicago will differ in a number of important respects. Each of these differences becomes a potential explanatory factor when the time comes to account for some intercommunity variation in political behavior. A glance at the two case studies shows that there are many factors in addition to the reputation for power of local industry that might have been singled out to account for the fact that Gary ignored its dirty air while East Chicago did not: for example, differences between the two towns in the strength and structures of local party organizations, differences in the ability of citizens to register complaints about dirty air, differences in the volume and nature of the political business that the two towns faced, differences in the political skill and experience of the people who attempted to promote the air pollution issue in the two cities, and differences in the parts that state and federal government played in the pollution politics of Gary and East Chicago. Any or all of these variations, as well as some others, could have contributed to the observed differences between the two cities' handling of the issue.

The problem here is that we cannot find out whether these inter-community variations actually did contribute to the difference that we are trying to explain or whether their connection with the difference in question is merely fortuitous. For example, it is possible that we may have been misled in our attempt to explain Gary's neglect of the dirty air issue in terms of the power reputation of local industry. The decisive factors here may have been the power of the Gary Democratic Party and its lack of interest in proposals advanced by political outsiders like Milton Roth or Albert Gavit. It may be that the reputation of U.S. Steel was just a distracting sidelight; it may be that industrial influence and political party influence were closely related. Perhaps U.S. Steel's reputation for power was itself actually dependent upon the power of the Democratic Party organization or on the fact that Gary was preoccupied with certain items of political business other than air pollution. The remedy for this uncertainty is an extension of our investigation to cities other than Gary and East Chicago—cities, for example, that share Gary's strong industrial community but East Chicago's weak party organization. We need to control for the effects of some explanatory variables so that we can isolate the effects of others. Expanding the scope of the investigation can also help us overcome the idiosyncrasies of Gary and East Chicago politics, so that we can construct a general explanation for the neglect of the air pollution issue.

The Gary and East Chicago findings are useful as a source of working hypotheses for this investigation. They suggest the kinds of factors which may be relevant to the life of the dirty air issue. They also indicate the kinds of political processes which mediate between the explanatory factors and the political career of an issue. Finally, they provide a concrete introduction to pollution politics—the kinds of people who participate in it and the kinds of policy questions that it involves. Our next task is to translate these specifics into a more general portrayal. We must know something about the over-all nature of the issue in order to make any sensible predictions about its life chances under political conditions not present in Gary and East Chicago, as well as to bring some order to the succession of hypotheses that will be advanced. A modest theoretical framework will therefore be supplied, within which the factors that affect the emergence of the issue can be located—a basis for prediction that is simpler and clearer than the unordered, idiosyncratic political experience of Gary and East Chicago.

III | Air Pollution and the Air Pollution Issue

By comparison with East Chicago's air pollution debate, Gary's dirty air issue was politically stunted. It matured only after a long and inhospitable season. But pollution politics in Gary, though slow to mature, were not entirely different from pollution politics in East Chicago. In fact, there were many respects in which Gary's encounter with the dirty air issue was simply a slow-motion replay of its neighbor's experience.

In both towns the people who promoted the air pollution debate were political outsiders. They remained more or less detached from what were probably the principal vehicles of community political action—the local Democratic Party organizations—and the Party organizations, for their part, remained more or less detached from the air pollution debate. Local Chambers of Commerce and industrial organizations, on the other hand, sooner or later became active participants in anti-pollution policymaking for both Gary and East Chicago. What opposition there was to local pollution control proposals came primarily from these business and industrial groups. But support for the pollution abatement programs was not consolidated within formal organizations. Albert Gavit's inconclusive attempt to accomplish such a consolidation only convinced Gary's political observers that the public was not concerned about the problem. In general, organized interest groups—neighborhood improvement associations, for example—were not effectively mobilized to protest the damage done to buildings, furnishings, or people by dirty air. Almost all of the "organized" backing for the two anti-pollution campaigns came from municipal administrators and, to a lesser extent, from local newspapers. In both towns, city bureaucrats framed the relevant legislative proposals and engineered their passage. Newspapers added their weight to the dirty air debate by their extensive coverage of the anti-pollution campaigns. Had it not been for their interest in the issue, it would have been much more difficult for us to reconstruct the sequence of events that led to the enactment of pollution ordinances in the two towns.

The air pollution issue, then, seems to have evoked roughly similar patterns of political activity in Gary and East Chicago. Opposition was concentrated in business and industrial organizations. Support, when it was visible, was usually unorganized, diffuse, and led by political outsiders or municipal bureaucrats. The interest of the local press probably reflected the diffuseness of the anti-pollution forces. Of all community organizations, the local newspaper is probably the institution whose clientele is most amorphous and difficult to identify, and the newspapers were among the very few community organizations in Gary and East Chicago who took an active and apparently positive interest in pollution control.

At least one more item might be added to the list of similarities between pollution politics in Gary and in East Chicago. In neither place was the dirty air controversy an especially intense one, though levels of intensity are difficult to determine. Certainly there was no head-on clash of organized interest groups, nor were there many instances of unyielding devotion to a particular proposal or point of view. Among the opponents of the pollution control programs, for example, there was almost no one who seriously proposed that local businessmen and industrialists ought to resist the passage of any and all pollution legislation. The inchoate character of the support for pollution control may have helped to maintain this restraint. There was no organized, concentrated assault upon the interests of local industrial concerns, and perhaps industry itself exercised restraint precisely because it did not want to risk activating and unifying the anti-pollution forces.

There is good reason to expect that we might find a similar pattern of political activity in the pollution debates of other cities. The configurations of political decisionmaking, after all, probably have something to do with the substance of decisionmaking—with the kinds of issues and policy questions that are involved. When the same issue arises in a number of different cities, there is likely to be some resemblance between the various local attempts to resolve that issue. Similar sets of groups and institutions will participate. In effect, each political issue may be said to have a typical "constituency," or set of constituencies, which is likely to be visible wherever the issue has made an appearance.

All of this is merely an extension of the pluralist proposition that political power is tied to political issues. The pluralists have argued that, as different local issues rise and subside, they tend to activate different sets of local decisionmakers. Unfortunately, the pluralists have never been able to tell us just which decisionmakers tend to be activated by what issues—not until after the issues have arisen and the decisionmakers have stepped forward. We know only that the distribution of political activity and power varies, in an apparently unpredictable way, with changes in the subjects of community political concern.

The predictability of these variations would obviously be increased if we could show that, when the same issue arises in different cities, it tends to trigger political activism among similar kinds of people and organizations—that it has a typical constituency. The composition of this constituency may reveal something about the kinds of political conditions that can prevent a potential political issue from making its appearance. Its constituency may be weak, or absent, or suffering from some internal imbalance that impairs its ability to promote the issue in question. The factors that affect the life chances of an issue will probably be reflected in the life of that issue, the pattern of political activity that it typically generates.

The evidence from Gary and East Chicago suggests that there may be such a pattern for the air pollution issue, a "typical" dirty air constituency. It should not be hard to understand why this is the case. The uniformities that we have observed in the politics of pollution probably reflect the fact that there are uniformities in the costs and benefits that pollution control offers to different communities. Confronted with similar social costs and benefits, different communities will generate somewhat similar patterns of political activity. A crude economic analysis of pollution control policy shows why we can generally expect it to elicit concentrated opposition and diffuse support.

For economists, dirty air is not just a nuisance or a health hazard: it represents a flaw in the economic system. In a perfectly functioning market economy, industries would pay some price for the fumes that they generate, burners of rubbish would pay a price for their smoke, and drivers of automobiles would foot the bill for their exhaust. In the absence of any pollution control regulations, polluters are not compelled to pay anything for the privilege of using the air as their dumping ground, and because the air that they use costs them virtually nothing, they treat it as though it were worthless. Their air resource costs fall not primarily on them but on the public at large, and the result is an inefficient allocation of air resources between those who use the air for waste disposal and those who use it for breathing. Polluters get more air than they ought to.[1]

In order to achieve an economically efficient allocation of air resources, it would be necessary to force the polluters to realize that the air is not costless—that its supply is limited and that it has uses other than waste disposal. Most pollution control proposals achieve this by compelling waste disposers to pay some price for using the air, either in the form of a fee or a fine.[2] Presumably, polluters would attempt to avoid these costs, if they were high enough, by substituting for them the costs of pollution control. While it is difficult to predict the final economic result of these proposals, it is fairly clear that what they all seek to achieve is a redistribution of pollution costs from the public at large to the polluters, from a "diffuse" group to a group whose membership is probably more limited and, in some of the most critical cases, certainly better organized. Anti-pollution proposals would therefore bestow socially diffuse benefits while imposing socially concentrated costs. The degree of concentration of costs is most readily apparent in the expenses that pollution abatement programs can impose upon industrial corporations. For example, in 1962, an electrostatic precipitator for a small open hearth furnace would probably have cost a steel manufacturer about $150,000. The furnace itself might have been worth only $50,000 more than that sum.[3] Faced with the prospect of such sizeable expenses, it is hardly surprising that the steel corporations of Gary and East Chicago eventually took an interest in the matter of air pollution control policy and that opposition to pollution control proposals in the two cities was concentrated within business and industrial organizations. By the same token, it is not surprising that support for the Gary and East Chicago programs was diffuse and largely unorganized: the prospective benefits of pollution control were relatively diffuse. Organizations with limited and well-defined constituencies were therefore not activated

---

[1] Goldman, *Controlling Pollution*, pp. 10–19.

[2] Edwin S. Mills, "Economic Incentives in Air Pollution Control," in *ibid.*, pp. 100–106.

[3] Robert L. Chass, "The Status of Engineering Knowledge for the Control of Air Pollution," p. 217.

on behalf of dirty air restrictions. The only organized backing for
pollution abatement came from institutions whose clienteles were
hazy and diffuse—certain local administrative agencies and the press.
In short, the pattern of political activity that emerged in connection
with the anti-pollution proposals appears to have mirrored the anticipated distribution of costs and benefits.

The costs and benefits of pollution control are only the most
obvious explanatory factors that might be used to account for the
similarity of pollution politics in Gary and East Chicago. We can add
something to the plausibility of the explanation by establishing that
the air pollution issue tends to arouse the same pattern of political
activity wherever it appears, and that this pattern is a distinctive one
which is not likely to be duplicated in issue-areas where the prospective distribution of costs and benefits is different.

The evidence for this generalization comes from a survey of
organizational officials in fifty-one American cities. Ten officials were
interviewed from each city, and four of the ten—the labor council
president, the editor of the largest newspaper, the president of the
Chamber of Commerce, and the president of the local bar association—were each asked a series of questions about community activity
on the air pollution issue and a series of questions on the federal
anti-poverty program. Each series began with a question worded like
this:

It's often said that there are two sides to every issue. But on some
matters, people may be divided into more than two sides. And in
those few cases where everyone agrees about a subject, there is really
only one side represented. How would you characterize the subject of
air pollution [anti-poverty program] as it has been discussed in
[name of city]? Has only one side been active, two sides, or more
than two?
1. no sides—the subject has never come up
2. one side—everyone agrees
3. two sides
4. more than two sides.

If the official reported that the subject had never come up, he was
not questioned further. Those respondents who reported that the
subject had been discussed (whether or not they reported general
agreement) were next asked to identify the "leading" people and
groups active in community discussions and to describe their positions
on the issue.

These inquiries are clearly less satisfactory instruments for examining local politics than are the case study procedures employed in many other investigations of community decisionmaking. It has been necessary to ask short and relatively simple questions about complex subjects, and the result has been to introduce some ambiguity into both the questions and the answers. There is good reason for uncertainty about what it means to "take sides" on an issue, and there may be considerable disagreement concerning the qualities that place a local organization among the "leading" groups in an issue-area. What is more, the method of inquiry suffers from the fact that although it was sometimes possible to address the questions directly to those people who participated in making the community's decisions, the intention was to select the sample from a group of people likely to be knowledgeable observers of decisionmaking activity, not necessarily actors in it.

The need for extensive information about political activity in many different cities makes shortcomings of this kind unavoidable. Of course, these investigative deficiencies oblige us to treat the responses of our informants with caution. The respondents' accounts tell us only about perceived activity and can be expected to supply only a crude profile of likely decisionmaking tendencies for cities in general. It is assumed that there is a rough correspondence between the perceptions of our respondents, taken as a group, and the facts of community decisionmaking.

Some of these collective perceptions are reported in Table III–1. The responses of the informants concerning individual and group activity in the fields of poverty and pollution were put into about sixty-five response categories. From these classifications nine mentioned with some frequency were selected. The nine categories are listed in the table in the order of the frequency with which they appeared in the replies to questions about active participants in the resolution of the dirty air issue.[4]

Perhaps the most revealing aspect of the table is what it indicates about the perceived activity of the "general public," a group more diffuse than any other. The 109 respondents who reported that pollution control was an issue resorted to this residual category with some frequency in describing its supporters, but it was never men-

[4] "Supporters" were those mentioned as active on the side recommending the "most extensive air pollution control program." "Opponents" were those mentioned as active on those sides demanding "less extensive" or the "least extensive" pollution control programs.

TABLE III-1: LEADING SUPPORTERS AND OPPONENTS OF AIR POLLUTION CONTROL AND ANTI-POVERTY PROGRAMS, AS SEEN BY COMMUNITY LEADERS, 51 AMERICAN CITIES

Group	Supports Air Pollution Control	Supports Anti-Poverty Program	Opposes Air Pollution Control	Opposes Anti-Poverty Program
Industrial corporations and	%	%	%	%
their executives	8.2	1.3	94.7	4.7
Chamber of Commerce	23.8	5.3	15.8	10.4
City and county administrators and their agencies	27.5	23.3	0.0	4.7
Local newspapers	15.5	4.7	2.6	15.1
"General public"	13.8	0.0	2.6	13.2
Labor organizations	4.6	20.0	0.0	2.8
Political parties	2.8	16.7	5.3	21.7
Churches, clergymen, and church-affiliated organizations	0.9	27.3	0.0	5.7
Ethnic groups and organizations (including civil rights groups)	0.0	42.0	0.0	2.8
	(109)	(150)	(38)	(106)

Note: Respondents were permitted to name as many groups as they pleased, so that percentages in this table do not add to 100. Throughout the tables, numbers in parentheses represent numbers of respondents.

tioned by the 150 respondents who reported support for the anti-poverty program and identified its supporters, which tends to confirm the earlier suggestion that support for pollution control is relatively diffuse, like the diffuse benefits likely to arise from it.

The pattern of opposition to pollution control is clearly quite different. The figures show that more than 90 per cent of the thirty-eight respondents who perceived opposition to pollution control cited industry as a leading antagonist. Chambers of Commerce ranked second, though only distantly, among its enemies. Thus almost all the perceived opposition was concentrated within two kinds of organized interest groups. The general public was named by only 2.8 per cent of the thirty-eight as a leading opponent of pollution control.

Opposition to the poverty program was viewed as somewhat less concentrated than opposition to air pollution. The general public, for example, was named as a leading opponent by 13.2 per cent of the 106 respondents who perceived opposition to the poverty program. The pattern of variation for this group and others again confirms the impression that opposition to air pollution control is relatively concentrated and support relatively diffuse. The configurations of political activity in both cases appear to reflect the kinds of costs and benefits that are at stake. The dirty air issue raises the prospect of socially concentrated costs and socially diffuse benefits, hence the concentrated opposition and diffuse support. The poverty issue, we might reasonably argue, involves costs and benefits of just the opposite kind—relatively diffuse costs and relatively concentrated benefits. The result of this reversal is a reversal in the pattern of political activity.

Table III–1 reveals one more notable difference between the politics of poverty and the politics of pollution. The breakdown of respondents at the bottom of the table indicates, not surprisingly, that air pollution is a much less controversial issue than the anti-poverty program. Of the 109 respondents who said that air pollution was a community issue, only 38 (slightly more than a third) perceived that anyone had taken a position in opposition to pollution control proposals. Of the 150 respondents who said that people in their towns had taken sides on the poverty program, over two-thirds (106) believed that the backers of the program faced opposition.

The relative non-controversiality of the dirty air issue is reflected in another of the survey findings. In each sample city the local health commissioner was asked to report on past efforts to enact pollution ordinances. Thirty of the fifty health commissioners interviewed said that air pollution ordinances had been introduced in their communities' city councils since 1950. None of the ordinances proposed was reported to have been defeated. Even if we allow for gaps in the administrators' memories and for the fact that many of the proposed ordinances were probably amended before being passed, the record is a remarkable one. Among other things, it suggests that the only way to prevent air pollution legislation from being enacted is to prevent the issue from coming up in the first place—that once dirty air legislation has been introduced in a city council, some anti-pollution regulations are almost sure to result. In the life history of an anti-pollution proposal, therefore, it appears that the most critical stage is not so much the passage through the decisionmaking process—the object of the pluralists' political investigations—but the journey through the prior process of non-decisionmaking in which a community sifts out subjects that will not be given political attention and so will never become key political issues.

At any rate, the findings in Table III–1 indicate that pollution politics everywhere is rather similar to pollution politics in Gary and East Chicago. Support for anti-pollution proposals tends not to be consolidated within identifiable interest groups. It is diffuse. When it does receive organized backing, that backing comes most often from local public bureaucracies, as in Gary and East Chicago. Opposition to pollution control, on the other hand, is highly concentrated within organized business and industrial groups. Finally, political parties seldom take an active interest in pollution control but remain, as in Gary and East Chicago, relatively detached from the dirty air debate. In general, the survey findings tell us that there is probably a relationship between the emergence of the air pollution issue and the appearance of a particular pattern of political activity—between the substance of political discussion and the configurations of the political process. This information can be useful in organizing the search for those factors that tend to diminish the "issue-ness" of air pollution. The survey results suggest that there are some organizations—industrial corporations, Chambers of Commerce, local administrative agencies, and newspapers—which seem to perceive that they have a stake in the resolution of the air pollution issue. To some groups the dirty air debate presents the possibility of organizational benefits, to others, the prospect of costs. In towns where organizations of the latter sort occupy dominant positions, we would hypothesize that the "issue-ness" of air pollution will be dampened. Organizations that can expect to lose something through the promotion of the dirty air issue will rarely initiate discussions of the problem themselves. We might also expect that in communities where these groups are especially influential, their prominence may deter other individuals from raising the issue. It might be predicted, for example, that among similarly polluted cities, there will be a negative relationship between the political influence of local industrial corporations and the issue-ness of air pollution.

Not all organizations behave as though they had a stake in the resolution of the dirty air issue, and perhaps they tend to reduce the life chances of the pollution issue simply because they have no interest in it. They are not members of the dirty air constituency. Political parties appear to fall in this category. Though party organizations were named with some frequency as active participants in the debate over poverty programs, they were almost never mentioned as participants in the dirty air debate. In towns where parties are powerful, where (as in Gary) they tend to monopolize the political initiatives of their communities, it is improbable that the air pollution issue will floursh. In other words, there will be a negative association between the influence of local political party organizations and the issue-ness of air pollution. Before this prediction can be tested, it is necessary to decide upon some acceptable means of measuring air pollution, issue-ness, and political influence.

MEASUREMENT OF BASIC VARIABLES

Air Pollution

Of the three items that call for quantification, dirty air is surely the most easily measured. There is broad agreement concerning the major components of urban air pollution, and it is no longer very hard to identify them. The most troublesome difficulties encountered in measuring the dirtiness of air are the occasional unavailability of pollution data and the problem of using these data to assess the "over-all pollution problem" of particular cities.

The U.S. Public Health Service has developed a procedure for ranking metropolitan areas according to the severity of overall air pollution.[5] The ranking attempts to take account of three different pollution factors, suspended particulates, sulfur oxides, and photochemical smog. These three ingredients will also be used here as measures of the severity of local air pollution problems. Wherever possible, the same sources of pollution data used by the P.H.S. to construct its ranking will be used.

Data on suspended particulates come from the surveillance stations of the National Air Sampling Network, which is maintained by the Public Health Service in cooperation with state and local governments. There are or have been N.A.S.N. stations in forty-one of the fifty-one sample cities. In each town the station is located within the central business district, at a distance of no more than 75 feet above ground. Pollution data from a single site naturally do not provide accurate information about particulate levels in outlying areas of the city, but investigations conducted by the Public Health Service indicate that "concentrations of pollutants at a center-city site bear a fairly consistent relationship to concentrations in residential and outlying areas." Because there is such a relationship, "the single center-city sampler does provide a valid index for comparing cities."[6]

[5] U.S. Public Health Service, Press Release (HEW-R43), 4 August 1967.
[6] McMullen et al., "Air Quality and Characteristic Community Parameters," pp. 2–3.

In compiling its own pollution ranking, the Public Health Service assembled the available particulate data for metropolitan areas and computed a particulate average for each area for the period 1961–1965. For the forty-one cities of the sample in which N.A.S.N. stations were located, the same procedure was followed, with two exceptions. First, particulate averages were computed for cities, not metropolitan areas. Second, the particulate data included in these averages cover the period 1957 to 1965. It was decided to make this second departure from the P.H.S. procedure because these pollution measures are intended to serve a slightly different purpose than the P.H.S. ranking. The P.H.S. seeks to make its index up to date, but we are interested in relating our own assessment of a city's air pollution problem to actions that sometimes have occurred over fairly long periods of time. It is therefore appropriate that we should take account of long-term pollution problems.

Of the ten cities that lacked N.A.S.N. sampling stations, seven had alternative sources of data which could be used. In four cases it was possible to use particulate data that had been collected at N.A.S.N. stations in neighboring cities. In none of these four instances was the relevant sampling station more than about three miles from the geographic center of the city for which particulate data was needed. In three other cases particulate information came from more distant sampling sites. These data were included in the computations only after consulting with metropolitan area pollution officials, who indicated that there was no reason to believe that there were sharp differences between pollution conditions in the cities for which information was needed and at the more distant sampling sites. There was no acceptable particulate data for the three remaining towns, and, unless otherwise noted, they have been excluded from all the statistical computations that follow.

The information on sulfur oxides used here is somewhat less complete than the data that the P.H.S. used. In order to construct the sulfur oxide component of its index, the P.H.S. combined data on ambient sulfur dioxide with sulfur oxide emission estimates. In constructing its index, the P.H.S. combined data on ambient sulfur dioxide with sulfur oxide emission estimates. Information on ambient sulfur dioxide levels is relatively scarce for the cities of our sample, and we will have to rely on the emission estimates alone, but this is not an especially serious revision of the P.H.S. procedure. The P.H.S. estimates of sulfur oxide emissions have been shown to be closely associated with measurements of ambient SO_2.[7]

Photochemical smog, the third factor to be included in any pollution index, is probably the most complex variety of dirty air. Its composition has only recently been revealed, and the techniques for measuring smog levels have only recently been developed. These measures have not yet been widely adopted, and the P.H.S. index therefore attempts to take account of photochemical smog levels by using an alternative indicator, an estimate of local gasoline consumption. Automobile exhaust is by far the most potent source of smog, and there is a substantial statistical relationship ($r = +.60$) between the amount of gasoline consumed in a city and such known components of smog as nitrogen dioxide.[8]

The data on suspended particulates, sulfur oxides, and gasoline consumption give us three pollution measures for each of the forty-eight cities finally selected. It remains to decide exactly what to do with these measurements. The P.H.S. has reluctantly chosen to combine its pollution measures, weighted equally, in a single index of the over-all severity of local dirty air problems. The trouble with this procedure, as the P.H.S. points out, is that it assumes that one form of pollution is as "severe" as another—that different varieties of dirty air all do approximately the same kinds and quantities of damage.[9] The assumption is obviously an unrealistic one.

As an alternative to the P.H.S. procedure, we might treat each one of the pollution measures as a separate index. To control for the effect of actual pollution levels upon the "issue-ness" of dirty air, we can simply control for three pollution indices instead of one. In addition to avoiding the pitfalls of the P.H.S. technique, this strategy has the positive advantage of allowing us to examine possible differences in the political impact of different types of pollution.

The "Issue-ness" of Air Pollution

A political issue has already been defined as a subject on which community leaders have taken public positions. The more leaders

[7] *Ibid.*, pp. 15–18; Ozolins and Smith, *Estimating Community Air Pollution Emissions.* McMullen and his associates report that the product-moment correlation coefficient between the P.H.S. sulfur oxide emission estimates and measurement of ambient sulfur dioxide is $+.74$. Sulfur oxide estimates refer to the total tonnage of all sulfur and oxygen compounds produced in a city.

[8] McMullen et al., "Air Quality and Characteristic Community Parameters," Appendix.

[9] U.S. Public Health Service, Press Release, 4 August 1967.

who take positions, the bigger the issue.[10] In order to measure
directly the "size" of an issue, it would therefore be necessary to
identify all the leaders of a town and somehow gauge the sum of
their positiontaking activities. The data do not permit a direct measurement of this sort. Instead, the positiontaking activities of just a
handful of formal leaders, representing a variety of community organizations and institutions, will be examined. The presumption here
is that the activities of these people and the organizations that they
head will reflect positiontaking activity in the community at large.
The assumption, as we shall soon see, is not a rash one.

Different organizations can be expected to act differently in order
to signify that they have taken positions on a matter of public concern.
For a political party, decisive action may take the form of a campaign
platform statement. For a newspaper, an editorial is the conventional
instrument for publicizing a position. An administrative officer's
action may be more guarded—perhaps a report that "lets the facts
speak for themselves." The interview schedules attempted to anticipate these probable variations in organizational behavior; different
respondents were asked different kinds of questions about action on
the matter of dirty air. Newspaper editors, Chamber of Commerce
presidents, and labor council presidents were asked, first, whether
they thought that their organizations had taken positions on air pollution control. They were also asked to describe specific activities which
their organizations had undertaken with respect to the dirty air problem. Only if the claim that a position was taken was accompanied by
some account of specific activities was the respondent's organization
counted as having taken a stand on the issue.

A somewhat different approach was used with local political party
chairmen, who were asked whether their organizations had taken
platform positions on air pollution control. For the purposes of the
issue-ness index, a town's political parties were counted as having
taken a position only if both parties reported platform statements on
dirty air. This requirement reflects the belief that a topic on which
only one party feels obliged to take a platform position cannot have
been a very serious campaign issue. For similar reasons, the other
respondents were required to back up their claims to have taken
positions on dirty air with some specific actions. The idea was to sift
out serious from frivolous instances of positiontaking. As it turned

[10] See above, pp. 29–31.

out, this approach did not make any great difference for the measurement of issue-ness. In most of the cities where one political party had taken a position on dirty air, the other had as well, and almost all the Chamber of Commerce presidents, newspaper editors, and labor council presidents who reported that their organizations had taken positions on air pollution could also report some specific organizational activity in the field of pollution abatement.

Local health commissioners were also asked for some evidence of activity in the matter of pollution control. Here the approach was more oblique because it was expected that their activities would be more oblique. We anticipated that they might regard themselves as impartial administrators whose effectiveness could be diminished by overt participation in policy disputes, that they would seldom perceive that their agencies had "taken positions" on matters of public concern, and that they would conceive their function to be provision of expert opinions and information to lawmaking and policymaking authorities. Even the act of dispensing information can be a species of positiontaking, however. A health commissioner who informs the residents of his town that they have a serious air pollution problem has, in effect, taken a position on the matter of air pollution control. His announcement carries an implied proposal that something ought to be done about dirty air. It was this discreet sort of positiontaking activity that we attempted to uncover.

The administrators were first asked whether they thought that their cities faced "very serious," "serious," or "not serious" air pollution problems. Those who perceived serious or very serious problems were next presented with a list of people and groups, both public and private, and asked to indicate which of them had been informed about the existence of the problem. Finally, the health commissioner was asked to identify the person or group who had pointed out the problem to each name on the list. If he named himself or his agency, his department was counted as having taken a position on air pollution.

The interviews with the health commissioners produced at least a hint that we may have underestimated their willingness to take explicit public positions on air pollution control. One health officer in a southern city commented, during the course of his interview, that he had come close to losing his job because of his vigorous efforts to secure the enactment of a local pollution law. In a midwestern city a health commissioner said that he had been at odds with some members of the local board of health because of his persistent and unsuccessful attempts to get the board's approval for an air pollution ordinance that he had drafted and wished to submit to the City Council. In both of these cases, health officers seem to have discarded their presumed administrative aloofness. It should be noted, however, that in both instances the administrators reported that they had also performed the information-dispensing function which had been expected of them.

For each city in the sample, the interview data yielded five indicators of organizational positiontaking, one each for the health department, the Chamber of Commerce, the AFL-CIO Council, and the largest local newspaper, and a single indicator for both local party organizations. Considered one by one, these reports of positiontaking activity could provide valuable information about the dirty air issue. For example, these data might be used, along with other pieces of information, to find out what kinds of local conditions induce Chambers of Commerce or labor councils or political parties to contribute to the discussion of the air pollution issue. Occasionally, that is precisely the sort of purpose for which the information is used. But it was also hoped that something more could be extracted from it—not merely an account of the positiontaking activities of particular organizations, but a general measure of the issue-ness of air pollution in different cities. If this can be done, then we must assume that the positiontaking responses of our informants are not just unconnected reports of organizational activity. In each city, they must all consistently reflect a single community attribute, the size of the local dirty air issue. Perhaps an analogy will show why it is sensible to assume that this is the case and reasonable to use this information about positiontaking to test the issue-ness of air pollution in different cities.

Suppose that people were being tested instead of cities and individual intelligence instead of issue-ness. We have an intelligence test consisting of five questions, and our first concern is to establish that the ability to answer these questions is an indication of *something*, that the test items do not call upon a haphazard collection of capacities but all tap the same dimension of individual ability. There is reason to suspect that the five questions are not all equally difficult. Some of them were answered correctly by most of the people to whom the test was administered. Others were successfully answered by just a handful of test-takers. By comparing the number of correct answers on one question with the number of correct answers on the other questions, all five test items can be arranged in a tentative order of difficulty, from easiest to hardest. If the easier and harder questions actually do tap the same dimension of individual ability, then we should find a certain kind of order in the responses of the people who take the test. Anyone who can answer the hardest question should also be able to answer all four of the easier questions. If he and others like him cannot, then we can conclude that the hardest question calls for a different kind of ability than do the easier questions. This line of reasoning can be extended to the other respondents and the other questions. Anyone answering the second hardest question ought to be able to answer the three easier questions. Anyone answering the third hardest question ought to answer the two easier ones, and so on. After the test performances of all the respondents had been canvassed, each test-taker could be classified in one of a limited number of response patterns.

The acceptable response configurations for the hypothetical intelligence test are set out in Table III–2. If these response patterns prevail, we can conclude that the five test items exhibit a characteristic called unidimensionality: they are all indicators of a single underlying quality or phenomenon. The reasons for this conclusion should be fairly clear. We expect the harder questions to demand greater intelligence (or visual acuity or education) than the easier questions. Anyone who can meet the large demands of the hard questions ought to be able to meet the smaller demands of the easy questions, provided that all these demands are for the same commodity, or, to put it another way, provided that the test items are unidimensional.

It may already be apparent that the examination of hypothetical questions and responses is more than a way to establish the unidimensionality of test items. It has also been shown that, taken together, the test questions constitute an ordinal scale of measurement.

TABLE III–2: ACCEPTABLE RESPONSE TYPES
FOR A PERFECT SCALE

Response Pattern	Test Question 1	2	3	4	5
0	−	−	−	−	−
1	+	−	−	−	−
2	+	+	−	−	−
3	+	+	+	−	−
4	+	+	+	+	−
5	+	+	+	+	+

Whoever can answer the third question in the scale, for example, possesses more of that underlying quality than a test-taker who can go only as far as the second question.

Indicators of organizational positiontaking can now be substituted for hypothetical test items and sample cities for test-takers. The criteria of scalability and unidimensionality are the same in this case as they were for the items on the intelligence test. We must first arrange the five indicators of organizational activity in order of difficulty, more precisely, in order of the frequency with which the five kinds of organizations took stands on dirty air. The organizations that come first in this array are the ones that most frequently took positions on air pollution. In a sense, these groups took stands on dirty air more "easily" than did the other kinds of organizations. At the end of the tentative scale comes the kind of group that was least likely to take a position, the most "difficult" group, in other words. Next, it is necessary to examine the response pattern for each of the cities in the sample. In this case, the response configuration is actually a pattern of organizational positiontaking. If the five indicators of organizational activity are scalable and unidimensional, then in any city where the most "difficult" group has taken a stand on dirty air, all of the "easier" groups will have taken positions as well. In general, the response patterns that we find should conform to the ideal patterns that appear in Table III–2.

Social statisticians have devised several methods for testing the over-all conformity of actual response patterns to ideal patterns, and they have suggested several conventional criteria for deciding whether a set of measurements, such as the organizational indicators, is sufficiently close to the ideal to qualify as scalable and unidimensional.[11] These tests have been applied to the positiontaking reports of the organizational officials, and the results show that the data do reach the minimum criteria, but just barely.[12] The five organizational indicators do roughly reflect a single underlying dimension, and they do provide a scale for measuring that dimension, but only with a fairly substantial chance of inaccuracy. The positiontaking scale and the ideal response patterns associated with it appear in Table III–3.

The ordering of the items in the scale tends to support the earlier conclusions concerning the pattern of political activity that emerges

[11] For criteria of scalability, see Samuel Stouffer et al., *Measurement and Prediction*, pp. 77–80.

[12] Coefficient of scalability = .67 (the conventional minimum is .60). Coefficient of reproducibility = .89 (the minimum is .90).

TABLE III–3: PROPOSED "ISSUE-NESS" SCALE

City Response Pattern	Organization Took Position on Air Pollution				
	Health Department	Largest Newspaper	Chamber of Commerce	Labor Council	Political Parties
0	No	No	No	No	No
1	Yes	No	No	No	No
2	Yes	Yes	No	No	No
3	Yes	Yes	Yes	No	No
4	Yes	Yes	Yes	Yes	No
5	Yes	Yes	Yes	No	Yes

in association with the air pollution issue. The scale shows that local health agencies, newspapers, and Chambers of Commerce were all more readily moved to take positions on dirty air than were labor councils or the two political parties. This pattern is generally consistent with the one that we discovered in our earlier survey findings concerning the respondents' perceptions of "leading" air pollution activists. The survey findings suggest that, had we attempted to use positiontaking reports to measure the issue-ness of the anti-poverty program, a different ordering of scale items than in the case of air pollution might have been found. Political parties and labor organizations might have surpassed the Chambers of Commerce and perhaps even local newspapers in their readiness to take a stand on urban anti-poverty efforts. Unfortunately, the necessary data to construct a positiontaking scale for the poverty program are not available, and there are problems enough in the scale that we have constructed for the air pollution issue.

Inconsistencies with the ideal scale pattern are not randomly distributed among the five items in this scale. Exactly half of these errors are attributable to a single item, the indicator of health department activity. This concentration of errors indicates that the measure of health department positiontaking may lie on a different dimension than do the other four items, or that it lies on the same dimension but on some other as well. The reason may be that health department representatives were asked different sorts of questions than were the other respondents. Perhaps they were the wrong questions, but there is at least a hint of another explanation.

Those health commissioners who produced inconsistencies in the scale did so because they reported that their agencies had not been responsible for informing any of the groups and organizations on our list about local air pollution problems. In every one of these cases, the health commissioner said that someone else had done the informing. And in several instances, the same kind of organization, a state administrative agency, was reported to have performed this information-dispensing function. What this uniformity suggests is that local health departments may be sensitive to state anti-pollution activity in a way that other local organizations are not. Where state authorities take the initiative in matters of air pollution, some local health departments appear to have retired from the field.

The effect of state intervention is even more clearly evident in some other pieces of information that have been collected. In each town the local health officer was asked to name the persons and organizations on whom he depended most for advice about air pollution problems. Of the fifty health commissioners who were interviewed, six could name no one on whom they depended for advice. Half of the remaining health officers mentioned state agencies as advice-givers, and these health commissioners were about five times as likely to produce inconsistencies in the scale as were those who reported some other source of advice about dirty air. Scale errors and state intervention appear to go together, as do state intervention and health department inaction. There is a modest negative association between health department positiontaking and reliance on state advice ($r = -.22$).

The existence of this relationship may signify that state action in the pollution field tends to discourage action by local health agencies, or it may mean that the failure of local agencies to take action helps to stimulate state intervention. Both interpretations are plausible, and the choice of an appropriate one will have to be deferred until we can examine some additional evidence. For the time being, it is sufficient to know that the indicator of health department positiontaking tends to be incompatible with the other four items in our scale, and it is probably wise to exclude it.[13] It reflects a different set of forces, perhaps a different underlying dimension, than do the other four indicators.

It remains to identify the underlying dimension that these four scale items reflect. Here, we are probably much better off than we would be if we were actually attempting to construct an intelligence test. The relationship between conventional notions of intelligence and the questions that appear on intelligence tests is seldom an immediately obvious one, but there is a fairly direct connection between

[13] Excluding the health department indicator from the scale raises the coefficient of scalability to .79 and the coefficient of reproducibility to .92.

the items that appear in our own scale of measurement and the concept of "issue-ness." Issue-ness has already been identified with positiontaking activity, and the items that are included in the scale were all selected precisely because they have to do with that kind of activity.

The scale constructed therefore provides a simple means for assessing the "issue-ness" of air pollution. By examining the response patterns of the cities in our sample, we can decide where each town belongs on the issue-ness scale. We could then attempt to find out how the scale positions of the cities are related to other local political characteristics. It turns out, however, that this research strategy is a statistically cumbersome one. It will usually be more convenient, and more informative, to dissolve the issue-ness scale into its constituent items—the original indicators of organizational positiontaking. We can then look for relationships between each of these items and other local characteristics. The results of this procedure are not the same as they would have been if we had simply set out to discover what kinds of local conditions induce particular kinds of organizations to take positions on dirty air. We know now that the various indicators of organizational positiontaking not only represent the actions of particular groups but roughly reflect various levels of the issue-ness of air pollution. We can therefore use these items in the effort to find out what kinds of factors tend to stunt the growth of the air pollution issue.

ISSUE-NESS AND AIR POLLUTION

Probably the simplest explanation for a community's neglect of the dirty air issue is that its air is not dirty. If this is the case, then there is no need to resort to any more exotic explanatory variables like the distribution of political influence or the structure of local government. Inter-city variations in the issue-ness of air pollution would be accounted for in the most obvious way, by referring to inter-city variations in the dirtiness of air.

The findings reported in Table III–4 show that this obvious explanation is useful but not sufficient. Each of the figures in the table is a product-moment correlation coefficient, a measure of the strength of the relationship between a particular measure of local air pollution and a particular indicator of issue-ness.[14] For example the first figure

---

[14] Concerning the statistical interpretation of these coefficients, see James S. Coleman, *Introduction to Mathematical Sociology.* pp. 263–68.

TABLE III–4: AIR POLLUTION AND THE ISSUE-NESS OF AIR POLLUTION

Pollution Indices	Issue-ness Scale Item			
	Newspapers	Chamber of Commerce	Labor Council	Political Parties
Suspended particulates	+.29	+.32	+.22	+.35
Sulfur oxide emissions	−.10	+.15	+.23	+.28
Gasoline consumption	−.09	−.14	−.19	−.06
	(47)	(48)	(46)	(47)

in the first column of the table shows that there is a modest positive association between the average concentration of suspended particulates in a city and the likelihood that the largest local newspaper will take a position on the matter of air pollution control. The other coefficients reported in the first row of the table show that there is a similar association between the concentration of suspended particulates and each of the other issue-ness indicators. The conclusion here is fairly obvious and understandable: the heavier the concentration of suspended particulates, the greater the likelihood that the air pollution issue will flourish. The relationship appears to hold at every level of issue-ness. There is no point at which the concentration of particulates becomes irrelevant to the further growth of the air pollution issue.

The other relationships reported in Table III–4 are not so congenial to common sense. The data show, for example, that there is a weak *negative* association between the level of sulfur oxide emissions and the likelihood that local newspapers will take positions on the dirty air issue. The relationship is so slight, however, that the only tenable inference to be drawn is that variations in sulfur oxide pollution make almost no difference for the positiontaking activities of local newspapers. The other correlation coefficients reported in Table III–4 show, as one might expect, that sulfur oxide emissions are positively related to positiontaking activity on the part of Chambers of Commerce, labor councils, and local party organizations, but none of these associations is especially strong. They suggest, at most, that sulfur oxide may contribute slightly to the growth of the dirty air issue, and even this limited contribution may be due in part to suspended particulates rather than sulfur oxides. Sulfur oxide levels are associated with suspended particulate rates ($r = +.30$). What appears as evidence of the political impact of sulfur oxides, therefore, may in fact reflect the influence of this associated form of pollution. By controlling for the level of suspended particulates, it is

TABLE III–5: SULFUR OXIDE POLLUTION AND THE ISSUE-NESS OF AIR POLLUTION, CONTROLLING FOR THE LEVEL OF SUSPENDED PARTICULATES

		Issue-ness Scale Item		
	Newspaper	Chamber of Commerce	Labor Council	Political Parties
Estimated sulfur oxide emissions	− .20 (47)	+ .06 (48)	+ .17 (46)	+ .19 (47)

possible to assess the independent effect of sulfur oxide pollution upon the issue-ness of dirty air. The results in Table III–5 suggest that its positive effects are negligible. Sulfur oxide pollution is probably just less noticeable than other kinds of air contamination. In its most common form it is colorless and, except in abnormally heavy concentrations, odorless as well, so that it is easy to understand why this relatively unobtrusive form of air pollution generally fails to trigger political action on the dirty air issue.[15]

The relationship between gasoline consumption and the issue-ness of dirty air is more consistent than the relationship between sulfur oxides and issue-ness, but it is also more difficult to understand. Table III–4 showed that there is a weak negative association between the gasoline consumption index and every one of the organizational positiontaking indicators. The implication is that there exists a very slight (and probably negligible) tendency for the issue-ness of air pollution to diminish as the severity of automotive pollution increases, a tendency directly opposed to common sense. It may be that faulty measurement accounts for these unexpected findings. Though the gasoline consumption data are probably the best available estimates of automotive pollution for the cities of the sample, it is clear that these estimates are less satisfactory than direct measurements of smog would be. They may not accurately reflect ambient air quality in the sample cities. Still, the gasoline measurements cannot be too seriously deficient, since previous investigations have shown them to be associated with other, more direct measures of automotive pollution.[16] It is therefore unlikely that measurement error accounts fully for the findings. Unlike sulfur oxide pollution, the pollutants from automobile exhaust are often easily noticed. Photochemical smog, the

[15] It should be pointed out that this conclusion is consistent with the findings of the St. Louis opinion survey that were reported in Chapter II. St. Louis residents, like those of the cities in the sample, seem to have been relatively insensitive to sulfur oxide pollution.

[16] See above, p. 94.

most notorious of these contaminants, is easily visible and physically irritating. Because it is noticeable, it might be expected to goad many communities into anti-pollution activities. The findings in Table III-4 suggest that it does not.

One possible explanation for the political impotence of automotive pollution in the sample cities is that local authorities are unable to cope with this kind of atmospheric contamination. Its major sources are both mobile and numerous and are therefore difficult to regulate. More important, regulation of the automobiles themselves would probably not produce any significant relief from automotive pollution. It would also be necessary to exercise some control over their manufacture. Recent state and federal legislation in the pollution field has recognized this necessity, but for local authorities, the necessity is a virtual impossibility. There are only a very few large cities (none of them included in our sample) which account for such a large portion of the motor vehicle market that they might conceivably demand that automobile manufacturers comply with local standards for automobile exhaust systems. To most localities automobile manufacturers are politically inaccessible. Since local solutions to automotive pollution are simply not feasible, local leaders may have refrained from taking positions on a problem that so clearly defies local solution, leaving it to political units that are more capable of dealing with it.

There is some support for an explanation of this kind. In the first place, it is apparent that local authorities who face severe automotive pollution problems are more likely to turn to higher levels of government for assistance than local officials who do not. Health commissioners in cities that scored high on the gasoline consumption index were more likely than others to say that they had relied on state officials for advice ($r = +.29$). This tendency was not apparent where other kinds of pollution, suspended particulates and sulfur oxides, were concerned.

Reliance upon state authorities, it will be remembered, was also associated with local health department inaction on the dirty air issue, and automotive pollution is the factor that appears to account for this relationship. Incapable of attacking the automotive pollution problem themselves, the local administrators turn to state authorities, who are better prepared to handle it. Having surrendered the problem to state agencies, the local officials tend to be inactive in the pollution field. Perhaps as a result of such a process, automotive pollution turns out to be unrelated to local political action in the pollution field.

Whatever the explanation, it appears that gasoline emissions, like sulfur oxide emissions, have almost no independent effect upon the issue-ness of air pollution. Sulfur oxides are not readily noticeable, and the problem of automotive pollution may not be locally soluble. For a complete description of local pollution problems, it may be important to take both forms of pollution into account, but because they have almost no local political impact, we will concentrate on the third major form of pollution, suspended particulates, which does appear to have a fairly substantial political effect. Even this politically efficacious form of pollution does not account fully for inter-city variations in the issue-ness of dirty air. The correlation coefficients in the first row of Table III–4 showed that there is no perfect correspondence between the level of suspended particulates and the local level of political activity on the pollution issue. Factors other than pollution itself may distort the translation of dirty air into a political issue, and the present attempt to identify the dirty air constituency provides a theoretical basis for locating some of these distorting factors. We have predicted that the political influence of certain local groups and organizations will be critical to the survival and growth of the dirty air issue and that these groups can be found where the costs and benefits of pollution control are likely to fall. The next chapter will test these predictions.

IV The Impact of Industrial Influence

Not all of the people and groups who are influential in community decisionmaking will necessarily be visibly active in local politics. Some will be able to exert their influence from points outside the range of observable political behavior. In Gary, for example, U.S. Steel seems to have been one of these offstage influentials. Though the corporation seldom intervened directly in the deliberations of the town's air pollution policymakers, it was nevertheless able to affect their scope and direction. This is what Robert Dahl has called "indirect influence."[1] Presumably, it is indirect because there is no observable interaction between the person being influenced and the influential to whom he responds. A political actor who is indirectly influenced adapts his behavior to his own perception of the preferences of others, tailoring his action to his expectation of the response that it will provoke among those whom he fears or respects.

The pluralist theory of community politics acknowledges the existence of indirect influence, but pluralist research does not make much of it. Pluralist political studies are concerned almost exclusively with the kinds of influence that may be exercised through direct participation in political decisionmaking.[2] What indirect influence adds to this direct influence, according to the pluralists, is a measure of democratic control. In any community, says Dahl, there will be a small minority of citizens who are much more highly involved in the town's political life than is the great bulk of the local population.

[1] Dahl, *Who Governs?*, p. 163.
[2] Pluralist research techniques are clearly designed for the investigation of those varieties of political influence which are revealed in observable political action (see *ibid.*, pp. 330–31).

107

Members of this small "political stratum" naturally exercise much greater direct influence over most local decisions than do ordinary citizens. Indirect influence is one of the things that prevents this minority rule from degenerating into oligarchy. Local political leaders, often taking their cues from the results of local elections, "keep the real or imagined preferences of constituents constantly in mind in deciding what policies to adopt or reject."[3] Thus, though most community residents take no active part in policy decisions, their presumed preferences will nevertheless be taken into account when those decisions are made. Though ordinary citizens possess little or no direct influence, most of them have a moderate amount of indirect influence, and their possession of it helps to reduce the mismatch in power between the minority who are members of the political stratum and the majority who are not.

Especially interesting for our purposes is the pluralist contention that indirect influence helps to convert the inarticulate discontents of apolitical citizens into political issues. Ordinary citizens, says Dahl, rarely generate political issues themselves. This job is usually performed by members of the political stratum, who anticipate and respond to the presumed concerns of their constituents by translating these worries, aggravations, and aspirations into items for the local political agenda.[4] Indirect influence therefore enhances the penetrability of local politics, its readiness to receive and nurture nascent political issues.

What Dahl has neglected to point out is that indirect influence may also have exactly the opposite effect: it may inhibit the introduction of new issues into local politics. Influence that is capable of stimulating action within the political stratum may also operate to prevent action, and though indirect influence may clear the path for some issues, it can raise a barrier to others. That possibility is illustrated by Gary's hesitant encounter with the dirty air issue. The Gary case history also suggests that indirect influence is not merely the mechanism by which the preferences of ordinary citizens are brought to bear upon the conduct of local politics. If indirect influence can work for ordinary community residents, then there is no reason why it cannot work for U.S. Steel or General Motors or bank presidents or members of families in the Social Register. There is nothing inherently democratic about indirect influence. It may just as easily serve the political

3 Ibid., p. 164.
4 Ibid., pp. 90–91.

interests of social or economic elites as the interest of the great mass of ordinary citizens. In fact, there is no reason to presume that indirect influence is any more democratically distributed than direct influence. Most important, there is the possibility that indirect influence may serve elite interests by restricting the penetrability of local politics, reducing its receptivity to potential political issues, and, incidentally, obstructing the political careers of the Milton Roths and Albert Gavits whose political fortunes happen to be tied to those issues. That, at least, is the possibility that the Gary case history suggests. It remains to determine whether Gary's experience is peculiar or typical of many American cities. At stake in this matter are both the pluralists' notion of political penetrability and their optimistic assertions concerning the democratic role of indirect influence.

These considerations raise what is probably one of the most frequently posed and difficult problems of social science: how is political influence to be measured. On the basis of the findings in Gary, it has been argued that the indirect influence of local industry is one of the factors which affects the political life chances of the dirty air issue. In order to test this hypothesis, it is necessary to find out who holds influence in the cities of our sample and in what amounts, though that is probably an oversimplification of the problem. It is oversimple, first, because it assumes that influence is "possessed" by people. Most students of the problem would maintain that it is a property not of a person but of a relationship between people. They would also be reluctant to speak about "amounts" of influence, as though all types of political influence could somehow be summed up to give us over-all influence scores for people, groups, and organizations. It is not at all clear that such a sum can be computed. For each influential, we would have to take account of several different and seemingly incommensurable dimensions of influence. We would want to know just how many people were under the sway of a given influential. We would want to find out just how deeply he could influence them. Could he induce them to give up their lives, their savings, or just a few minutes of their time? Finally, we would want to find out just what kinds of decisions he had the ability to influence. Could he make his weight felt in matters of taxation, military strategy, public education, urban renewal, or in all of these and others as well? Once all this information is gathered, there is the problem of deciding how to combine it in an index of influence.

Simple arithmetic procedures seem inappropriate for accomplishing this amalgamation. Perhaps the notion of amalgamation is itself inappropriate.

One school of community political research has sought to bypass these difficulties by transferring the problems of influence measurement from the observers of political influence to the people who have actually influenced others or themselves been influenced. Adherents of the "reputational" approach attempt to locate and measure influence simply by asking selected members of a town's political stratum to identify their community's most influential residents. People who are frequently cited as influentials are judged to possess more influence than those who are less frequently mentioned.[5]

The reputational strategy suggests one obvious solution to the problem of assigning weights to the various dimensions of influence and combining them in an over-all influence index. Members of the political stratum are themselves given this task, at least implicitly. If anyone is qualified to assess over-all influence, it is they, because they have actually felt its weight. Of course, they may also feel the pressure of things other than political influence. They may be impressed by a man's wealth or social status. This combination of "real" influence with other elements creates difficulties for the reputational strategy. Nelson Polsby has stated the problem thus:

Presumably what is being determined when judges are asked to identify influentials is who has a *reputation* for being influential. The reputation can be divided into that part which is justified by behavior and part which is not so justified. It is clearly those in the community whose behavior in the main justifies their reputation as leaders whom social scientists would want to call the "real" leaders in the community. In other words, asking about reputations is asking, at a remove, about behavior. It can be argued that the researcher should make it his business to study behavior directly rather than depend on the opinions of secondhand sources.[6]

Polsby's criticism is probably a sound one, but only so far as direct influence is concerned. Here it is true that the only "real" leaders are the ones whose reputations for leadership are justified by their actions. But indirect influence does not operate through political action. People who are indirectly influenced respond not to the exercise of power but to the perception of power, and, whatever its

---

[5] Floyd Hunter, *Community Power Structure*, p. 258.
[6] Polsby, *Community Power and Political Theory*, pp. 50–51.

shortcomings, the reputational approach, as Polsby points out, allows us to identify those people who have a reputation for being influential. The reputational technique, then, will be used here for the limited purpose of helping to identify those communities in which local industry is reputed to have influence. If the findings from Gary are not misleading, we should discover that in such towns the life chances of the dirty air issue are diminished. Such a discovery would help to substantiate the contention that active influentials are not the only "real" community leaders. The reputation for power, as well as its exercise, can influence the course of local politics in a particularly significant way, not simply by affecting the resolution of political issues but by controlling their emergence.

The reputational technique still requires some reworking to meet pluralist objections before it is useful for the present purpose. Pluralist critics have pointed out certain shortcomings in the method which impair even its ability to uncover the reputation for power. First, they argue that it makes the unwarranted assumption that every community really does have some leading influentials. When an investigator asks local residents "Who runs this town?" he presupposes that there is someone who runs the town, when, in fact, no person or group of people may really be in charge. Thus when local informants are asked to identify their town's influentials, they must be given a clear opportunity to answer that there are no influentials.[7] The method used here gave respondents this option, and a number of them chose to take it.

A second objection to the reputational technique is that it ignores variations in the distribution of influence that may occur from one issue-area to another.[8] A leader who is influential in municipal elections may carry no weight when questions of urban renewal arise. People who are concerned with municipal elections will probably regard him as an influential leader. Informants who are concerned about urban renewal will probably be less likely to cite him as a leader. Neither group of respondents, it might be argued, has provided an accurate indication of his influence, and combining their answers does not produce a satisfactory solution either. The resulting influence index would overstate his urban renewal influence and understate his municipal election influence. Of course, this index

[7] Herbert Kaufman and Victor Jones, "The Mystery of Power," p. 207; Polsby, *Community Power and Political Theory*, p. 113.

[8] Polsby, *Community Power and Political Theory*, pp. 68, 113–14.

might be regarded as a measure of his "average" influence. But this facile solution fails to address the question of whether election influence and urban renewal influence are really equivalent and therefore susceptible to being averaged. Not only might this average influence index be inaccurate, but it would also be unsuited to our particular research purposes. Our concern is not simply with influence in general, but with influence in a specific issue-area, the field of air pollution control. People who are perceived to be quite powerful in the matter of pollution control may not score high on an index of general influence, and by considering only the general influence of local leaders, we may overlook those very people who are most relevant to the emergence and resolution of the dirty air issue. When local informants are asked to identify their community's influentials, the question should therefore refer to a specific issue-area. Only questions of this kind were used in the present study.

There remains one more major problem that some critics have cited as a weakness of the reputational approach. Raymond Wolfinger has identified it as the "difficulty of making sure that the researcher and the respondent share the same definition of power."[9] "Power" and "influence" are terms with multiple meanings, and investigators who use these terms run a high risk of introducing ambiguity into the questions that they ask and, more important, into the answers that they receive. The possibility of disparity between the interviewer's notion of power and his respondent's conception of it is one more reason for an investigator "to study behavior directly rather than depend on the opinions of secondhand sources," as Polsby says. In fact, the problem here is quite similar to the one that Polsby has in mind when he warns against the confusion of "real" leadership (i.e., leadership that is justified by behavior) with the mere reputation for leadership (leadership as the informants see it). Wolfinger's criticism might be answered in much the same way as Polsby's was: the criticism is well taken when direct influence is the object of inquiry but is irrelevant to the study of indirect influence as the pluralists themselves would define it. For our purposes, whatever an informant regards as influence is influence. We are interested primarily in his perception of local politics and, for the present at least, not in the reality that lies beyond that perception.

Though the answer is probably appropriate to Wolfinger's com-

9 "Reputation and Reality in the Study of 'Community Power,' " p. 638.

ment, it does not constitute a complete response to his criticism. "Power" and "influence" remain ambiguous terms, and they could conceivably introduce some confusion into our inquiries. There is no reason to insist that the questions asked of respondents be imprecise, and an attempt has been made to minimize the possibility by employing terms that are somewhat less abstract than "power" and "influence." The chance for misunderstanding remains, as it would in any question addressed to an informant, but it is hoped that it has been reduced.

In each of the sample cities, our modified reputational questions were addressed to a set of seven organizational officials. The panel of influence judges included the presidents of the largest local bank, the Chamber of Commerce, the bar association, the AFL-CIO Council, the editor of the largest newspaper, and the chairmen of the Democratic and Republican Party organizations. Each of these respondents was given a list of fifteen groups and organizations and was then asked a series of questions about the distribution of influence among these groups for different issue-areas. He was asked, for example, to go down the list of organizations and "tell me for each whether their support is essential for the success of a program of air pollution control, whether their support is important but not essential, or whether their support is not important." It should be noted that the question gives the respondent a clear opportunity to answer that no one is influential, it specifies the issue-area in which the survey is interested, and it avoids the use of abstract words like power and influence. Even so, it may reasonably be argued that some of the terms employed in the question have uncertain meanings. For example, different respondents may have different notions of "success" in the field of air pollution control. It may mean, as it seems to have meant to Milton Roth, the successful enactment of an anti-pollution ordinance, or it may mean the successful enforcement of pollution regulations, as it did to Chris Angelidis. Here, as before, the informant's definition, whatever it may be, is acceptable. If he believes that the passage of an air pollution ordinance is the critical step in a dirty air program, then we want to know whose influence he perceives to be relevant at that step. We are interested, for the moment, in political reality as the respondent perceives it. The questions call upon these perceptions, and not upon the objective facts of a situation.

What is needed next is some means for converting the individual perceptions of the respondents into indices of influence for the cities in the sample. The first piece of information that we require is a measure of perceived industrial influence on the air pollution issue. If the Gary case history is a representative one, then industry's power reputation is probably more critical for the life chances of the dirty air issue than is any other political variable. A rather straightforward index of perceived industrial power could be constructed by simply summing up the number of informants in each city who mentioned industry as either "important" or "essential" to the success of a pollution control program. This total could then serve as a measure of perceived industrial influence on the dirty air issue. The procedure appears to take account of the three major dimensions of influence that were mentioned earlier. It clearly reflects the substantive aspect of influence—the kind of decision or issue to which it is relevant. Second, it appears to take account of the extent of influence, the number of people who respond to it. Finally, it attempts a threshold measurement of the "depth" or intensity of influence, distinguishing as it does between those respondents who regard industry as unimportant in the pollution field and those who regard it either as essential or important.

There are two important shortcomings in this tentative strategy for measuring perceived industrial influence. First, the threshold level that we have chosen to gauge the intensity of industrial influence may be the logical one, but, as a practical matter, it is simply too low. Only a little more than 12 per cent of the respondents thought that industry was unimportant on the air pollution issue. The exact figures for perceived industrial power in this issue-area and in the others for which we asked questions of the reputational type are presented in Table IV–1. The findings suggest that the dirty air issue is a peculiar one as far as industrial influence is concerned. In no other decisionmaking area were the respondents so likely to say that local industry was either an essential or an important political actor.

If we choose to distinguish between these answers and the ones in which industry was mentioned as unimportant, then we will have very little to make distinctions about. There are only a few cities in which anyone regarded industry as unimportant to the fate of a local pollution control program. The obvious solution to this problem is to raise our standards for industrial influence. We shall therefore construct the industrial influence index for a city by summing up only

TABLE IV–1: PERCEPTIONS OF INDUSTRIAL INFLUENCE IN SELECTED ISSUE-AREAS

| Issue-Area | Industry Support Is | | | |
	"Essential"	"Important"	"Not Important"	Total
	%	%	%	%
Air pollution control programs	49.8	37.7	12.5	100.0 (329)
Urban renewal projects	31.7	52.2	16.1	100.0 (341)
Municipal bond referenda	25.4	54.2	20.3	99.9 (330)
Mayoral elections	13.3	57.7	29.0	100.0 (338)
School board appointments/elections	5.9	43.4	50.7	100.0 (341)

Note: Throughout the tables, numbers in parentheses represent total respondents in each category.

those responses in which industry was named as "essential" to the success of an air pollution control program.

There is one further difficulty in the perceived influence index as it now stands. Suppose that all of the informants in a city to whom the list of fifteen groups and organizations was presented answered that all of the groups on the list were essential to the success of a local pollution control effort. Suppose that in another city every respondent mentioned industry support as essential to pollution control but judged all of the remaining fourteen groups to be unimportant. In both cities local industry would have received the same number of "essential" votes, but it is clear that its influence in the first city ought not to be regarded as equal to its influence in the second city. In one town industry is perceived to be no more influential than any other group; in the other, it is undeniably pre-eminent in the field of pollution control. In other words, influence is relative, but the present measure of industrial influence does not take that relativity into account.

It is clear that in attempting to measure industrial influence on the air pollution issue, we must also take account of the influence that other groups enjoy in this field. We must know not only how many "essential" votes industry has received but also how many of these votes have gone to other organizations on our list. In order to accomplish this, the perceived influence index has been modified in the following way: for each city, the "essential" votes of all respondents for all groups were summed up. Next, industry's share of this total was computed as a percentage. The median share for industry was 15 per cent. Where industry's portion of the "essential" votes was greater than this, it was considered to be highly influential on the air pollution issue. Where industry's portion was 15 per cent or less, it was judged to have relatively little influence.

It should be apparent that the index has not been used to make any exact measures of industrial influence. It allows us only to distinguish between "high" and "low" industrial influence. The reason, quite simply, is that the index is probably not a reliable indicator of any finer variations in power. No claim is made for it as an exact and final solution to the problem of measuring influence. Like other uses of the reputational method, it is probably best regarded as little more than "a systematic first step in studying a city's political system rather than a comprehensive technique of discovering the distribution of power."[10] Strictly speaking, the index does not even provide a rough measure of indirect influence, but only of the reputation for power. In order to establish the existence of indirect influence, it is necessary to show not only that a particular person or group is perceived to be influential, but that this perception has somehow affected the course of political events.

INDUSTRIAL INFLUENCE AND THE GROWTH OF THE POLLUTION ISSUE

Local polities in which industry is perceived to be highly influential on the matter of air pollution control will be relatively impenetrable to the dirty air issue—at least, that is the prediction one would be inclined to make on the basis of Gary's experience. Local political actors, it might be argued, will have no difficulty in perceiving that the resolution of the dirty air debate may be quite costly for local industrial corporations. If they also perceive that industry is politically powerful, they will hesitate even to initiate the debate. In statistical terms, the hypothesis is simply that, if we control for variations in local pollution levels, we will find a negative association between the index of perceived industrial influence and each of the various indicators of the issue-ness of dirty air. The correlation coefficients,

10 *Ibid.*, p. 637.

Table IV–2: Perceived Industrial Influence and the Issue-ness of Air Pollution, Controlling for Suspended Particulate Level

| | Issue-ness Scale Item | | | |
	Newspaper	Chamber of Commerce	Labor Council	Political Parties
Industrial influence on air pollution	−.11 (45)	−.01 (46)	−.09 (44)	−.15 (45)

presented in Table IV–2, show that when this is done there is a general negative association between industrial influence and the issue-ness of air pollution, but most of the relationships are very weak. Industry's reputation for power does not appear to make any substantial difference for the life chances of the dirty air issue.

But a closer look at the data tells a somewhat different story. The cities of the sample were divided into two groups, those with above-average scores on the suspended particulate index and those with average or below-average scores. For each group a separate measure of association for the relationship between industrial influence and the issue-ness of air pollution was calculated, again controlling for the exact level of air pollution. The results, given in Table IV–3, make it readily apparent why the correlation coefficients in Table IV–2 were so low. Newspaper positiontaking, for example, is negatively associated with industrial influence among the high-pollution cities, but there is a slight positive association between the two variables among the low-pollution cities. In effect, one relationship cancels out the other, and the result is a low over-all association between industrial influence and newspaper positiontaking, as was seen in Table IV–2. The same kind of canceling-out process appears to have occurred for each of the other issue-ness indicators.

Table IV–3: Industrial Influence and the Issue-ness of Air Pollution, Controlling for Suspended Particulate Level

| | | Issue-ness Scale Item | | | |
		Newspaper	Chamber of Commerce	Labor Council	Political Parties
Industrial influence on air pollution	High-pollution cities	−.34 (18)	−.23 (18)	+.07 (18)	+.03 (17)
	Low-pollution cities	+.05 (27)	+.30 (28)	−.24 (26)	−.36 (28)

The statistical explanation for the findings is not difficult, but a substantive explanation is no easy matter. The only thing that is clear is that the impact of industrial influence upon the issue-ness of air pollution turns out to be much more complex than anticipated. In heavily polluted cities industrial influence does seem to operate as a deterrent to the growth of the political issue, but its deterrent effects do not extend to all of the local organizations which appear in the issue-ness scale. The positiontaking activities of local newspapers and Chambers of Commerce do seem to be inhibited by industrial influence; the activities of local labor councils and political parties do not. Because the indicators of organizational positiontaking have been ranked in a scale, it is possible to locate the impact of industrial influence not only with respect to various community organizations but also within the life history of the dirty air issue. We know that positiontaking by newspapers and Chambers of Commerce tends to occur at an earlier stage in the development of the issue than does positiontaking by labor councils and political parties.[11] The suscepti-bility of the former to industrial influence therefore suggests that, in heavily polluted cities, industry's reputation for power is brought to bear on the dirty air debate at a relatively early period in its develop-ment. In the low-pollution cities, industrial influence also appears to retard the development of the issue, but the deterrent effect is felt only at a relatively late stage. Here labor councils and political parties (but not newspapers or Chambers of Commerce) are vulnerable to industry's inhibiting influence. In short, where air pollution is rela-tively severe, industrial influence tends to inhibit the early growth of the dirty air issue. Where pollution is less severe, industrial influence tends to block the later development of the issue.

The earlier consideration of the costs and benefits of pollution control supplies at least the hint of an explanation for this pattern. It was predicted that local industry would be likely to attempt to prevent the emergence of the dirty air issue because pollution control might be costly for manufacturers. No attempt was made to take account of variations in its cost, however. It was implicitly assumed that the burden imposed on industry by dirty air regulations would be roughly the same everywhere, which is obviously unrealistic. There is good reason to believe that the expenses of pollution control weigh more heavily on industrial corporations in cities where pollution itself

11 See above, p. 100.

is heavy. The level of industrial activity in a community is associated with the level of pollution,[12] reflecting the obvious fact that industry contributes to that pollution. Where the air is highly polluted, industrial emissions are likely to be high, and the cost of controlling them is likely to be both relatively large and relatively obvious. Thus the influence of industry quickly becomes relevant to the political life of the air pollution issue. Its impact is evident during the early stages of the issue's development. In low-pollution cities, where the costs of controlling industrial emissions are likely to be lower, the inhibiting influence of industrial power reputations does not become evident until a later stage in the growth of the issue. If this is the case, it remains unclear why, in heavily polluted cities, industrial influence should cease to affect the development of the dirty air debate in its later stages—why, if the issue can survive its early days, industrial influence should become irrelevant to its further development.

Perhaps this phenomenon has something to do not with the costs of pollution control, but with its perceived benefits. Its benefits, like its costs, can be expected to vary with the severity of pollution. Where the air is not very dirty to begin with, little can be gained by cleaning it, and there is relatively little to sustain the issue in the face of clear political obstacles. In high-pollution cities, on the other hand, the benefits of cleaning the air will be relatively large. What is important, of course, is that these benefits be recognized by community residents and their leaders. That recognition may come only after the pollution issue has begun to emerge, after the attention of the community has been called to it, and general solutions have been proposed. At this point the severity of pollution itself may provide stimulus to the growth of the dirty air issue effective enough to override political deterrents like industrial influence.

In short, the peculiar pattern of negative associations that appear in Table IV–3 may be the result of a complex interaction between the perceived costs and the perceived benefits of pollution control. In low-pollution cities the costs to industry of pollution control are likely to be small, and, as a result, perceived industrial influence does not prevent the issue from taking root. Once the pollution problem has been brought to the community's attention, however, its ability to elicit a broad response is diminished by the very fact that local pol-

[12] The correlation coefficient for the association between the proportion of the local work force employed in manufacturing and the level of suspended particulates is $+.25$.

lution conditions are not especially serious, and the perceived benefits of pollution regulation are relatively small. In high-pollution cities just the opposite conditions hold. Pollution control is likely to impose relatively heavy costs upon local industry, and those costs will probably be obvious to local political actors. Perceived industrial influence will therefore be an immediate obstacle. Once the dirty air issue has become established, however, its growth prospects are enhanced by the severity of local pollution. Having once been called to the attention of the community, the issue is not so easily forgotten.

E. E. Schattschneider calls attention to phenomena of this kind when he points out that the course of a political conflict is largely determined by its scope. The balance of forces in a dispute is decisively affected by the extent to which the "audience" becomes involved in it.[13] In the present case, it appears that the introduction of the dirty air issue into a heavily polluted city may mobilize the audience more effectively than its introduction into a low-pollution city. The result is a subsequent difference in the balance of forces which are at work in the dirty air issue. In low-pollution cities industrial influence tips the balance during the later stages of the issue's development; in high-pollution cities it does not.

This interpretation suffers from all the uncertainties that go with any post hoc rationalization of empirical findings. The data are not sufficient to establish the general accuracy of the explanation. Perhaps its greatest merit is that it is theoretically parsimonious. The same kinds of considerations that produced the original prediction about industrial influence and the issue-ness of air pollution have provided the materials necessary to modify that prediction. We have not had to discard the framework of anticipated costs and benefits. Even so, the explanation must remain a provisional one. The only conclusion that is well justified is this: industrial influence does inhibit the growth of the air pollution issue, but the nature of this inhibiting effect depends upon the actual level of pollution.

There is other evidence that supports this conclusion. The respondents were asked not only whether their own organizations had taken positions on dirty air but also whether any people in their communities had "taken sides" on the matter. Their responses to this question and others were discussed above in an attempt to find out what patterns of political activity emerge in conjunction with the air

13 Schattschneider, *The Semisovereign People*, pp. 1–2.

pollution issue. We can use those responses now to construct an additional measure for the issue-ness of dirty air, more precisely, a measure of its perceived issue ness.

"Taking sides" is just the sort of activity that we have identified with the emergence of a political issue. When local informants say that their fellow residents have taken sides on dirty air, they are reporting, in effect, that the subject of air pollution has crossed the boundary of the political system. They perceive that it has become an issue. We would expect that perceptions of this kind would occur less frequently in cities where industrial influence is high than where it is low. That expectation is modified somewhat by the previous finding that variations in actual pollution levels have something to do with the operation of industrial influence. In high-pollution cities the efficacy of industrial influence appears to be restricted to the early days of the dirty air debate.

It is this "early" influence that we would expect to be most evident in the present case. When we try to find out whether anyone in a community has taken sides on dirty air, what we are attempting is a threshold measurement of the issue-ness of air pollution. The previous findings suggest that only in high-pollution cities does industrial influence tend to bar the threshold of the political system against the entry of the issue. Only in high-pollution cities, therefore, should we find evidence that industrial influence has a substantial effect upon the respondents' answers to our questions about people taking sides on dirty air. In fact, in high-pollution cities there was a strong negative association ($r = -.61$) between the measures of local industrial influence on the air pollution issue and the number of informants in a town who reported that their fellow residents had taken sides on dirty air. In the low-pollution cities there was a weak positive association ($r = +.15$) between industrial influence and "perceived issue-ness."

DIRECT VS. INDIRECT INFLUENCE

So far, the evidence indicates that the distribution of perceived influence within a local political system has something to do with the penetrability of that system. Where industrial corporations are thought to be powerful in the matter of anti-pollution policy, either the emergence or the growth of the dirty air issue is likely to be hindered.

The obvious conclusion is that industry's reputation for power reduces the viability of the air pollution issue, but before we can make that inference, it is important to know just what part of industry's power reputation we have been examining—whether it is, in Polsby's words, "that part which is justified by behavior" or the "part which is not so justified."

If it is industry's "unjustified" power reputation that prevents the air pollution issue from flowering, then we have established that manufacturing corporations enjoy indirect influence in the matter of pollution control. Like U.S. Steel in Gary, they can diminish the survival prospects of the dirty air issue without taking action on it. In this case, industry's reputation for power, unsupported by acts of power, would be sufficient to inhibit the efforts of would-be air pollution policymakers. There is another possibility, however. Perhaps what we have been regarding as industry's reputation for power on the air pollution issue is really a simple and direct reflection of actions that it has taken. In other words, the reputation may be "justified by behavior." In this case, it might be argued, industry's reputation for power is not the real obstacle to the emergence of the air pollution issue. The actions that lie behind that reputation are the things that deter the emergence of the dirty air debate. In short, we have an example of direct, not indirect, influence.

In order to find out whether political action was the source of industry's reputation, we asked several of our informants whether they or other officers of their organizations had ever talked with industrial executives about the air pollution problem. Conversation, after all, is one form of political action, perhaps the most common form, and a possible medium for the exercise of direct influence. Through such conversations, industrial executives might dissuade an informant's organization from taking a public position on air pollution control. If talking to industrial executives actually had this result, then it would be established that industry had exercised direct influence to block the emergence of the air pollution issue. This exercise of influence might also serve to enhance industry's reputation for power in the matter of pollution control, thus accounting for the negative relationship that exists between the perceived influence of industry and the issue-ness of dirty air.

Two pieces of statistical evidence are necessary to sustain this explanation. First, it must be shown that there is a positive association between perceived industrial influence and the occurrence of conversations about pollution between our informants and industrial executives. This statistical relationship could establish that industry's power reputation in the pollution field was a reflection of its actions in this area. Second, industry's actions on air pollution must be shown to be responsible for inhibiting the emergence of the dirty air issue. We would need to show that organizations whose officers had discussed the air pollution problem with industry were less likely to take positions on air pollution than those organizations whose officers had not had these conversations.

The findings reported in Tables IV–4 and IV–5 show that the evidence does not fulfill the requirements of the direct influence argument. The coefficients in Table IV–4 indicate that industry's participation in dirty air discussions with the editor of the largest newspaper and the presidents of the Chamber of Commerce and labor council was not positively associated with its reputation for power. In fact, there were several cases in which industry's power reputation was *negatively* associated with its participation in these discussions. The findings in Table IV–5 show that, when representatives of industry did discuss dirty air with the informants' organizations, it did not discourage these community groups from taking a position on the issue. Industrial participation in such discussions is positively associated with position-taking in the pollution field.

Thus the survey evidence not only fails to support the direct influence argument but pretty consistently contradicts this line of explanation. The data show that industry's perceived influence is not a reflection of its actions. If any aspect of industrial behavior underlies industry's power reputation, it is industrial inaction, as was the case in Gary. That much is suggested by the negative correlation coefficients in Table IV–4. They indicate that where industry remains silent on the dirty air issue, it is likely to be thought of as highly

TABLE IV–4: PERCEIVED INDUSTRIAL INFLUENCE AND OCCURRENCE OF CONVERSATIONS WITH INDUSTRIAL EXECUTIVES ABOUT AIR POLLUTION, CONTROLLING FOR SUSPENDED PARTICULATE LEVEL

		Newspaper Talked with Industry	Chamber of Commerce Talked with Industry	Labor Council Talked with Industry
Perceived industrial influence	High-pollution cities	− .44 (18)	+ .10 (18)	− .05 (18)
	Low-pollution cities	− .06 (26)	+ .25 (27)	− .34 (25)

TABLE IV–5: CONVERSATIONS WITH INDUSTRIAL EXECUTIVES ABOUT AIR POLLUTION AND TAKING A POSITION ON AIR POLLUTION, CONTROLLING FOR SUSPENDED PARTICULATE LEVEL

		Newspaper Took Position	Chamber of Commerce Took Position	Labor Council Took Position
Talked to industry	High-pollution cities	+.32 (18)	+.51 (18)	+.44 (18)
	Low-pollution cities	+.39 (26)	+.45 (27)	+.45 (25)

influential in the pollution field. We might conclude that industry's power reputation in anti-pollution matters tends to be an "unjustified" one, and, since that is the case, it follows that the neglect of the air pollution issue is largely a consequence of industry's indirect influence, not its direct influence. The mere reputation for power, unsupported by acts of power, has been sufficient to inhibit the emergence of the dirty air issue.

The survey evidence also indicates that, where industrial action does occur, it does not prevent the expansion of the dirty air debate. Here again, industrial inaction appears to be the critical factor. The positive coefficients in Table IV–5 indicate that when industry speaks up on the matter of dirty air, the growth prospects of the air pollution issue are enhanced. It follows that when industry remains silent about dirty air, the life chances of the pollution issue are likely to be diminished.

Industrial behavior may deserve some place in the attempt to account for the neglect of the dirty air issue, but it is industrial in-action and not industrial action that proves to be the critical form of behavior. Perceived industrial influence, industrial inaction, and the neglect of the dirty air issue go together, although it is difficult to say exactly how. We might maintain, for example, that industrial inaction is a simple by-product of the neglect of the dirty air issue. Where industry's perceived influence has enforced inaction on the air pollution issue, manufacturing executives, like everyone else, have little to say about the problem. On the other hand, it may be that industry's inaction is an important link in the relationship between perceived industrial influence and the neglect of the air pollution issue. There is some support for this line of argument in the Gary case history, where U.S. Steel's silence on the matter appears to have been a major source of frustration to promoters of the air pollution issue because they perceived that the company's inaction was a critical obstacle to the development of the dirty air debate: "If only there had been a fight, then something might have been accomplished."

U.S. Steel could afford to remain inactive on the pollution issue because its power reputation deterred others from contributing to the growth of the issue. So long as the maturation of the dirty air debate could be retarded, there was no need for industry to take defensive action against the anticipated costs of a pollution control program. As long as industry took no defensive action, the issue was stalled at a very early stage of its development. It appears that industrial action or "neutrality" may serve as a strategic device for blocking the emergence of the air pollution issue, but it is a device that can be used successfully only when industry enjoys an impressive reputation for power. In effect, the possession of indirect influence permits industry to refrain from exercising its direct influence. In East Chicago industry's "unjustified" power reputation was apparently not sufficient to halt the emergence of the issue, and industrialists were compelled to take to the field as political activists in order to protect themselves from the possibility of excessive pollution control costs. When they did, they naturally hastened the development of the issue.

INDIRECT INFLUENCE AND DEMOCRACY

To say that industrial influence has contributed to the impenetrability of local political systems is implicitly to assert that it has prevented the political process from accurately reflecting the concerns of citizens. Specifically, the assumption is that local residents really are irritated by air pollution and that industry's reputation for power has inhibited them from expressing that irritation. But it may be that cities in which industry enjoys a reputation for power also happen to have residents who are relatively indifferent to the quality of the air they breathe. As a matter of fact, there may be more than a fortuitous connection between public indifference and industrial influence. One might argue that only where the public is unconcerned about dirty air is it possible for local industry to enjoy a reputation for power in the pollution field. Industry may receive its prominence by default because local residents have failed to take an interest in the pollution problem. Obviously, such public indifference may also lead to the neglect of the dirty air issue. The statistical connection that we have observed between industrial influence and the neglect of the dirty air issue may have appeared only because they were both dependent upon the same third factor, the character of public opinion and interest. If this were the case, it could no longer be asserted that industrial influence obstructed the entry of the issue into local politics because there was really nothing to obstruct—no movement to be resisted, no pressure to be counteracted. Industry's apparent ability to prevent air pollution from becoming a key political issue could be explained away by the fact that, in cities where industry was perceived to be influential, dirty air was simply not a matter of public concern.

In order to decide whether this explanation is accurate, it is necessary to know something about the level of popular interest in the dirty air problem. If the explanation is a sound one, then there should be a positive relationship between popular indifference and industrial influence, and public indifference should also be associated with the neglect of the issue. If we find these two things, we will also find a third: when we control for popular interest in the dirty air problem the relationship originally observed between industrial influence and the issue-ness of air pollution will tend to disappear. In effect, its disappearance is the sign that the statistical connection between industrial influence and issue-ness merely reflected the fact that both these things are dependent upon the control variable, public opinion.

Unfortunately, the evidence necessary to conduct this test of the relationship between industry's power reputation and the neglect of the dirty air issue is not available, since it has been impossible to collect information about public opinion in all the sample cities. However, some data concerning public attitudes toward air pollution in one city, St. Louis, are available. The factors, in addition to air pollution itself, that helped to determine whether or not a citizen felt that dirty air was bothersome were discussed in Chapter I, where the age, income, education, and race of the respondents were shown to be the most important. The St. Louis findings suggest that these four items, as well as the actual level of pollution, can serve us as rough substitutes for direct measures of public opinion about dirty air. By controlling for each of them, along with a measure of actual pollution, we can attempt to control for the local level of public concern about air pollution.[14] In each of the four sections of Table IV–6 one of the

14 Normally, it would be desirable to control for pollution levels and the four population characteristics simultaneously. In the present case, that strategy is probably an undesirable one. The problem here is that we have few cases but many variables. This combination tends to inflate correlation coefficients.

TABLE IV–6: PERCEIVED INDUSTRIAL INFLUENCE AND THE ISSUE-NESS OF AIR POLLU-
TION, CONTROLLING FOR SUSPENDED PARTICULATE LEVEL AND SELECTED POPULATION
CHARACTERISTIC

Population Characteristic Held Constant	Issue-ness Scale Item			
	Newspapers	Chamber of Commerce	Labor Council	Political Parties
Median education				
High-pollution cities	− .32	− .28	+ .01	− .14
	(18)	(18)	(18)	(17)
Low-pollution cities	+ .08	+ .30	− .14	− .35
	(27)	(28)	(26)	(28)
Median income				
High-pollution cities	− .32	− .21	+ .10	+ .07
	(18)	(18)	(18)	(17)
Low-pollution cities	+ .09	+ .25	− .19	− .40
	(27)	(28)	(26)	(28)
Median age				
High-pollution cities	− .34	− .23	+ .08	+ .03
	(18)	(18)	(18)	(17)
Low-pollution cities	+ .05	+ .34	− .24	− .35
	(27)	(28)	(26)	(28)
Percentage non-white				
High-pollution cities	− .35	− .22	+ .08	− .01
	(18)	(18)	(18)	(17)
Low-pollution cities	+ .05	+ .28	− .23	− .39
	(27)	(28)	(26)	(28)

four population characteristics has been held constant, as has the level
of suspended particulates. The results show that when relevant demo-
graphic factors are introduced as control variables, the pattern of
association between industrial influence and issue-ness does not dissolve. The introduction of these controls makes only a very few note-
worthy differences for the nature or strength of this relationship. This
finding does not prove that public opinion has no effect upon the
efficacy of perceived industrial influence, but it does indicate that
popular sentiment about air pollution probably does little to soften
the impact of industry's reputation for power.

INDIRECT INFLUENCE AND PLURALISM

It is presumably a sign of the pluralism of local politics that the
distribution of influence within one issue-area is seldom reproduced
exactly within others. Though local industry may figure prominently
in the pollution field, its power will not necessarily extend to matters
of urban renewal or local bond referenda or municipal elections. The
converse is also true. Industrial influence in urban renewal or bond

referenda or elections is not necessarily accompanied by industrial influence in the pollution field. The survey evidence is consistent with the presence of this variability in the distribution of influence. The findings reported in Table IV–1 showed that perceived industrial influence varies widely from one issue-area to another. Pluralist theory anticipates these results.

But pluralist theory would not lead us to expect that industrial influence in urban renewal or in other matters might be relevant for the course of political events in the pollution field. Yet it is certainly not outlandish to suppose that such transfers of influence do occur. Would-be pollution activists, though not directly confronted by the perception of industrial power, may be deterred from taking action against dirty air because they are apprehensive about coping with industry in matters of urban renewal or municipal bond referenda or in any field where industry does have a reputation for power. If this were the case, it would be possible for industry to affect the course of pollution politics even though it enjoyed neither a reputation for power nor any direct influence within the pollution field itself. An industrial reputation for power established in matters of urban renewal or in municipal bond referenda or elsewhere could cast its shadow across the politics of air pollution. Where industry enjoys a reputation for power in some fields besides air pollution, it may more effectively influence the life chances of the dirty air issue than if it had to rely exclusively on its reputation in the pollution field. To the extent that power reputations are transferable in this way from one issue-area to another, the apparent pluralism of local politics would be diminished. The independence of each policymaking area would be reduced, as would the political significance of variations, from one policymaking region to the next, in the distribution of direct influence.

The survey evidence indicates that, to some extent, transfers of influence from one issue-area to another actually do occur. Industry's reputation for power in urban renewal, mayoral elections, municipal bond referenda, and school board appointments was gauged in just the same way used earlier to measure its perceived influence in the pollution field. Several of these other measures of industrial influence turned out to be associated with the issue-ness of air pollution, and these associations were independent of the one observed earlier between industry's reputation for power in pollution matters and the life chances of the dirty air issue. In other words, perceived industrial influence in urban renewal or mayoral elections or bond referenda

TABLE IV-7: PERCEIVED INDUSTRIAL INFLUENCE IN SELECTED ISSUE-AREAS AND THE
ISSUE-NESS OF AIR POLLUTION, CONTROLLING FOR SUSPENDED PARTICULATE LEVEL
AND PERCEIVED INDUSTRIAL INFLUENCE ON THE AIR POLLUTION ISSUE

Issue-Area	Issue-ness Scale Item			
	Newspaper	Chamber of Commerce	Labor Council	Political Parties
Urban renewal				
High-pollution cities	−.17	−.58	−.24	+.01
	(18)	(18)	(18)	(17)
Low-pollution cities	−.12	+.28	−.08	−.08
	(27)	(28)	(26)	(28)
Municipal bond referenda				
High-pollution cities	−.23	−.40	−.20	+.17
	(17)	(17)	(17)	(16)
Low-pollution cities	−.38	−.04	+.03	−.28
	(27)	(28)	(26)	(28)
School board appointments				
High-pollution cities	−.07	−.45	−.05	+.22
	(18)	(18)	(18)	(17)
Low-pollution cities	−.02	+.04	+.11	+.40
	(27)	(28)	(26)	(28)
Mayoral elections				
High-pollution cities	+.13	−.34	−.07	+.16
	(18)	(18)	(18)	(17)
Low-pollution cities	+.17	+.31	+.07	−.02
	(27)	(28)	(26)	(28)

subtracts something more from the life chances of the dirty air issue
than is subtracted by industry's reputation for power in the pollution
field alone. The relevant partial correlation coefficients are presented
in Table IV–7, where not only the level of suspended particulates
but also the index of perceived industrial power on the dirty air issue
were held constant. If industrial reputations for power are transferable
to the pollution field from other issue-areas, then the resulting partial
correlation coefficients should be negative. Some of them are. It is
evident, as it was earlier, that perceived industrial influence does
operate to obstruct the emergence of the pollution issue, but only
under certain conditions. It is primarily in the high-pollution cities,
where the costs of pollution control are likely to be high, that
industry's perceived power appears to be regularly transferable to
the pollution field from other areas. Not all types of industrial influence are equally relevant to the life chances of the dirty air issue,
however. The pollution issue appears to be more vulnerable to
industry's reputation for power in the field of urban renewal and in
bond referenda than to its reputation in mayoral elections or in
school board appointments. To put it more abstractly, industry's
reputation for power seems to be most effective when it arises in a

policy-area that involves the distribution of material resources, rather than in the appointment of government personnel.

CONCLUSION

It should come as no great surprise that the political power of polluters operates to diminish the survival and growth prospects of the pollution issue. Anyone who bothers to reflect on the political sources of inaction in the pollution field could probably predict these findings, but very few investigators have thought it worth while to inquire about the political origins of political inaction. The evidence, then, provides some fairly obvious answers to a not-so-obvious question. The question has been overlooked, in part, because of a conviction that the sources of political neglect are not themselves political. It has been maintained that, if citizens really are bothered by some local problem, no politically imposed inhibitions will bar the conversion of their private discontents into a public issue. The visible heterogeneity of local politics is thought to assure that the polity will not overlook genuine citizen concerns; diversity, it is argued, is a sign of responsiveness to diverse interests. But the findings of this study indicate that this heterogeneity is not all that it has appeared to be. The visible fragmentation of political power among issue-areas does not necessarily obstruct the exercise of indirect influence across issue-areas. This means, among other things, that influence established in one issue may operate to prevent another, emergent issue from securing its place in the sun. The operation of indirect influence thus undermines the apparent pluralism of local politics by reducing the independence of one issue-area from another and prevents the enrichment of even this diluted pluralism by imposing restrictions on the emergence of new issues and issue-areas.

Uncovering these restrictive operations of indirect influence has demonstrated that political neglect is not a politically random phenomenon, at least where the air pollution issue is concerned. In this field, an element of political consistency in the occurrence of non-decisionmaking has been found. If non-decisionmaking is not a politically random occurrence, then decisionmaking cannot be politically random either. It follows that any investigation of community affairs which confines itself to the study of decisionmaking events will have founded its research conclusions upon a politically biased sample of phenomena. The bias is a serious one. Suppose, for example, that this investigation of pollution politics had been restricted to those cities in which the dirty air problem had developed into what the pluralists have called a "key political issue," towns where pollution had been a potent stimulus to decisionmaking activity. The findings suggest that these towns would tend to be ones in which industry's reputation for power was relatively puny. Evidence from these cities would provide an unsound foundation for inferences about industry's role in the politics of air pollution.

A similar bias can infuse more general conclusions about community affairs. It was pointed out earlier that the penetrability of local politics is likely to be exaggerated by investigators who confine their attentions to those political issues which have stimulated decisionmaking activity. These issues, after all, are precisely the ones that have succeeded in penetrating local politics, and the study of these successful penetrations alone will understandably lead to the conclusion that the boundaries of the political system are easily pierced. It is necessary to consider the politically unsuccessful as well as the politically successful issues, political inaction as well as action.

Actions, by themselves, are probably misleading guides to political analysis: alone, they fully reveal neither the impenetrability of local politics nor the location of political power. We have already seen some evidence, for instance, that there is a disjunction between industry's political actions and its political influence and that the mere perception of industrial power, unsupported by industrial actions, is sufficient to affect the survival prospects of the pollution issue. Of course, industry's reputation for power is not the only political factor on which the fate of the issue depends. Some of the other political determinants will be considered in the next chapter.

V Political Parties and the Pollution Issue

Industry's reputation for power has proved to be a useful explanatory variable, but a mysterious one. We know that it can help to make political inaction a more comprehensible phenomenon, but industry's reputation for power itself remains fundamentally incomprehensible. Perceived industrial influence in the pollution field does not grow, as one would expect, from industry's actions in this area. For that reason, it may be argued, there is something arbitrary or unjustified in the informants' perceptions of industrial influence. To say that the life chances of the dirty air issue are dependent upon industry's power reputation may mean only that they are related in a systematic way to the random imaginings of our respondents.

Yet these imaginings do have tangible political effects, and it would be a mistake to dismiss them as phantoms. What is more, they are not random. Certain kinds of cities appear to provide especially congenial environments for industrial power reputations. Where local elections are partisan, for example, industry is more likely to qualify as highly influential on the pollution issue than in towns where they are non-partisan ($r = +.33$). Cities without civil service regulations also appear to be hospitable breeding grounds for industrial power reputations. Where major municipal employee groups remain outside the coverage of civil service laws, industry is more likely to be regarded as highly influential than in towns where city bureaucrats are civil service employees ($r = +.33$). In short, industry's reputation for power tends to flourish where local government bears some of the formal earmarks of traditional machine politics—where local candidates for office carry partisan labels and municipal jobs are legally available for distribution as patronage.[1]

There are several possible explanations for this affinity between industrial influence and the characteristic signs of machine politics. Industrial influence, we might argue, is likely to be substantial where industrial operations are extensive. Such operations presuppose a local labor force that is largely blue-collar, and blue-collar populations have traditionally been inclined toward machine politics—hence the relationship between industrial influence and the formal trappings of the machine.

The trouble with this plausible explanation is that the data do not support it. It is true that industrial influence and blue-collar populations tend to go together. The larger the blue-collar fraction of a town's labor force, the greater the likelihood that industry will be highly influential on the pollution issue, but the connection is so weak ($r = +.08$) that it cannot carry the weight of our argument. It is necessary to look for some alternative explanations.

Alternative explanations are not hard to find, but they suffer from old age. More than fifty years ago Lincoln Steffens, Moise Ostrogorski,[2] and other observers of American urban affairs perceived that there was a symbiotic relationship between big business and the political machine. Businessmen, it was argued, sought special privileges from local governments—low tax assessments, franchises, licenses, and favors of all sorts. Of course, they were not unique in this respect. Most organized groups seek concessions of some kind from governmental authorities. What distinguished the businessmen were the large monetary rewards which they could offer for the fulfillment of their political desires. In effect, these capitalists sought to extend the incentive system of business to politics, and the appearance of the political machine signaled their success. Its distinguishing characteristic as a political organization was its extensive use of specific, material incentives to maintain the reliability of its employees.[3] Private business organizations provided the wherewithal to sustain the machine; the machine used these resources to secure con-

---

[1] It should be pointed out that partisanship and patronage are not the only manifestations of machine politics. A third characteristic of the machine is its ability to control the party primary (see Edward C. Banfield and James Q. Wilson, *City Politics*, p. 117). Unfortunately, it was not possible to collect sufficient primary election data to test for machine control of the primaries.

[2] Lincoln Steffens, *Autobiography*, chap. 27; Moise Ostrogorski, *Democracy and the Party System in the United States*, pp. 268–80.

[3] Banfield and Wilson, *City Politics*, p. 115.

trol of government; the businessmen were repaid with the privileges that they desired.

Under such an arrangement, the incentive system of the machine would make the polity particularly responsive to the wishes of business. In the field of pollution control, for example, the machine polity would be especially receptive to the demands of local industry, and this special receptivity might account for the fact that industrial influence in the pollution field and the formal traits of machine politics tend to appear in tandem. This, at least, is the explanation that Steffens or Ostrogorski would probably have favored.

But the conclusions of Steffens and Ostrogorski are founded upon the observation of urban political institutions as they existed more than half a century ago, and, by all accounts, urban affairs have undergone a substantial change since then. Today, it is held, businessmen rarely distribute their riches among local politicians. In fact, many who built their enterprises with the assistance of the machine subsequently became the backers of local reform movements, attracted by the prospect of a stable, predictable, and professional municipal bureaucracy.[4] The view is widely held that the old connection between local business and the machine has been weakened substantially, if not severed; it is therefore peculiar that we should continue to find some fairly strong hints that the old pattern of deference still persists. Perhaps what we have found is only a cultural vestige of a bygone political arrangement: the material connection between business and the machine may have withered, but the political perceptions that it engendered have survived. There is reason to believe, however, that the deference of machine polities to industrial interests is based on something more substantial than a memory, at least where the air pollution issue is concerned. It is not the cash contribution of the industrialist that maintains this deference but the party organization's way of doing business and the nature of that business. In order to understand why this is the case, it is necessary to give these matters rather extensive consideration.

THE POLITICAL PARTY AS A BROKERAGE OPERATION

In spite of its abuses, the traditional machine performed an important political function. In order to provide his businessmen-clients

[4] *Ibid.*, p. 265.

with the privileges and protection that they demanded, the political boss had to establish control over the city government. In most cities the formal apparatus of government was (and still is) a rather disjointed affair, sometimes paralyzed by the constitutional decentralization of formal authority. The boss and his machine overcame this fragmentation. Behind a constitutional façade they attempted to establish a more centralized, orderly, and informal government, and urban party organizations are still engaged in this task.

Neither the traditional machine nor its modern counterpart have attempted to achieve the desired consolidation of influence by lining up adherents behind a charismatic leader or a popular ideology. They proceed more quietly, by "purchasing" small pieces of influence and authority from the people who own them. These purchases are often made with no specific use, no policy or ideological commitment, in mind. The party boss, according to Banfield and Wilson, is merely a broker in the power business, and "much of what the political broker gathers up is on speculation: he does not know exactly how it will be used, but he is confident that someone will need a large block of power."[5] Someone is sure to find that the fractionation of local authority obstructs the achievement of a desired objective.

The boss obviously needs resources to make such purchases of power. In the heyday of the machine he seems to have relied heavily on cash and patronage, but it is generally acknowledged that municipal reform and the loss of businessmen-clients have caused a considerable shrinkage in his supply of these inducements. Today, he must acquire his purchasing power from alternative sources, and it is public policy that generates the new political currency. The party leader uses the costs and benefits of public policy to purchase bits of influence.[6]

Not all public policies have an equal exchange value for the party leader. Their worth will naturally vary with the magnitude of the costs and benefits that they create. But it is also important to take account

[5] *Ibid.*, p. 104.

[6] One interesting possibility that arises from these considerations is that the federal government, through its urban grant and subsidy programs, may be providing a large part of the resources that now sustain the operations of party politicians. These federally funded programs, though they seldom yield much in the way of traditional patronage, may supply politicians with reservoirs of policy costs and benefits, which can be used to "purchase" bits of influence. Of course, a broker can purchase power only from people who already have it. If left to his own devices, he is therefore likely to dispense federal largesse to those who are already influential in his community. He is not likely to use federal programs to achieve any significant redistribution of local political power.

of the nature of those costs and benefits. In general, "collective" benefits will be less valuable to the party leader than "specific" benefits. Clean air is an excellent example of a collective benefit, collective because there is no way to control or restrict its distribution among the residents of a city. If the local Democrats get clean air, they cannot deny its use to Republicans or Independents. Collective benefits are indivisible and cannot be captured by any social grouping whose membership does not include the whole community. The distinguishing quality of these benefits is that "they must be available to everyone if they are available to anyone."[7]

There are two reasons why control over collective benefits does not give the influence broker as much purchasing power as control over specific benefits. Because collective benefits must be available to everyone in a community, there is no way to restrict their distribution to people who have paid for them. It is understandable that many people—perhaps most people—would like to be included among those who receive without paying. People who own pieces of influence, therefore, will not readily exchange them for collective benefits. It is more profitable to be a freeloader. Nevertheless, there are some people who ignore narrow considerations of personal profit and willingly pay for the enjoyment of collective benefits. In return for a promise of clean air, for example, they may voluntarily surrender their time, energy, votes, money, or influence. Their willingness to make these sacrifices in return for a collective good, as Mancur Olson has pointed out,[8] cannot be attributed to the desire for material profit alone. Devotion to principle, program, ideology, or a sense of public obligation probably plays some part in the behavior of most clean air advocates. Their precise motivations need not concern us for the present. The important thing to note is that they surrender the influence that they possess in return for a combination of material benefits (clean air) and non-material inducements (moral or ideological gratifications). An influence broker might conceivably buy the influence of these program- or principle-oriented people by simply committing himself to their "collective" objective, thus giving them the ideological or moral gratifications that they desire in addition to the material benefit of clean air. But influence that is purchased in this way is not the kind that is likely to be most useful to an influence broker. It must certainly be counted as a political asset, but

[7] Mancur Olson, *The Logic of Collective Action*, p. 14.
[8] *Ibid.*, pp. 10–11.

it is not an especially fluid asset because the broker's title to it is likely to be encumbered with non-material commitments.

The second reason why collective benefits are not especially useful to influence brokers, then, is that they are not fluid. Fluid assets are essential to a brokerage operation. Resources acquired in one transaction must be used in other transactions to acquire still more valuable resources. The influence broker overcomes the fragmentation of local influence by assembling bits and pieces of power that he has purchased in a variety of political transactions and applying them to a single political objective. A politician who extends a favor in the field of urban renewal, for example, may demand repayment in the form of support for a municipal bond issue. In this way, he makes himself useful to those who have a stake in the achievement of a political objective and "purchases" their labor and support for any subsequent political enterprises which he may undertake.

Influence purchased with collective benefits will not exhibit the kind of fluidity that is essential for these transactions. It will tend to be tied to a relatively restricted range of principles, policies, or objectives.[9] Outside this range, the influence sellers will not receive the moral or ideological gratifications that were part of the original purchase price. Once these inducements are withdrawn, the sales contract is broken, and the sellers are likely to withdraw their support. A political leader whose assets are tied down by moral or ideological commitments will therefore find it difficult to behave like an influence broker, and a leader who "purchases" support with collective benefits is likely to find himself in just such a situation.

A leader who dispenses specific benefits in exchange for pieces of influence is much more likely to maintain the fluidity of his political holdings. His title to these assets is likely to be less encumbered because the people who surrender their influence in return for specific benefits need not be paid off with non-material inducements such as programmatic or ideological commitments. A desire for personal profit is sufficient to make people respond to specific benefits, and this is why influence purchased with these benefits is a more fluid political asset than influence purchased with collective benefits. It can be applied to political projects in which the seller has no interest or commitment. The practice of log-rolling depends on this kind of fluidity and provides a good illustration of what it means for political

[9] See James Q. Wilson and Peter Clark, "Incentive Systems: A Theory of Organization."

assets to be fluid. A log-roller creates political obligations by bestowing specific benefits on other political actors. Later, he can call in these political debts on behalf of enterprises to which the influence sellers may be completely indifferent or even antagonistic. Log-rolling is an operation that maximizes the convertibility of political assets. It tends to prevail, as some observers have noted, where the political stakes are highly specific, and this is probably no accident.[10]

Because specific benefits have greater purchasing power than collective benefits and because they yield more fluid political assets, they are likely to be attractive to people who are influence brokers—in American cities, usually the party politician. The preference for specific benefits probably has much to do with his behavior. It may explain, for example, why he usually purchases influence in bits and pieces rather than in wholesale lots.[11] It may help to account for some of the policy preferences of party men. It has been noted, for instance, that politicians tend to be antagonistic toward urban planning because "the politician's way at the municipal level seems to be usually slanted toward segmental approaches and special interests."[12] The segmental bias is certainly more congenial to a specific than to a collective incentive system.

The same kind of bias may be responsible for the connection that we have observed between perceived industrial influence on the air pollution issue and the formal characteristics of the machine. Because party organizations are not inclined toward collective benefits, we can expect that political machines will be relatively uninterested in the benefits of pollution control policy. Clean air, a collective benefit, will not add much to the resources that party influence brokers require to sustain their political operations. On the other hand, the costs of pollution control—its negative benefits—are clearly not of the collective variety. It is not the case that if these costs fall on anyone, they must fall on everyone. A large portion of them can be "captured" by a group whose membership is quite limited. In short, the costs of pollution control constitute a specific, negative benefit of public policy that might be used to carry on the operations of a political brokerage. These costs fall most noticeably on local industry, and it is for that reason, perhaps, that a machine polity is more likely

10 Theodore Lowi, "American Business, Public Policy, Case-Studies and Political Theory."
11 Edward C. Banfield, *Political Influence*, pp. 241–42.
12 David Wallace, "Renaissancemanship," p. 174.

than others to turn toward industry where the air pollution issue is concerned. It is there that the politician's entrepreneurial opportunities lie. By manipulating the costs of pollution control, he may be able to purchase the kind of influence that is most useful in overcoming the formal fragmentation of urban authority.

The inclination toward industry is evident not only in machine politics, but among party men generally. The findings reported in Table V–1 show political party chairmen more likely than most other informants to perceive that industry would have an essential role in any local anti-pollution efforts. It can be argued that this result reflects the interest of the party politician in maintaining or enhancing the brokerage operations of his organization. He turns toward industry in the matter of pollution control because it is there that he can use specific inducements to acquire relatively fluid political assets. Of course the "brokerage" interpretation is not the only one that might be offered to account for the political perceptions of party men or for the conjunction of perceived industrial influence with machine politics. What makes this interpretation a particularly attractive one is the fact that it is consistent with both of these findings and with others as well. Because it lends coherence to many bits of evidence, it is useful, and probably correct.

Many characteristics of pollution politics in Gary and East Chicago can be understood in terms of the party politician's preference for specific rather than for collective policy benefits. It is probably sig-

TABLE V–1: PERCEPTIONS OF INDUSTRIAL INFLUENCE ON AIR POLLUTION CONTROL

Group	Industrial Support Is "Essential"
	%
Labor council presidents	58.5
	(46)
Political party chairmen	55.9
	(92)
Newspaper editors	51.1
	(47)
Chamber of Commerce presidents	47.9
	(48)
Bar association presidents	37.2
	(43)
Bank presidents	35.0
	(48)

Note: Numbers in parentheses represent respondents in each category; total respondents, 336, of which 12 were n.a.

nificant, for example, that the promoters of pollution control proposals in both towns were not party organization men. The advocates
of clean air appeared outside the party organizations because the
party incentive systems, relying as they did on specific benefits, were
probably not congenial to men who sought collective goods.

The behavior of party politicians during the course of the dirty air
debate may also reflect the bias of the party system. Local politicians
seldom intervened in local discussions of the pollution problem, but
when they did, it was often to represent the interests of industrial
corporations. Mayor Migas, at the request of some East Chicago
industrial executives, delayed the introduction of Loyd Cohen's dirty
air ordinance. Mayor Chacharis, when he spoke out on the pollution
problem, counseled caution in the campaign against dirty air lest an
excessively strict regulation of industrial emissions do damage to the
economic interests of U.S. Steel and perhaps to the economic well-
being of Gary. It may be that these kindnesses to local manufacturers
represented attempts to manipulate the costs of pollution control and
thereby purchase bits of industrial influence.

PARTIES AND THE LIFE CHANCES OF THE POLLUTION ISSUE

Because of the nature of his political operations, the broker-
politician will probably respond more readily to requests for specific
benefits than he will to requests for collective benefits. Where he is
a prominent figure, his favoritism can be expected to have some effect
upon the kinds of demands that rise to the surface of local politics.
"Collective" demands will tend to be filtered out of the political system because they cannot be made to serve his purposes so easily as
specific demands. In politics dominated by party organizations, then,
we can expect that the demand for clean air will tend to be shunted
aside, and pollution politics in Gary and East Chicago provide a
possible illustration of this phenomenon.

In East Chicago during the late 1940's the local Democratic Party
organization was torn by factional rivalries. Mayor Frank Migas, the
party chairman, was under political siege. He could not attract a
majority vote in the primaries, and it was not long before an opposition faction ejected him, first from the party chairmanship and later
from the mayor's office as well. It was during this period of party
debilitation that Loyd Cohen successfully mobilized East Chicagoans

for the campaign against dirty air and managed, with no great difficulty, to place the air pollution problem on the community's political agenda.

There may have been more than a coincidental connection between the temporary confusion in East Chicago's dominant party and Cohen's success. Cohen did not feel obliged to take his anti-pollution proposals to the party politicians, and his effectiveness, one might argue, depended in part upon his circumvention of these broker-politicians. He did not rely on political middlemen to assemble the bits of influence that were needed for his project: he himself secured the acquiescence of local industrialists; he activated public support for his anti-pollution campaign. He was his own political broker, and his political self-reliance meant that the dirty air issue, in its rise to prominence, would skirt the party organization and the organizational bias which inclines politicians toward policies that generate specific benefits.

The Democratic Party, as the evidence in Chapter II indicates, was probably more powerful and tightly organized in Gary during the late 1950's than it was in East Chicago during the late 1940's. When Milton Roth raised the dirty air issue with Mayor Mandich, Gary's Democratic organization was in the midst of a political consolidation, and by the time that Albert Gavit attempted to reopen the dirty air debate, the consolidation appears to have been complete. Mayor Chacharis had been able to command more than 80 per cent of the vote in the Democratic primary of 1959. The robust condition of the party may have been one of the factors that obstructed the emergence of the air pollution issue. If obstruction did occur, it was not the result of any active attempt to suppress the issue. Party leaders were simply uninterested in it, perhaps because it originated with political outsiders like Albert Gavit and Milton Roth, possibly because the issue did not seem to be particularly profitable. Their disinterest was a crucial factor in the progress of the pollution issue because Gary's pollution activists, unlike Loyd Cohen, seem to have thought it necessary to turn to them for assistance. Albert Gavit was especially sensitive to this need: his anti-pollution efforts were designed, for the most part, to activate party politicians on behalf of clean air. When the party men remained unmoved after his repeated attempts to mobilize them, Gavit finally gave up. He believed that the anti-pollution campaign was a hopeless effort so long as it did not number them among its backers.

In East Chicago, then, where the party organization was temporarily disorganized and pollution activists did not rely on its brokerage services, the dirty air issue flourished. In Gary, where the party organization was strong and pollution activists turned to it for assistance, the issue floundered. It was not until Mayor Chacharis went to jail, and the party hierarchy was momentarily disorganized, that the pollution issue began to rise toward a position of prominence on Gary's political agenda. This coincidence and others like it suggest that where local party organizations are strong and unified, the life chances of the pollution issue will be diminished. Clean air, we might argue, simply does not yield the kinds of political assets that party organizations are likely to find attractive, and its irrelevance to party interests is sufficient to diminish the force of demands for pollution control in cities where parties monopolize the political initiatives of their communities.

If this is an accurate analysis of pollution politics in Gary and East Chicago, then we ought to find some support for it in other cities of our sample. We ought to find that where members of local political strata turn to political parties for a solution to the dirty air problem, the size of the pollution issue is diminished. People who "turn to the parties" are those who believe that party support is essential to the success of a local pollution control program. It was a similar belief that we looked for when measuring perceived industrial influence—the belief that industrial support would be essential for a campaign against dirty air. The present object of measurement, therefore, is really "perceived party influence," and it has been measured in the same way, using the same reputational question and the same index of influence.[13] For the time being, no distinction will be made between Republican and Democratic influence. The party influence measurement combines reputational votes for both parties in a single index. Political parties in a city qualify as highly influential on the air pollution issue if their joint share of the "essential" votes on this issue is greater than the median two-party share.

The nature of political party operations and the evidence from Gary and East Chicago lead us to expect that, among towns with similar pollution levels, there will be a negative relationship between party influence in the matter and the life chances of the pollution issue. The findings reported in Table V–2 do not support these expectations:

[13] See above, pp. 113–16.

TABLE V-2: PERCEIVED PARTY INFLUENCE AND THE ISSUE-NESS OF AIR POLLUTION, CONTROLLING FOR SUSPENDED PARTICULATE LEVEL

| | Issue-ness Scale Item | | | |
	Newspaper	Chamber of Commerce	Labor Council	Political Parties
Party influence on air pollution	$-.19*$ (45)	$-.02$ (46)	$+.02$ (44)	$+.11$ (45)

* Partial correlation coefficients.

after controlling for variations in local pollution levels, there is only a weak and uneven association between the power reputation of local parties and the various indicators of positiontaking on dirty air.

There are, however, some local conditions that accentuate the impact of party influence upon the survival and growth prospects of the pollution issue. As in the case of industrial influence, the operation of perceived party power appears to be affected by the local pollution level. In low-pollution towns party influence does seem to inhibit the early growth of the issue; in high-pollution towns it does not. The finding is an understandable one. In low-pollution towns, the prospective benefits of pollution control are relatively small. The party's need for specific inducements can therefore be expected to override the need for pollution abatement. In high-pollution towns, on the other hand, the benefits of pollution abatement are relatively large, and the dirty air issue can therefore be expected to overcome the party bias against "collective" policies.

Low pollution is not the only condition that appears to activate the deterrent capacity of perceived party influence. Another and more important catalytic factor is the absence of perceived industrial power. The operation of this factor is notable not only because it accentuates the impact of party influence but because it most effectively reveals the nature of the political party's organizational bias. It has been argued here that this bias inclines the party toward public policies that are likely to generate specific, capturable benefits because control over such benefits enables the party organization to sustain itself as a political brokerage. Control over collective benefits, on the other hand, is not likely to provide the party with the kind of purchasing power that it needs to acquire the fluid political assets that are essential to a brokerage operation. This is why the benefits of pollution abatement policy fail to arouse the interest of broker-politicians. They are collective benefits. But the costs of pollution control policy may well stimulate the party politician's entrepreneurial appetite. These negative benefits of public policy are relatively specific. They fall heavily upon a social grouping whose membership is limited—the local industrial community. Because this is the case, they may provide the party politician with the sorts of inducements that he needs to carry on his brokerage activities. He may manipulate the costs of pollution control in order to purchase useful bits of industrial influence, provided, of course, that industry is perceived to have influence to sell. In towns where industry enjoys a reputation for power, therefore, we should find that perceived party influence operates to enhance the life chances of the pollution issue because the dirty air debate will appear to offer entrepreneurial opportunities to political parties.

Where industry does not enjoy a reputation for power, the pollution issue can supply the party politician with little that is useful to his organization. We can therefore expect that party influence will operate to inhibit the emergence of the dirty air issue. That is precisely what we find. The results in Table V–3 show that among cities where industry does not enjoy a reputation for power in the pollution field, perceived party influence is negatively associated with most of the indicators of issue-ness. Here, the party's influence appears to reduce the life chances of the pollution issue. Among cities where industry does enjoy a reputation for power, however, party influence seems to operate to enhance the life chances of the dirty air debate.

It was found earlier that the air pollution issue tends not to flourish in cities where industry enjoys a reputation for power. These new findings suggest, in addition, that where industry does enjoy that reputation, the life chances of the air pollution issue will be greater in cities where political parties are influential than where they are not. This finding, like several of the previous ones, can be subsumed under

TABLE V–3: PERCEIVED PARTY INFLUENCE AND THE ISSUE-NESS OF AIR POLLUTION, CONTROLLING FOR PERCEIVED INDUSTRIAL INFLUENCE AND SUSPENDED PARTICULATE LEVEL

| | | Issue-ness Scale Item | | | |
		Newspaper	Chamber of Commerce	Labor Council	Political Parties
Perceived party influence	High industrial influence	− .06 (19)	+ .13 (20)	+ .48 (19)	+ .40 (20)
	Low industrial influence	− .44 (26)	− .20 (26)	− .20 (25)	+ .01 (25)

the "brokerage" interpretation of political party operations. It seems to reflect the interest that party organizations have in using the air pollution issue to "purchase" industrial influence—when that influence is available.

The impact of party influence could not be explained away by referring to local population characteristics like median age, educational level, income, or racial composition—factors that were previously found to affect the level of public concern about dirty air. It is likely, then, that the workings of party influence do not simply reflect public preferences in the matter of air pollution. They represent a response to organizational, not just popular, demands. The consideration of local population characteristics therefore fails to alter the assessment that party influence can have an important effect upon the penetrability of community political systems.

Nor is this assessment much altered when a distinction is made between Democratic and Republican parties. Both parties appear to affect the life chances of the pollution issue in roughly the same way, as Tables V–4 and V–5 indicate. They show that Democratic Party influence and Republican Party influence both operate according to the "brokerage" pattern. They promote the emergence of the pollu-

TABLE V–4: PERCEIVED DEMOCRATIC PARTY INFLUENCE AND THE ISSUE-NESS OF AIR POLLUTION, CONTROLLING FOR PERCEIVED INDUSTRIAL INFLUENCE AND SUSPENDED PARTICULATE LEVEL

| | | Issue-ness Scale Item | | | |
		Newspaper	Chamber of Commerce	Labor Council	Political Parties
Perceived Democratic influence	High industrial influence	+.23 (19)	+.18 (20)	+.56 (19)	+.14 (20)
	Low industrial influence	−.44 (26)	−.20 (26)	−.20 (25)	−.01 (25)

TABLE V–5: PERCEIVED REPUBLICAN PARTY INFLUENCE AND THE ISSUE-NESS OF AIR POLLUTION, CONTROLLING FOR PERCEIVED INDUSTRIAL INFLUENCE AND SUSPENDED PARTICULATE LEVEL

| | | Issue-ness Scale Item | | | |
		Newspaper	Chamber of Commerce	Labor Council	Political Parties
Perceived Republican influence	High industrial influence	−.16 (19)	+.08 (20)	+.53 (19)	+.38 (20)
	Low industrial influence	−.27 (26)	−.01 (26)	−.21 (25)	−.18 (25)

tion issue in those cities where industry has a reputation for power—where it is perceived to have influence to sell; they inhibit the emergence of the issue in towns where industry does not enjoy a reputation for power and does not have influence to sell. The small differences that do appear between the effects of Democratic and Republican influence suggest that the operation of Democratic Party influence may adhere somewhat more consistently to the "brokerage" pattern than Republican Party influence.

THE NATURE OF PARTY INFLUENCE

It should not be difficult to understand how the built-in biases of the political party may affect the treatment that the pollution issue receives at the hands of party organizations. However, it remains unclear just why party bias should also affect the responsiveness to the pollution problem of local newspapers, Chambers of Commerce, and labor organizations. We do not know how perceived party influence is brought to bear on these organizations nor why they respond to it. The survey data do not provide clear answers to either of these questions. It is uncertain, in the first place, whether the party exercises its influence through observable political actions or whether its "unjustified" reputation for influence affects the behavior of other organizations—in other words, whether the party's influence is direct or indirect.

The problem here is to discover whether or not perceived party influence in the pollution field is based on party behavior in the area, and an attempt has been made to solve the problem in the same way as the earlier attempt to determine whether perceived industrial influence was a reflection of industrial action.[14] In this case, however, the inquiry produced uncertain results. The weight of the evidence is divided about evenly between the conclusion that party influence is direct and the conclusion that it is indirect. It is probable, therefore, that it is a mixture of both.

We can only speculate about the ways in which the two kinds of party influence manage to affect the behavior of civic activists, but the speculations are supported at some points by bits of evidence. For example, the findings from Gary and East Chicago suggest that, if party support is thought to be essential to a pollution control campaign, then the expressed disinterest of party politicians in the pollu-

[14] For a more complete discussion of this problem, see above, pp. 121–24.

tion problem could have a decisive effect upon the career of the issue. Local pollution activists might abandon their efforts on behalf of clean air and turn their attention to projects that appear to have more favorable political prospects. Few people like to waste their effort on enterprises that seem doomed to failure.

The prospect of failure seems to have had something to do with the slow development of Gary's dirty air debate. Party politicians were able to influence the growth of the anti-pollution campaign by diminishing the optimism of some pollution activists. Because the politicians were thought to be essential to the anti-pollution effort, their actions in this matter were critical signs of the chances for success. The cues that they gave to other political actors could influence the distribution of energy and attention among alternative civic enterprises.

The party's reputation for power, however, is probably not the only thing that may induce a civic activist to take his cues from party politicians. The politician, after all, has traditionally been regarded as expert in the evaluation of political possibilities, and it is understandable that people should rely on his judgment where questions of political success and failure are involved. As a political broker, it is his business to know which political projects are likely to yield a return on investment and which ones are not. His evaluation of a civic enterprise can therefore make it more or less attractive to other political actors. Its stock may rise or fall according to his judgment. Of course, if he is not regarded as an effective influence broker, his judgments will probably carry little weight with other political actors, but where he has a reputation for power, there is an especially good chance that it will be accompanied by a reputation for political expertise.

There is another, more indirect avenue of party influence which may also help to carry the party's organizational bias into the activities of newspapers, labor organizations, and Chambers of Commerce. The connection between the party and these other organizations may be an "ecological" one such as Norton Long describes when he suggests that communities may be regarded as an ecology of games.[15] The ecological interpretation of urban affairs emphasizes the interconnectedness of various local institutions and organizations. Like the plants and animals in a natural ecological system, the elements of

15 Norton Long, "The Local Community as an Ecology of Games."

a local organizational ecology use one another in order to maintain themselves. The fruits of one organization provide other organizations with sustenance.

The ecological approach to local politics calls attention to these interdependent relationships and to the continuous mutual adjustments that they are likely to entail. Organizations, like the creatures of a natural ecological system, modify their life habits so as to make use of the resources generated by their neighbors, and an ecological system that includes a strong party organization is likely to be characterized by modifications of a particular sort. We have seen that the resources that a strong party typically makes available to its organizational neighbors are specific benefits, and we can expect that these neighbors will adjust their incentive systems so that, in their own efforts to keep and attract members or adherents, they can make use of the inducements that the party provides. These adjustments are likely to have a visible impact upon organizational behavior. The nature of an organization's incentive system, as James Wilson and Peter Clark have pointed out, is likely to be reflected in the character of organizational strategy, in the configurations of organizational conflicts, and in leadership behavior.[16] It is also likely to have some effect upon the kinds of political demands that an organization generates or nurtures. If its incentive system is fueled by specific benefits, it will tend to make relatively few collective demands because collective benefits will not effectively serve its own maintenance and enhancement interests.

Political parties, therefore, may influence the activities of other organizations by affecting the character of the organizational resources that happen to be available within a local community. The very existence of a strong party organization may induce other local groups to shift their survival strategies and their political behavior. For example, Chambers of Commerce in strong party towns will probably differ in a systematic way from Chambers in weak party towns. In a strong party town we would expect the Chamber to stress "specific" services to its members. In a weak party town we would expect the Chamber to concentrate on more diffuse, intangible inducements, like appeals to the spirit of civic boosterism or local pride.[17]

[16] "Incentive Systems."

[17] An "ecological" explanation of this sort seems to provide the most promising way to account for James Q. Wilson's findings that the organization of Negro politics in a community generally comes to resemble the organization of white politics. Negro political organization is heavily influenced by the organizational resources available,

The adaptation of its organizational neighbors to the existence of the party is something like the adaptation of giraffes to the existence of tall trees. In both cases the adaptation functions to enhance growth and survival prospects, and in both cases the adaptors acquire a limited resemblance to the objects that have induced their adjustments. Party indifference to clean air and to collective benefits generally is likely to be transferred to other organizations within its environment. This hypothesis might explain why, under certain conditions, perceived party influence seems to deter local newspapers, Chambers of Commerce, and labor organizations from taking positions on the dirty air issue. The party's influence may operate to create or reinforce organizational incentive systems that are inhospitable to such collective benefits.

But there are also some situations in which party influence seems to have just the opposite effect. In towns where industry enjoys a reputation for power, perceived party influence operates to enhance the survival prospects of the pollution issue. This result, as has been pointed out, is quite consistent with the organizational needs of political parties, reflecting their interest in using specific policy benefits (in this case, negative benefits) to purchase bits of industrial influence. In towns where industry has influence to sell, it is understandable that parties themselves might attempt to promote the pollution issue. But it is not quite understandable why, in these same towns, party influence should induce other organizations to promote the issue. The "ecological" bias that strong parties engender would presumably diminish the interest of these other organizations in the quest for collective benefits like clean air. How can party influence operate to reverse this bias?

A partial answer is that the party does not uniformly succeed in doing so. A look at the top row of Table V–3 shows that local newspapers and Chambers of Commerce are not especially responsive to party influence in towns where industry enjoys a reputation for power. Only local labor organizations seem to be sensitive to their influence, and it is a notable coincidence that only in the case of labor organizations can we conclude that the operation of party influence is

---

and the nature of those resources is influenced, in turn, by the character of white political organizations. Chicago provides a good illustration of the ecological relationship that may exist between white and Negro political organizations. Here, it appears, the emergence of the Dawson machine within the black ghetto was in large part a response to the availability of organizational resources that were generated by Chicago's white machine, chiefly patronage, favors, and cash (see James Q. Wilson, *Negro Politics*, pp. 22–24, 48–76).

largely direct rather than indirect. The responsiveness of labor councils to party influence can be explained in terms of observable party action in the matter of dirty air.[18]

This coincidence suggests that we may be able to describe the operations of party influence like this: where the pollution issue is irrelevant to the party's organizational interests, the party's indirect, "ecological" influence will operate to diminish the life chances of the issue. Where it is advantageous for the party to promote the debate, it must exercise its influence directly in order to overcome the community bias that it has created indirectly: it must take some positive action if the issue is to develop. The party organization can then bargain about it with local industrial corporations. Influence brokers may purchase bits of industrial influence by making concessions to industrial interests.

Two points concerning this description ought to be kept in mind. First, it is highly tentative, though it is occasionally supported by uncertain hints in the survey data or in the case study materials. Second, even if the speculative nature of the description is discounted, it must be recognized that the portrayal is onesided. It attempts to reveal the ways in which a strong party organization may affect the behavior of its organizational neighbors but neglects to take account of the reciprocal influence that neighboring organizations may exert upon the operations of a political party. The possibility of mutual adaptation, not just onesided adjustment, is implied by the ecological analogy used here.

The debut of the political machine, which was discussed earlier, provides a good illustration of the way in which the party may adjust to its organizational neighbors. If the classic account is reliable, the appearance of the machine can be regarded as the party's response to the emergence of large-scale, capitalist enterprise. Party organizations adapted their operations and their incentive systems so that they could make use of the resources that local capitalists were able to provide. The growth of the machine represented an "ecological" adjustment of the party to other organizations in its environment.

Another sign of party adjustment is the impact of reputedly powerful manufacturing firms upon the operation of party influence. The presence of these industrial corporations seems to make a difference

[18] Specifically, there is a positive relationship between perceived party power and the occurrence of dirty air discussions between labor council officials and party officials ($r = +.28$) and another positive association between the occurrence of these discussions and positiontaking by labor on the issue ($r = +.40$).

in the way the party works, and community newspapers appear to have a somewhat similar capacity to affect party operations. Newspapers, like industrial corporations, are profitmaking organizations, but in the newspaper business "profit" will very probably include diffuse, intangible rewards as well as hard cash. If publishers were singlemindedly devoted to financial advancement, they would probably not be in the newspaper business.[19] Among the intangible returns that help to sustain the newspaper as a community organization, moral and ideological gratifications figure prominently. Newspapermen like to think of themselves as public crusaders or as guardians of the public welfare, and the fact that the newspaper claims the public in general as its constituency, and things in general as its field of competence, reinforces these self-conceptions. It is, as Norton Long points out, one of the few local institutions with a long-term interest in the community as a whole.[20]

The newspaper's claim to represent the whole community will probably incline it, more than other local organizations, toward public policies whose benefits accrue to the whole community. Its advocacy of collective causes may help to justify its institutional pretensions and to strengthen its ability to employ moral or ideological inducements to maintain itself and its following. We should therefore expect to find local newspapers among the leading advocates of collective benefits such as clean air, and the findings reported in Chapter III confirm those expectations.[21] We might also anticipate that the presence of an influential newspaper within a community would affect the operations of local political parties. The newspaper is probably less responsive than most other local organizations to specific inducements, the broker-politician's stock in trade, so that where the newspaper is influential, the party politician may have to change his way of doing business. In order to purchase newspaper support for his civic enterprises or to forestall its opposition, the politician may find it necessary to employ non-material or collective incentives. In doing so, he would of course depart from the normal operating procedures of an influence broker.

Perhaps more important than newspaper influence itself is what newspaper prominence reveals about the character of a community and its residents. Where newspapers enjoy a reputation for power,

[19] Banfield and Wilson, *City Politics*, pp. 319–21.
[20] Long, "The Local Community as an Ecology of Games," pp. 259–61.
[21] See above, p. 89.

it is likely that a large segment of the local population is responsive to the moral or ideological inducements that newspapers can employ. When this is the case, the party politician will find it difficult to play the role of an influence broker. He will frequently discover that specific policy benefits do not provide him with much purchasing power because the sellers of influence demand moral or ideological gratifications in exchange for their support or cooperation. To the extent that the politician meets those demands, he leaves the influence brokerage business.

In short, newspaper influence and the things that go with it could conceivably modify the operations of political party organizations in a way that might be significant for the life chances of the pollution issue. In the presence of a reputedly powerful newspaper, the party bias against clean air might dissolve. This change could be brought about in much the same way that industrial influence can induce a shift in the party's treatment of the pollution issue. Where newspapers are perceived to be powerful, party politicians may see some profit in promoting the dirty air issue. They can use the benefits of pollution control to purchase newspaper influence, which they can then use to sustain their own operations. Where newspapers are not perceived to be powerful, however, the air pollution issue will not present these entrepreneurial advantages. An uninfluential newspaper has nothing of political value to offer in exchange for the benefits of pollution control. In such a situation, the party's organizational biases will not be softened, and party influence will operate to diminish the force of clean air campaigns.

Unfortunately, the data do not bear out these reasonable expectations. The power reputations of local newspapers have no consistent effect upon the operation of party influence. Newspaper prominence is reflected less in the operation than in the level of perceived party power, and there is a good reason for this result. Newspaper influence tends, as suggested above, to be encumbered with moral or ideological commitments and is not an especially fluid political asset. This is not to say that it is completely irrelevant to the dealings of a party influence broker, however. It is significant that party organizations do not thrive on the kind of influence that they can buy from newspapers or their adherents. Newspapers do not contribute much to their sustenance. Where newspapers occupy a prominent place in the local ecology of organizations, we can therefore expect that political parties will find it relatively difficult to collect the kind of political influence

TABLE V-6: PERCEIVED NEWSPAPER INFLUENCE AND PERCEIVED PARTY INFLUENCE

		Newspaper Influence in				
		Air Pollution	Municipal Bond Referenda	Urban Renewal	School Board Appointments	Mayoral Elections
	Air pollution		−.19	−.26	−.14	−.19
	Municipal bond referenda	−.20		−.38	−.15	−.38
Party influence in	Urban renewal	−.35	−.29		−.05	−.18
	School board appointments	−.31	−.21	−.22		−.31
	Mayoral elections	−.13	−.22	−.40	−.10	

which makes them grow strong. Newspapers and political parties tend not to flourish as influential actors within the same ecological system; that, at least, is the implication of the findings presented in Table V-6.[22] The table shows that perceived newspaper influence in any issue-area is negatively associated with perceived party power in any other issue-area. The relationship between these two local institutions appears to be competitive, not symbiotic.

CONCLUSION

Edward Banfield has argued that local political issues grow out of the maintenance and enhancement needs of a city's large formal organizations.[23] In this chapter and the preceding one an attempt has been made to elaborate on the mirror image of this hypothesis. The argument, in effect, is that the neglect of potential political issues can

[22] The associations between newspaper power in one issue-area and party power in that issue-area have been purposely omitted from Table V-6. The reason, briefly, is that the influence measures for the two kinds of local organizations are based upon each organization's share of the reputational votes cast within particular issue-areas. The larger the newspaper's share of the votes within an issue-area, the smaller the party's share is likely to be, and vice versa. In other words, there will tend to be an artificially induced negative relationship between the index of party influence in an issue-area and the index of newspaper influence within that issue-area. This artificial association tends to inflate the negative correlation between perceived party power and perceived newspaper power. The same problem does not exist when we compare perceived party influence in one issue-area with perceived newspaper influence in another issue-area. In this case, the two local organizations would be drawing on different pools of reputational votes.

[23] *Political Influence*, p. 263.

be traced to their incompatibility with the maintenance and enhancement needs of large organizations.

Where industry is powerful, for example, the life chances of the
pollution issue are diminished, and it is not difficult to understand
why. Industrial corporations are sustained by profits, and the pollution issue poses a possible threat to profits. Industrial influence therefore operates to inhibit the growth of the dirty air issue. The impact
of political parties is somewhat more subtle. Parties maintain themselves by exchanging specific benefits for pieces of influence, and
there are some circumstances in which the pollution issue fails to
generate benefits that can be employed in these exchanges. In such
situations, party influence operates to obstruct the entry of the issue
into local politics.

In a sense, the source of this obstruction is not the political party
itself, but political pluralism. The party's operating procedures, as
well as its organizational biases, are derived from the need to do business in polities where a variety of independent political elites hold the
power to frustrate successful political action. Were it not for this
fractionation of influence, there would be little demand for the
brokerage services that American political parties have traditionally
provided, and were it not for the imperatives of its brokerage operations, the political party would probably not have maintained its
indifference toward collective goods. In pluralism, it appears, there
is a built-in potential for political bias, and influential party organizations help to realize that potential. The bias is quite similar to the
one that seems to have roused muckrakers fifty years ago to complain
that American politics and politicians accorded special advantages to
"special interests." Some of the muckraking journalists, like Lincoln
Steffens, went on to point out that this inclination toward special
interests did not originate in the moral degeneracy of party politicians
but was built into the business of American politics. The preference
for specific benefits has a similar kind of origin, and perhaps it is
a descendant or a continuation of the political bias that Steffens and
others perceived. At any rate, it may constitute an important limita-
tion upon the alleged openness of pluralistic political systems, tending
to obstruct the expression of collective interests and the political
progress of collective issues.

In general, a political issue tends to be ignored if there is a mismatch between the kinds of benefits that it is likely to create and the
kinds of inducements that influential community organizations need

in order to survive and grow. This elementary generalization, however, leaves some important things unsaid. It suggests that the life chances of a political issue will depend in part upon the kinds of policy benefits that are at stake in it, but the proposition says nothing about the criteria that might be used to distinguish one kind of benefit from another. It would not be hard to assemble a long list of ways in which we might classify policy benefits. The problem is to identify those dimensions of variability that are worthy of attention, and it is to that problem, among others, that recent investigations in "policy theory" have addressed themselves. The one element common to most of these efforts is the distinction, presented under various labels, between collective and specific benefits. Theodore Lowi, for example, has called attention to the "disaggregability" of public policies—the divisibility of the costs and benefits that they entail. Lewis Froman, relying on the work of Lowi and others, has drawn a distinction between "segmental" and "areal" policies—policies that affect particular groups within a community vs. policies that affect the whole local population.[24]

The same kind of distinction has occasionally been employed by organization theorists in their efforts to classify organizational incentive systems. Something like the collective-specific dimension appears to underlie the division that Wilson and Clark make between organizations with purpose-oriented incentive systems, on the one hand, and organizations with solidary or material incentive systems on the other. The difference between collective and specific also seems to be one element in Amitai Etzioni's distinction between "expressive" and "utilitarian" organizations.[25] Organizational incentives, like policy benefits, can be arranged on the continuum from collective to specific. More important, the location of an organization's incentive system on this continuum has something to do with organizational practices and propensities. The classificatory efforts of the organization theorists would have been wasted if they did not show that the character of an organization's incentive system makes a difference in its behavior.

In the present effort to relate the maintenance and enhancement needs of organizations to the costs and benefits of political issues, the attempt has been made to capitalize upon the analytic tendencies that

24 Lowi, "American Business, Public Policy"; Lewis A. Froman, Jr., "An Analysis of Public Policies in Cities."
25 Wilson and Clark, "Incentive Systems"; Amitai Etzioni, *A Comparative Analysis of Complex Organizations.*

are shared by both organization theory and policy theory and to merge the categories implicit in organizational analysis with the categories of policy analysis. Collective organizations, it is argued, will tend to attach themselves to collective issues, specific organizations to specific issues. The fortunes of a political issue can be expected to vary with the prominence of its organizational patrons.

Policy theory and organization theory are drawn together by more than the similarity that exists between their respective classification schemes. There is also some resemblance between the ways in which these two enterprises use the classification systems that they have developed. Policy theorists seek not only to categorize policy characteristics but to relate these characteristics to patterns of political activity—to uncover the connection between the substance of policy and the process of policymaking. That has been one concern here as well. In Chapter III an attempt was made to find out whether the air pollution issue regularly evoked some distinctive pattern of political activity, and it was argued that, where dirty air was concerned, different cities tend to move toward a single pattern of political decisionmaking. The costs and benefits that are at stake in the pollution issue are everywhere similar, and this similarity in the political stakes is responsible for inter-city similarities in the political process. The line of reasoning here is quite similar to the one that Wilson and Clark follow in their attempt to relate organizational behavior to organizational incentive systems. Like the policy theorists, they hope to discover some systematic relationship between patterns of activity and the types of inducements which stimulate and sustain those activities. In this respect, policy theory and organization theory seem to run parallel. In fact, the phenomena themselves, as well as the analytic approaches to them, exhibit some notable similarities.

Issues and policies are not simply pieces of political subject matter. To say that an issue has arisen is to announce the emergence of an informal organization, a body of would-be decisionmakers who interact with one another in their efforts to deal with some common concern. Political issues, then, have an organizational aspect. When policy theorists try to relate the characteristics of a policy to the pattern of political activity which it has generated, they are attempting, in effect, to establish a connection between the kinds of inducements that are distributed by an informal organization and the internal practices of that organization. We have been looking at issues as organizations, but we have been less concerned with their internal operations than with their external relations. As organizations, issues are dependent upon their environments for the fulfillment of their maintenance and enhancement needs. They are elements in the same local ecological systems which contain Chambers of Commerce or political parties.

What has been said about the local ecology of organizations suggests that a certain kind of coherence or unity will tend to develop within such a system. To the extent that it is possible, groups will adapt their operations so as to make use of the resources that are provided by other, influential groups. When such adaptations are not consistent with the maintenance and enhancement needs of an organization, its prominence can be expected to decline. This seems to be the fate of a political party that finds itself confronted with a highly influential newspaper. The end result of all these organizational adjustments is a degree of consistency among the operations and inclinations of organizations that are locally influential. In this way, organizational biases may be translated into a general community bias.

As members of the local ecological system, issues and issue-areas can be expected to partake of this bias. This means that we may expect to find some consistency or unity among the political issues that flourish in a community, just as we would expect to find a similar consistency among the influential organizations of a town. In part, this common tie among issues may reflect the consistency which has been presumed to exist among the inclinations of locally influential organizations. In part, it may be the result of "ecological" interactions among the issues themselves. The existence, the sources, and the nature of this unity among issues are the concerns of the next chapter.

VI | Air Pollution and Political Agendas

If dirty air were the only problem demanding the attention of urban political leaders, we would almost certainly be breathing more easily than we do. But cleaning up the air is obviously just one of the many civic projects that draw upon the political energies of American cities, and because it is just one concern among many, it is understandable that it should sometimes be overlooked. Cities may ignore their dirty air simply because they have other things to worry about.

Local leaders, it might be argued, are able to cope with just so many political issues at one time. To the extent that they become interested in some matters, they must ignore others. In Gary, for example, Mayor Mandich was so busy with the matter of downtown public parking that he was unable to make the necessary preparations for the Armour Research Institute's air pollution survey.[1] One political issue distracted attention from the other, and this was probably not the only instance in which the progress of Gary's clean air campaign had been retarded by the existence of political distractions. The town, after all, faced many problems that seemed to demand the attention of its political leaders. Public housing, traffic, race relations, and population growth could have diverted the attention of Gary's political activists from the cloud of grit and smoke that hung above them.

This explanation is a popular one among Gary civic leaders. The long neglect of the air pollution problem, they argue, was the "natural" result of inherent limitations in human attentiveness, one of those unavoidable oversights that can be expected to occur whenever people are trying to do several things at once. Unavoidable or

[1] See above, p. 62.

not, the oversight and the explanation of it have some important implications for the theory of community politics. They suggest that political issues are not independent of one another, but compete for allocations of political attention. When one issue gains in prominence, others must lose. The life chances of one issue are therefore bound up with the life chances of others.

The insights of Gary's civic activists are not universally endorsed by community political theorists. Members of the pluralist school, at least, do not admit the assumption that different political issues must draw their sustenance from a single, fixed reservoir of political energy. The assumption is a critical one for the notion of issue competition. If different issues do not depend on the same pool of resources, then there is no need for them to compete with one another, and it is the contention of the pluralists that they do not depend upon the same resources. A town's political resources, the pluralists argue, are likely to be fragmented, and different issues will tend to draw their sustenance from different fragments. Moreover, the pluralists maintain that a community's usable political resources are not fixed. There are slack resources which can be brought into play when the situation demands it.[2] When one issue rises to prominence, therefore, it need not do so at the expense of others.

The fragmentation to which the pluralists refer is probably most clearly evident in the organization of political manpower. Civic activists tend to specialize in the affairs of different policy-areas, and the division of activists among political specialties probably reduces rivalry among issues. Political specialization, like bureaucratic specialization, may enhance the capacity of a community to deal with many different items of business at the same time, so that one piece of public business need not interfere with the conduct of other public business.

Other elements in pluralist theory would also seem to contribute to the mutual independence of different political issues and so reduce the possibility of competition among them. The pluralists would probably be quick to point out, for example, that if civic activists are so busy with some issues that they lack the time or energy to deal with others, additional activists may arise to cope with the neglected subjects. This infusion of new political manpower, or the threat of it, could reduce both the need for issues to compete with one another

2 Dahl, *Who Governs?*, pp. 191, 228, 305.

and the likelihood that any significant topic will be neglected. The alleged openness of pluralistic polities—their receptivity to new civic activists—and the presence of unused political resources may therefore help to reduce the extent to which the political fortunes of one issue are influenced by the political fortunes of others.

The essential themes of pluralist theory are all consistent with one another on the matter of issue competition. Political fragmentation, specialization, openness, and the underutilization of political resources are all factors which can be expected to minimize the importance of this competition. In fact, they appear to minimize the likelihood of any sort of interconnectedness among political issues. In pluralist theory only the notion of "issue-area" seems to suggest that issues may be tied to one another, and even here the ties do not appear to be very strong or to extend very far. An issue-area is a subject matter category. Issues that fall within the same category, the pluralists argue, will often be handled by the same group of civic leaders. They will all depend upon the same reservoir of political manpower. Because this is the case, there is reason to expect that the issues in an issue-area will be tied to one another in some way. The salience of one issue will be related to the salience of others. But if such relationships do exist, the pluralists give no account of them. What is more, they provide very little advice that might be useful in locating the boundaries of an issue-area. Nowhere have the pluralists clearly stated the criteria by which one identifies an issue-area. The upshot of all this is that issue-areas are not very tight or coherent groupings of political agenda items. In the pluralist view, the linkages between different political issues are few and weak.

RELATIONS AMONG ISSUES

If the pluralist view is an accurate one, we should find little or no association between the prominence of one issue and the prominence of others. At most, we may expect to discover a weak relationship between the political fortunes of issues that fall under the same subject matter heading. In the eyes of Gary's civic activists, however, a different kind of arrangement prevails. There is a rivalry among political issues. As one issue moves to the center of attention, others must retire to the sidelines. If this view is an adequate portrayal of the connections that exist among political issues, then we should often find that the prominence of one issue is negatively related to the prominence of others.

In fact, there is some evidence to support the pluralist view, some to support the competitive view, some that supports neither. The evidence comes once again from interviews with formal community leaders. Eight respondents in each town were asked, in an open-ended question at the very beginning of the interview, to name the most important problems that their cities had faced since 1960. The answers to this question have been used to construct measures—admittedly crude—of the prominence of the air pollution issue and of eighteen other kinds of issues that were mentioned by the informants. The measure itself is quite simple. After classifying the various policy concerns that were named by the respondents, we computed, for each city, the proportion of informants who had cited each of the nineteen types of concerns. Next, the median proportion for each kind of issue was determined. In cities that scored above the median on an item, the problem in question was judged to have achieved relative political prominence.

This attempt to measure the political salience of different issues represents a research short cut, made unavoidable by the need to examine the relationships that exist among a rather large number of items. It would have been better, perhaps, to ask more precise questions about positiontaking activity on each of the nineteen issues, but that would have demanded too much of the project's finances and of the respondents' patience. Instead, the informants were simply asked to describe the civic problems that happen to have been uppermost in their minds during the past few years, on the assumption that these thoughts reflect the composition of recent local political agendas. By making the question an open-ended one and by placing it at the very beginning of the interview schedule, it was hoped that the interviewers' influence over the responses would be minimized.

The strategy seems to have worked rather well. One sign of its effectiveness is the fact that it produced results that are consistent with the earlier and more elaborate attempts to measure the issue-ness of dirty air. The open-ended question yields an index of the prominence of the dirty air issue which is associated with all of the positiontaking indicators that we have been using. More important, the new index is related in a consistent way to the issue-ness scale constructed earlier. If it had been sensible to do so, this item might have been incorporated into the scale, where it would have fallen at the midpoint, between the indicator for Chambers of Commerce and the one for labor councils.[3]

There is a second sign that the open-ended question has worked as it was intended to. If the informants' answers really do reflect the nature of local political concerns, then we may expect that respondents from the same town will give the same kinds of answers. The absence of such local unanimity would lead us to suspect that their reports do not accurately reflect community political conditions. But unanimity is not absent. Though they were free to mention any urban problems that came to mind, informants tended to cite problems that had also been named by other respondents in their towns. As a result, if we select any particular problem, we will find that it gets mentioned a disproportionate number of times in some towns and not at all in others. For example, almost 80 per cent of the "votes" for the air pollution problem came from just 20 per cent of the cities in the sample. Responses for all of the other community problems were concentrated in the same way, though the degree of concentration was not always so high. This element of unanimity among respondents from the same town suggests that a common body of experiences or events stands behind the answers that all of them have given. Their replies appear to reflect, not just their private concerns, but the concerns of their community—its political agenda.

The data reveal some notable regularities in the composition of these agendas. Some issues, for example, very rarely share space on the same agenda, while others quite regularly travel together. There appear to be some fairly consistent patterns of attraction and repulsion among issues, and the existence of these patterns would seem to contradict the pluralist view that different political enterprises tend to remain mutually independent. But the contradiction may be an illusory one. Suppose, for example, that there were a positive relationship between the prominence of the air pollution issue and the prominence of the water pollution issue. It might reasonably be argued that this connection signifies not a political kinship between the two concerns but a relationship between the physical conditions that create those concerns. The two issues may go together only because dirty air and dirty water tend to go together. If this were the case, we would have found not a relationship between political issues, but a connection among the objective, non-political conditions that generate those

[3] Had this item actually been included in the scale of issue-ness, the coefficient of reproducibility would have been .91.

TABLE VI-1: THE PROMINENCE OF THE AIR POLLUTION PROBLEM AND THE SALIENCE OF OTHER CIVIC PROBLEMS, CONTROLLING FOR SUSPENDED PARTICULATE LEVEL

Civic Problem	Association with the Prominence of Air Pollution as a Civic Problem
Government reorganization	+.42
Water pollution and sewage disposal	+.39
Mass transit	+.25
Crime, police and fire protection	+.20
Race relations	+.17
Loss of taxpaying residents	+.14
Municipal revenue and taxes	+.07
Public education	+.06
Recreation and parks	+.03
Unemployment	−.01
Wages and working conditions of public employees	−.02
Central business district renewal	−.03
Building and zoning codes	−.05
Traffic, streets, and parking	−.06
Housing	−.09
General conflict and public mistrust	−.11
Poverty and welfare	−.15
Business and industrial development	−.37

issues. As political enterprises, the two concerns might remain quite independent of each other.

This possibility would naturally introduce some uncertainty into the task of drawing a conclusion from the association between the air pollution issue and the water pollution issue, but most of this uncertainty can be eliminated by simply controlling for the dirtiness of local air. By holding constant the level of local air pollution, we can, in effect, cancel out its tendency to vary in conjunction with the severity of water pollution or with any other local problem. The correlation coefficients that appear in Table VI-1 have been computed in this way. They show how the prominence of the dirty air issue was related to the prominence of each of eighteen other issues that the respondents mentioned. In all eighteen cases, the actual level of air pollution has been held constant, which means that the associations do not reflect any of the relationships that may exist between dirty air and other issue-creating conditions.

Many of the relationships reported in the table appear to support the pluralist view that different issues tend to be politically independent of one another. For example, there is almost no association between air pollution as a civic concern and public education or unemployment or central business district renewal. The prominence of these issues neither enhances or reduces the life chances of the pollution issue. There are several other matters that do seem to have some bearing upon the political prominence of the dirty air problem, however.

The correlation coefficient reported at the bottom of Table VI–1 shows that where business and industrial development is a topic of local concern, the dirty air problem tends to be ignored. The prominence of one issue appears to be connected with the subordination of the other, and the existence of this connection calls into question the pluralist view that different political issues tend to rise and subside independently. But the relationship is precisely the sort that the informants in Gary anticipated when they suggested that different issues compete with one another for attention. In this view, the negative association between the air pollution and economic development issues stands as evidence of the rivalry that exists among political issues—the general tendency for one issue to gain its political prominence at the expense of other issues. But the other associations reported in the table suggest that the rivalry among issues is not a widespread phenomenon. It occurs only within certain pairs of issues, and it should not be difficult to understand why the two issues now under consideration should constitute one of those competitive pairs. Business and industrial development and air pollution control are civic projects which can be expected to impose contradictory demands upon a community. Pollution control is likely to require an increase in the operating costs of local industrial corporations. Efforts at business and industrial development are likely to call for a reduction of those costs, so as to make the community a more attractive site for manufacturing firms. A local polity that is occupied with the task of business and industrial development will therefore tend to be "impenetrable" where the air pollution issue is concerned. Its political interests and commitments are sharply inconsistent with the commitments that are demanded by a clean air campaign.

A city does not ignore its dirty air simply because it is busy with other things but because its other concerns are incompatible with the pursuit of clean air. That, at least, is one conclusion suggested by the table, but there is another possible conclusion. The real obstacle to the growth of the air pollution issue, it might be argued, is not the civic commitment to business and industrial development but the concentration of political influence that stands behind that commitment. We would expect that a town devoted to the cause of business and industrial development might generally defer to the interests of industrial corporations. In such a community, industry would be likely to enjoy a reputation for power, and perceived industrial influence in the pollution field tends to diminish the survival prospects of the dirty air issue. Perhaps it is not the concern for economic development that reduces the prominence of the pollution issue, but the industrial influence which is likely to go with that concern.

The evidence, however, fails to support this alternative explanation. There is no association between industry's power reputation in the pollution field and the civic prominence of efforts at economic development ($r = -.05$). If any kind of influence supports business and industrial development, it is that of political parties ($r = +.21$), and this finding is an understandable one.

Business and industrial development is a civic project that is likely to generate a large supply of specific, capturable benefits. It is true that the economic development effort may eventually profit a whole community, but it is important to note that this profit is not bestowed on the community as a whole. Tax reductions for business firms, free or underpriced land, special exemptions from zoning regulations, reduced charges for municipal services, public loans—these are all instruments of local economic development policy, and they all represent dividends for particular people or corporations. It is possible to exercise a degree of control over the distribution of these specific benefits: they can be given to some people and not to others. All of these things are likely to make business and industrial development attractive to party politicians. It is an enterprise which can yield the sorts of policy benefits that parties need in order to sustain their political brokerage operations.

The very things that make business and industrial development attractive to party politicians set it apart from the quest for pollution control. Clean air is a collective, indivisible benefit, while economic development policy generates specific, capturable benefits. The apparent rivalry that exists between these two concerns may reflect fundamentally different orientations toward public policy. Communities that exhibit one of these orientations will be unlikely to support a political enterprise that presupposes the contrary inclination. Cities that have spawned "specific" issues will be relatively inhospitable to clean air campaigns.

It would seem to follow from this that polities which have exhibited a concern for clean air will also tend to be concerned about other collective issues, and this brings us to the issues that are listed near the top of Table VI–1, those topics which appear to be congenial to the growth of dirty air deliberations. Government reorganization, water pollution, mass transit, crime, and race relations are all civic concerns whose prominence is positively associated with the salience of the air pollution issue. One thing that all of these congenial topics have in common is that they are all relatively "collective" concerns.

Consider, for example, the matter of government reorganization. Almost all of the items that fell within this category had to do with the creation or renovation of governing bodies for metropolitan areas, not cities. The respondents mentioned proposals for the creation of metro governments, for transferring municipal functions to county governments, for the annexation of suburban areas, and for the establishment of special district authorities to handle certain governmental functions for entire metropolitan regions. All of these proposals seem to presuppose a certain insufficiency in existing municipal government. It is insufficient, the argument goes, because today's urban problems are metropolitan in nature, not municipal, and their solution requires a government apparatus which is metropolitan in scope.

What is it about an urban problem that makes it "metropolitan"? One answer, it seems, is that the problem is a collective one. Neither the costs that it imposes nor the benefits that would arise from its solution can be captured by individual municipalities within a metropolitan area. The costs and benefits are indivisible and collective, and a "collective" form of government is needed in order to deal with such an issue. Of course, it may also be needed in order to deal with certain "specific" commodities. Some adherents of metro government, for example, perceive it as an instrument for equalizing the distribution of specific benefits between the deprived residents of central cities and more fortunate inhabitants of suburbs. In effect, they would use this governmental arrangement to change the character of the dividends that are distributed by local government. By dispensing these benefits through a metropolitan area organization, they hope to make them less specific—less susceptible to capture by limited social groupings and more nearly indivisible. Under metro government, it is argued, what one receives, all receive. In short, metro government and kindred arrangements represent an inclination to frame public policy in collective terms. They are intended, first, to generate benefits that are collective by nature, clean air, for example; second, they are intended to allocate benefits that are not collective by nature in a way that is collective by design.

When the respondents mentioned government reorganization, therefore, they were talking about a relatively "collective" concern. It shares something of this collective character with water pollution, mass transit, police and fire protection, crime, and race relations— all civic concerns whose prominence is positively associated with the salience of the air pollution issue. In each of these policy areas, the benefits dispensed are comparatively collective ones. For example, the benefits of mass transit are collective by comparison with the benefits of other approaches to urban transportation, but they are not collective in any absolute sense. The very fact that people can be required to pay for individual bus or subway rides indicates that the benefits of mass transit need not defy division and controlled distribution, but it is important to note that these specific benefits are bestowed in wholesale lots. If mass transit is made available to one urbanite, then it must also be made available to a large number of his fellow citizens, often to the whole population of a city, unlike other varieties of urban transportation policy. The "traffic, streets, and parking" category in Table VI–1 is the receptacle for these other approaches, and it represents a class of policies which offer relatively specific remedies for urban transportation problems—parking lots, widened or one-way streets, new traffic signals, and the like. All of these devices can be used in a practical way to benefit the residents of particular neighborhoods or even the people who live around a particular intersection. They generate benefits that are rather specific and capturable. Of course, there are other policy concerns within the "traffic, streets, and parking" category which are not so specific, of which the urban expressway is a notable example. If one citydweller enjoys the advantages of expressway transportation, then a large number of his fellow citizens must be able to enjoy them too. Like the benefits of mass transit, the dividends of expressway construction are seldom doled out in small pieces. Nevertheless, the expressway probably represents a somewhat less collective public benefit than does mass transit. Its primary dividends, after all, are not available to the residents of a whole community, but only to those who own cars. The "mass transit" and the "traffic, streets, and parking" categories, then, represent two kinds of civic responses to the same kind of urban problem. Neither of these responses is purely collective or purely specific, but mass transit, it might be argued, is generally the more collective of the two approaches. It is also the one whose political prominence is positively associated with the salience of the air pollution issue.

"Race relations" is another civic agenda item that tends to appear together with the dirty air issue, and it also represents a set of relatively collective concerns. Most of these concerns have to do with the achievement of racial equality through racial integration in housing, employment, schools, and public accommodations. Racial integration is not the only way in which communities seek to reduce social and economic inequality, and the items included in the "poverty and welfare" category of the table have to do with some of the other means for diminishing these inequities. There are a number of distinctions that might be drawn between these other methods and the integrationist approach. One of them is this: under the integrationist approach, general benefits are conceded to Negroes as a group. Poverty and welfare policies, on the other hand, would distribute benefits, and costs, in small pieces to individuals. In other words, integration is a more collective policy than is poverty and welfare, and it is notable that the salience of integrationist concerns is positively associated with the prominence of the pollution issue ($r = +.17$). But between the pollution issue, on the one hand, and poverty and welfare issues on the other, there is a slight negative association ($r = -.15$).

In general, air pollution tends to be found in the company of other relatively collective issues. Its closest companions are those topics that are most clearly collective ones, government reorganization ($r = +.42$) and water pollution ($r = +.39$). It exhibits a lesser affinity for issues whose collective character is less pronounced, issues like mass transit ($r = +.25$), crime ($r = +.20$), and race relations ($r = +.17$). Even this mild affinity disappears when issues of mixed or uncertain character are concerned, and it turns to aversion where the issues in question are highly specific ones, like poverty and welfare ($r = -.15$) or business and industrial development ($r = -.37$). In short, it appears that there is some regularity in the attachments of the dirty air issue. The more collective an issue, the closer its connections with the air pollution issue. That, at least, is the pattern to which these findings correspond, if only roughly. Because of the difficulty of determining just how collective an issue is, there must remain considerable uncertainty on the matter.

Some things, however, are less doubtful. It is fairly clear that these findings are inconsistent with the pluralist portrayal of community politics. Issues do not constitute mutually independent areas of activity. Action in one issue-area may have some bearing on the level of activity in other areas. Civic leaders who promote the economic development issue, for example, may thereby discourage the promotion of the dirty air issue. The influence of these political activists extends beyond the field of their visible actions to other issues and would-be issues. Thus community politics may be somewhat less fragmented than the study of political action alone would indicate. Several issue-areas may, in effect, be subject to the influence of local leaders who are visibly active in only a single field of public concern, and this influence may operate to reduce the penetrability of community political systems. By promoting one political agenda item, civic activists may succeed in driving other issues away. These findings and their implications cannot be accommodated within the pluralist theory of local politics, nor were they anticipated by the informants from Gary, who contended that issues compete with one another for attention. The research results seem to call for a third view of the relationships that exist among political issues.

COMMUNITY POLITICS AS AN ECOLOGY OF ISSUES

Political issues produce other political issues, not randomly, but with a measure of order and even rationality. One political demand may trigger a series of rationally related demands for things that facilitate the achievement, distribution, or enjoyment of the benefit that was originally requested. It is rational, for example, that a community which has turned its attention to the problem of unemployment should also exhibit some interest in the matter of business and industrial development. The two subjects are related to one another as problem and solution, and it is therefore not surprising that unemployment and economic development should often share space on the same political agendas ($r = +.25$). It is also understandable that where civic leaders are interested in economic development, they tend to be concerned about building and zoning regulations as well ($r = +.29$). A town that wants to attract business and industrial corporations, after all, must find some place to put them. The effort at business and industrial development may therefore set off a reshuffling of local land uses and generate demands for the revision of municipal building and zoning codes. Rezoning may serve as a means to the end of economic development.

In many other cases, the empirical connections that exist between political issues may also be interpreted as means-end relationships. The positive association between the issues of air pollution and government reorganization is one such connection. Atmospheric contamination is seldom a condition that begins and ends within the jurisdiction of a single municipality. It tends to be a regional or metropolitan-area problem, and its solution may require a regional or metropolitan-area form of government. Concern about dirty air might therefore lead to demands for government renovation and to reorganization proposals such as the respondents mentioned, proposals that would create or invigorate governing bodies for metropolitan regions, and so provide organizational instruments adequate to the task of cleaning up the air. It is also possible that a commitment to these organizational instruments may create the demand for clean air. Once they have taken up the cause of metropolitan-area government, civic activists may search out those urban problems for which metro government offers an appropriate solution. Where government reorganization is a salient political issue, therefore, air pollution also tends to become a matter of civic concern, and so does water pollution. Like the dirty air problem, the dirty water problem is one that is likely to call for metropolitan-area action. The water pollution issue and the government reorganization issue therefore tend to go together ($r = +.39$). In general, the promotion of one political issue may lead rationally to the promotion, or the neglect, of others.

To say that issues lead to other issues also says something about the role that political issues play within local politics. It suggests, first, that issues ought not to be regarded as safety valves for purging a community of discontent. The emergence of one issue, rather than preparing the way for the discharge of social tension—and the resolution of underlying conflict—may actually generate new foci of discontent. It may call attention to discomforts and deprivations that previously went unnoticed or were not regarded as fit subjects for public discussion. To put it another way, political issues can create political consciousness.

They also tend to shape or restrict that consciousness. Political agenda items like the economic development issue do not produce a general expansion in the scope of political discussion, but expansion only in certain directions. The same kind of means-end rationality that leads from the promotion of one issue to the promotion of others may also lead from the promotion of one issue to the avoidance of others. The negative relationship between the economic development and air pollution issues is a case in point. A clean air campaign, we might reasonably argue, is likely to interfere with the promotion of a business and industrial development program. It is therefore rational for a community which has committed itself to economic development to avoid the air pollution issue. To sum up, the means-end connections that exist among political issues may help to guide the growth of local political agendas. A community that commits itself to the consideration of one local concern may, in effect, commit itself to a whole chain of rationally related issues and diminish its ability to consider rationally antagonistic issues.

The problem with this rational view of the composition of political agendas is that it does not go far enough. Means-end rationality does seem to account for some of the negative and positive relationships between issues, but there are far more empirical relationships between issues than there are plausible means-end explanations. For example, it is not difficult to perceive the rational inconsistency between the air pollution and economic development issues, but how do we explain the empirical estrangement that exists between the economic development issue and the matters of government reorganization ($r = -.32$), mass transit ($r = -.30$), race relations ($r = -.25$), crime ($r = -.14$), and water pollution ($r = -.13$)? It is not easy to see how the economic development issue might be rationally inconsistent with all of these matters. There is no obvious reason, for example, why local concern for mass transit or government reorganization should interfere with a community's effort to make itself attractive to business and industrial firms. It is certainly possible that there may be some rational contradiction between the economic development issue and each of these other matters, but the contradictions, if they do exist, are obscure and probably not likely to produce the kind of estrangement that was observed. One thing is not so obscure. The economic development issue turns out to be negatively associated with every one of the political agenda items identified as a relatively collective issue. There are no other items on the list of community concerns to which the economic development issue is so inhospitable. Issues that involve the disposition of relatively specific goods—topics like economic development, unemployment, and building and zoning regulation—tend to appear together, but not in the company of relatively collective issues. Collective issues, on the other hand, tend to keep company with other relatively collective issues. Table VI–2 gives evidence, for example, of a positive

TABLE VI–2: INTERCORRELATION AMONG SELECTED ITEMS ON POLITICAL AGENDAS

	1	2	3	4	5	6	7	8	9
1. Crime		+.11	+.29	+.27	−.04	−.06	−.01	−.11	−.14
2. Mass transit			+.35	+.26	−.04	−.03	−.01	−.05	−.30
3. Race relations				+.21	+.12	−.06	+.16	+.04	−.25
4. Air pollution					+.30	+.34	−.03	−.18	−.41
5. Water pollution						+.39	+.01	.00	−.13
6. Government re-organization							−.03	−.11	−.32
7. Unemployment								+.11	+.25
8. Building and zoning codes									+.29
9. Business and industrial development									

association among the matters of air pollution, mass transit, crime, and race relations, all relatively collective issues. Government re-organization, water pollution, and air pollution seem to make up another possible cluster of collective agenda items. These subjects, too, are all positively related to one another.

Having dealt with one collective issue, a city is more likely to turn its attention to another collective issue than to a specific issue. This means that a community's political agenda will not constitute a random sample of political concerns. It will exhibit a general bias toward relatively specific or toward relatively collective issues. Means-end rationality, as was noted, does not fully account for the existence of this general bias. The process by which issues create political consciousness and bring other issues to the surface of local politics is not fully rational, or so it appears. There is, however, a certain consistency in its operation. Collective issues tend to trigger other collective issues, and specific issues tend to lead to other specific issues. This regularity suggests that the process may reflect means-end rationality of a more comprehensive sort than the kind that seems to operate within scattered pairs and trios of political issues. Specifically, it may reflect the rationality that comes with political ideology. The issues on a political agenda may all be rationally linked, not to one another, but to some comprehensive political ideal or principle that transcends the agenda—an ideological vision of the political system.[4]

[4] Some of the coefficients in Table VI–2 differ from the comparable coefficients in Table VI–1. The reason for these differences is that the coefficients in Table VI–1 were partial correlation coefficients (computed so as to control for the level of suspended particulates), while the ones in Table VI–2 were computed without any controls for pollution levels. Pollution levels were held constant in the first case in order to

In order to support this interpretation of the findings, it would be necessary to show that, among local political actors, there exist at least two widespread ideological tendencies, each of which would have to be rationally connected with one of the two general biases that we have detected in the composition of local political agendas, the bias toward collective and the bias toward specific issues. Previous inquiries into the nature of local political ideology have strongly suggested that there are two such tendencies. Banfield and Wilson have identified a "public-regarding ethos" and a "private-regarding ethos."[5] Public-regarding citizens are distinguished by the habit of framing and justifying their political decisions in terms of some conception of the public interest. This intellectual habit naturally assumes that there is a public interest, a collective good which is distinct from the private wants of individual citizens. Collective issues seem to presuppose this conception, and certainly the lack of it would constitute a logically significant impediment to the conduct of political discussions about collective benefits. For citizens who partake of the "private-regarding ethos" there exists no public interest. Public policy does not serve a community interest, but the private interests of individuals and groups within the community. In other words, the political process operates to distribute specific rather than collective benefits.

The public-regarding ethos and the private-regarding ethos appear to be something less than political ideologies. They represent two very broad, imprecise, and seldom articulated orientations toward politics, but they are likely to be connected with other views of the political system that lie closer to the surface of consciousness. Among members of the political stratum, it is especially likely that ethos will be translated into ideology. According to Robert Dahl, members of the political stratum will usually be more self-conscious, precise, and consistent in their political beliefs than other people.[6] Compared to their fellow citizens, political activists are ideologues. Agger, Goldrich, and Swanson have found a similar tendency toward ideology among

---

cancel out the effects of any relationship that might exist between dirty air and other issue-producing conditions. The intention was to isolate the relationships between issues from any connections that might exist among the non-political conditions that created those issues. These controls were omitted from the second table not because they were undesirable, but because it was impossible to control for the underlying, issue-producing conditions in relationships among political issues like mass transit, race relations, or business and industrial development.

[5] Edward C. Banfield and James Q. Wilson, "Public-Regardingness as a Value Premise in Voting Behavior."

[6] *Who Governs?*, pp. 90–91.

community political leaders and have devised a scheme for classifying the various ideological preferences among civic activists. In one of its more important aspects, this typology appears to mirror the distinction that Banfield and Wilson make between public-regardingness and private-regardingness: Agger and his associates found that one important axis of ideological variation has to do with the conception of a community that is embodied in a political creed. Some civic activists see the community as an aggregation of conflicting private interests, and they see some of those interests—usually their own—as appropriate guides to the making of public policy. Other political leaders "view the community as a collectivity—an organism with a common interest," and believe that this common interest is a proper and practical guide for political decisionmakers.[7]

Collective issues presuppose this organic view; they promise to bestow indivisible public goods upon the community as a whole. A general bias toward collective issues might therefore be the rational product of the collectivist principle. A rationally consistent political actor of the collectivist persuasion might be expected to enlist in one collectivist cause after another. The bias that is evident in his personal political agenda proceeds rationally from his devotion to a particular ideological vision or principle. But it would be a mistake to assert that bias in community political agendas arises in precisely the same way. Communities are not rational; individuals are. Communities do not adhere to ideological principles; individuals do. Rather than impute ideological rationality to communities it is necessary to find out how the ideological consistency of individuals is translated into community bias, the kind of bias that leads a town from one issue to others of the same species.

Issues create not only other political issues, but political activists as well. The kinds of issues that a community produces will probably have something to do with the kinds of people who enter the political stratum. The makeup of the political stratum—its ideological leanings—will have something to do with the subsequent composition of the community's political agenda. One issue can therefore affect the life chances of other issues by affecting the character of a town's political manpower, and this may be the way in which biases are introduced into community political agendas.

[7] Robert E. Agger, Daniel Goldrich, and Bert Swanson, *The Rulers and the Ruled*, pp. 17–21.

The manpower supply that is created by a collective issue will tend to differ in a systematic way from the manpower that is mobilized for a specific issue. Citizens who spend their energies in the quest for a collective good are more likely than other political actors to accept non-material, moral gratifications as compensation and, because of their public-regarding predispositions, are likely to contribute to the growth of other collective issues. A collective issue, then, can be expected to cultivate public-regardingness within a town's political stratum, and the result is to increase the political stratum's receptivity to other collective issues and to create a bias in the composition of the local political agenda. In effect, political issues provide one another with sustenance. Political manpower, the by-product of one political issue, becomes a political resource for other, related issues. The same kinds of ecological relationships that exist among community organizations may also exist among community political issues, and the existence of these relationships may help to account for the existence of bias in local political agendas. Whether they actually do so remains uncertain. There is evidence of bias in the makeup of local agendas, but no sure indication how it got there.

VII   Does Pluralism Fail Democracy?

It would misrepresent the findings of this study to refer to them all as conclusions because they are not really conclusive. The investigation has provided some highly probable, but not definitive, explanations for the fact that some towns ignore their dirty air. Even if these explanations were absolutely certain, they would not account fully for local neglect of the issue. Taken together, they do not explain all of the inter-city variation in its prominence. Finally, even if we could offer an exhaustive explanation for the neglect of the air pollution problem, we would not have accounted for political neglect in general. The air pollution issue is not representative of all community political issues. It may be easier to overlook than other matters of public concern, and the factors that promote neglect in the pollution field are undoubtedly different from the factors that consign other policy-areas to political oblivion. Granting all of these shortcomings, the findings still have some important implications for the study of local politics—and particularly for the pluralist view of community politics.

The findings, stated in their most elementary form, are these: first, community political power may consist of something other than the ability to influence the resolution of local political issues; there is also the ability to prevent some topics from ever becoming issues and to obstruct the growth of emergent issues. Second, this power need not be exercised in order to be effective. The mere reputation for power, unsupported by acts of power, can be sufficient to restrict the scope of local decisionmaking. Even people and groups who do not actively participate in a community's political deliberations may influence their content. Likewise, the "victims" of political power may remain politically invisible—indeed, invisibility may constitute their response to the power of non-decisionmaking. The actions or power reputations of other political actors may deter these would-be actors from making their way into the political arena. The operation of political power, therefore, is not always revealed in observable political action, nor do community political decisions reveal the full range of local policymaking. One must also consider the non-decisions. To put it simply, there is more to local politics than meets the eye.

What does meet the eye is the disjointedness of community affairs. Studies of local political activity undertaken by political scientists have disclosed that community decisionmaking is a highly fragmented process. In fact, it is not a single process at all, but an array of relatively independent processes each set in motion by a different political issue. Different issues tend to activate different groups of political decisionmakers, different kinds of political alignments, and different styles of policymaking. In effect, each political issue brings into being its own species of political order, and the result is a high degree of political disorder. Political issues are transitory, episodic phenomena, and because the political life of a community tends to be organized around issues, it too tends to be episodic and unordered.

But our findings indicate that the emergence of the issues themselves may be politically regulated or coordinated, and while this does not change the facts of observable political activity, it does alter the impression of disjointedness that those facts convey. The issues on a community's political agenda are not a random selection. The visible political activities of a community are more ordered and inhibited than an inspection of the activities alone would lead us to believe. There are politically imposed limitations upon the scope of decisionmaking. Within the area that is bounded by these restrictions, political power appears to be fragmented and political decisionmaking uncoordinated. But there is a general bias or direction in this disjointedness. Decisionmaking activity is channeled and restricted by the process of non-decisionmaking. The power reputations of people and groups within a community may deter action on certain sensitive or politically unprofitable issues. Activity in one issue-area may tend to foreclose action in certain other issue-areas, as the findings reported in Chapter VI suggest. Decisionmaking restrictions such as these impart a degree of bias and unity to the political activities of a community.

Moreover, it takes a degree of unity to maintain the restrictions themselves. The political stratum of a community will seldom behave "pluralistically" toward issues which fall victim to these restrictions. On such matters there will be virtually no disagreement, no competition, no bargaining. No groups of specialist decisionmakers will arise to deal with them. In short, a polity that is pluralistic in its decision-making can be unified in its non-decisionmaking.

It is not necessarily the case that this unity will be created or maintained by the power of some small, cohesive elite. Members of the political stratum may be unanimous in their avoidance of certain political issues, but this does not mean that they are all acting at the direction of a single political control center or that the neglect of every proscribed issue can be attributed to the same small clique of "non-decisionmakers." The power to enforce inaction, it might be argued, is almost as fragmented as the power to command action. The perceived influence of local industry, for example, tends to obstruct the political career of the air pollution issue, but it may be the perceived influence of local real estate agents that blocks the emergence of the fair housing issue or the power reputation of the local teachers' union that enforces silence on the matter of educational reorganization. It is quite likely that no single person or group sets the limits of a community's decisionmaking activities. It might be argued, therefore, that the process of non-decisionmaking is really not much different from the process of decisionmaking. In both political operations, power is distributed among a variety of people and groups. Non-decisionmaking, it seems, simply adds another dimension to political pluralism.

While there is no logical flaw in this conclusion, it misses the point. Although the fragmentation of political power is the distinguishing trait of a pluralistic political system, it is a characteristic worthy of attention only because it is seen to have momentous consequences for the nature of the polity, and the occurrence of non-decisionmaking calls some of these consequences into question.

Pluralism, the argument goes, helps to assure that popular senti-ment will be brought to bear on a community's decisionmakers. It is a guarantee that the small minorities of citizens who exercise direct influence over most decisions in most American cities will remain responsive to the local majorities who are politically inactive. Where there is pluralism, it is argued, there is likely to be competition among political leaders, and where leaders must compete with one another, they will actively seek the support of constituents. A leader who fails to cultivate public support runs the risk of being thrust aside by his rivals when the time comes to submit himself and his policies to the judgment of the electorate. The politically quiescent non-leaders will therefore acquire considerable indirect influence over policymaking because leaders will keep popular preferences in mind when they are making policy decisions, not so much to protect themselves from public wrath as from their rivals, who might promote and profit from that wrath. The pluralistic organization of the political elite, therefore, helps to assure that the great bulk of the population will enjoy a substantial amount of indirect influence in the making of almost all public decisions, even though it seldom participates directly in the making of any public decision.

Pluralism, then, acquires much of its importance from its presumed relationship with democracy. But the evidence concerning non-decisionmaking suggests that this relationship may be a tenuous one. First, there is the matter of competition among political elites and its contribution to the democratic responsibility of local leaders. Political competition is undoubtedly important for the maintenance of popular control over political elites, but much depends on just what the competition is about. If popular sovereignty is contingent upon leadership competition, then it will not extend to those matters on which leaders choose not to compete. Restrictions on the scope of competition therefore diminish the field of democratic control, provided that the restrictions themselves are not dictated by the popular will, and the restrictions that have occupied our attention probably are not. In other words, the limited democracy that is apparent in the decision-making activities of a pluralistic political system may be limited still further by the occurrence of non-decisionmaking. Visible political competition does not necessarily signify that a community's leadership is generally vulnerable to public opinion. Contrary to the contentions of Robert Dahl and others, competition among ruling minorities does not necessarily lead to government by the majority.

A pluralistic system which is not also an open system has ceased to perform some of the functions that make pluralism valuable. It is not only responsiveness to majority sentiment that may have been diminished. Restrictions upon the scope of decisionmaking may also deny minorities the opportunity to grow to majorities. For representatives of minority opinion, a political issue is not just a piece of public business. It can serve as a soapbox or a pulpit, a critical opportunity to communicate with the public, to persuade them, and perhaps to arouse them to action. When issues are excluded from a community's political agenda, minority opinions are likely to be denied their moment in the spotlight. Restrictions upon the scope of local decision-making, then, may also stunt the political consciousness of the local public, and it is not political consciousness alone that may be stunted. The pluralists rightly point out that political power is tied to political issues. When issues are shunted aside, therefore, it is likely that some would-be leaders will lose their opportunities to achieve prominence. A political challenger like Milton Roth, for example, will lose a chance for a public showdown with established economic or political leaders. In the process, the public loses an alternative source of information and opinion concerning the policies of the government.

Pluralism is no guarantee of political openness or popular sovereignty. We may celebrate the diversity of the decisionmaking groups that comprise a town's political stratum, but it should be remembered that this visible diversity tells us nothing about those groups and issues which may have been shut out of a town's political life, and, for that reason, there may be something fatuous in the celebration. The only sure inference that can be drawn from the visible diversity of a political system is that it is visibly diverse. It need be no more open and tolerant than the private club that proudly accepts members of all religious creeds but excludes Negroes, women, and people with unorthodox political opinions. Similarly, where diverse citizen concerns become the subjects of political decisionmaking, it need not follow that local political leaders are responsive to all or even most popular demands. The scope of their democratic responsiveness may in fact be seriously restricted. Matters of considerable importance to the people of a community can be placed beyond the limits of political debate and competition. While political diversity may count for something in itself, it does not constitute political democracy.

The curious thing about all of these observations is that they rely upon the same theoretical concept as do the pluralist contentions that visible diversity promotes democracy, the notion of indirect influence. It has been argued here that undemocratic restrictions on the scope of local political activity are the products of indirect influence. They are not the results of suppressive acts or directly applied pressure but are responses to the power reputations of various local groups, organizations, and individuals. Likewise, the pluralists argue that the democracy of a pluralistic political system is not evident in the influential acts of the demos, but in its indirect influence. In the pluralistic political systems of American communities the demos enjoys a reputation for power that is sufficiently impressive to control the behavior of politically active minorities. Though most policy decisions are actually made by political elites, they roughly reflect the preferences of a larger public. Consequently, indirect influence is more democratically distributed than observable, direct influence. While this assertion helps to soften the apparent inconsistency between democratic political principles and the visible facts of community decisionmaking, it introduces a disturbing paradox into the pluralists' approach to the study of local politics. On the one hand, they urge us to attribute no more power to reputed political elites than we can actually see them exercise. On the other, they maintain that the power of non-elites is really much greater than their observable actions would indicate.

Beyond this methodological inconsistency, there lies a more serious problem. How do we know that in pluralistic polities indirect influence is more democratically distributed than direct influence? Partisans of the pluralist view have never bothered to gather the evidence to substantiate this claim. In order to do so, they would have to depart from pluralist research techniques. It would be necessary to find out something about reputations for power, not just acts of power. The pluralists would have to make use of the very mode of investigation that they have explicitly rejected, the reputational method. More important still, investigations which have employed the reputational technique tend to detract from the plausibility of the pluralist contention. They suggest that perceived influence may be less democratically distributed than actively exercised influence. This finding does not necessarily refute the pluralist claim. It is still necessary to find out whether this oligarchic influence actually affects the course of political activity. If it does not, then it cannot properly be called influence. But the findings of this study indicate that it does. We have already seen that the perceived influence of political and economic elites can have an important effect upon the level of political activity in the field of air pollution.

The present investigation of non-decisionmaking does not deny pluralism, but it does cast doubt on some of the most important claims that are made on its behalf. Pluralism does not guarantee that every dissatisfied group of citizens will find a place to roost within the political stratum, nor does it assure that political competition and discussion will extend to all or even most areas of citizen concern. Finally, there is a good reason to doubt that the competition engendered by pluralism really inflates the indirect influence that the ruled have over their rulers. Political openness and democratic responsiveness are likely to exist to the extent that citizens find it possible to intervene directly in the political process. We cannot rely upon the mere plurality of political elites to secure the values of a liberal democracy. Even a diversity of competing political elites can exhibit collective biases against some kinds of issues. These biases appear to grow out of the organizational maintenance and enhancement needs of local elites, and it seems probable that they may be transmitted from one dominant organization to others by a series of "ecological" adjustments. Non-decisionmaking is the end result, but it is not inevitable. The case of Gary, for example, suggests that federal or state intervention in local affairs may sometimes suspend local biases and help to bring formerly neglected issues to the fore. In effect, political actors who find the local polity unresponsive to their demands can occasionally carry their case to another political arena whose biases are more favorable to their cause.

In the air pollution field, successive pieces of national legislation have made it progressively easier for a community's clear air advocates to introduce the federal government into local dirty air debates. The Federal Clean Air Act of 1967, passed a few months after the data for this study were collected, may well have altered the list of factors that affect the life chances of the dirty air issue in local communities. Increased federal activity in urban affairs has undoubtedly altered the life prospects of many would-be community issues other than air pollution. This does not mean that organizational biases are banished from politics; it means that henceforth the biases will be different. The ecological systems that bring bias to bear upon the composition of political agendas will no longer be local ones, but federal-state-local.

Bias is an inescapable feature of political systems. "All forms of political organization," writes E. E. Schattschneider, "have a bias in favor of the exploitation of some kinds of conflict and the suppression of others *because organization is the mobilization of bias.*"[1] All forms of political organization can therefore be expected to produce non-decisions. Of course, some systems may be less inclined toward non-decisionmaking than others. It has been suggested, for example, that the frequency of non-decisionmaking may be diminished by increasing the direct intervention of citizens in the political process.

[1] *The Semisovereign People*, p. 71.

But, in the end, the mere frequency of non-decisionmaking is not of critical importance. The crucial question is not how many non-decisions a political system makes but what kinds, and how significant they are.

The main issue in the evaluation of a political system is not simply how much bias it exhibits, but whether that bias is good or bad, whether the issues that it neglects are worthy or unworthy. That is clearly a matter for moral, not scientific, judgment, but the judgment need not be an unreasoned one. It is possible to advance reasons for believing that a proscribed issue is not trivial. It might be pointed out, for example, that the air pollution issue is one that bears directly upon the comfort, health, and even the survival of many citizens, and air pollution is not the only topic of seeming importance that may succumb to non-decisionmaking. More than one observer of the American political scene has been struck by its glaring oversights and omissions. "The most significant fact about the distribution of power in America," writes Robert Wolff, "is not who makes such decisions as are made, but rather how many matters of the greatest social importance are not the objects of anyone's decision at all."[2] Conversely, the most significant fact about these non-decisions is that many—perhaps most—of them have something to do with the distribution of power. They are not all politically random oversights but instances of politically enforced neglect.

2 Robert Paul Wolff, *The Poverty of Liberalism*, p. 118.

Appendixes

Appendix 1

SAMPLE CITIES AND THEIR SUSPENDED PARTICULATE RATES

City	Suspended Particulate Rate*	City	Suspended Particulate Rate*
Akron, Ohio	124	Memphis, Tennessee	101
Albany, New York	76	Milwaukee, Wisconsin	134
Amarillo, Texas	63	Minneapolis, Minnesota	85
Atlanta, Georgia	97	Newark, New Jersey	103
Berkeley, California	69	Palo Alto, California	101†
Birmingham, Alabama	125	Pasadena, California	133
Bloomington, Minnesota	85†	Phoenix, Arizona	194
Boston, Massachusetts	129	Pittsburgh, Pennsylvania	157
Buffalo, New York	112	St. Louis, Missouri	147
Cambridge, Massachusetts	87	St. Paul, Minnesota	94
Charlotte, North Carolina	107	St. Petersburg, Florida	43
Clifton, New Jersey	92†	Salt Lake City, Utah	112
Duluth, Minnesota	67	San Francisco, California	63
Fort Worth, Texas	86	Santa Ana, California	99
Fullerton, California	99†	San Jose, California	101
Gary, Indiana	214	Schenectady, New York	76
Hamilton, Ohio	99	Seattle, Washington	73
Hammond, Indiana	133	South Bend, Indiana	111
Indianapolis, Indiana	156	Tampa, Florida	84
Irvington, New Jersey	103†	Tyler, Texas	60
Jacksonville, Florida	73	Utica, New York	97
Long Beach, California	135	Waco, Texas	83
Malden, Massachusetts	71†	Waterbury, Connecticut	83
Manchester, New Hampshire	59	Waukegan, Illinois	82†

* Average concentration of suspended particulates in micrograms per cubic meter of air.

† Computed from data collected at a nearby air sampling station (see Chapter III, p. 93, for details).

Appendix 2

NATIONAL OPINION RESEARCH CENTER
INTERVIEW SCHEDULE FOR PANEL OF
COMMUNITY LEADERS

Name of Respondent _____

Position _____

City and State _____

Time Interview Began _____

1. A. What do you personally think has been the most important problem which (city   ) has had to face since 1960?

———

B. What other problems have been very important during this time period (1960–1966)?

2. Here is a list of subjects which sometimes pose problems for cities in the United States. (HAND RESPONDENT CARD 1.) Would you tell me which of these have been very serious problems in (city   ), which have been fairly serious problems in (city   ), and which have not been serious problems in (city   )?

	Very Serious	Fairly Serious	Not Serious
A. Industrial and economic development (new plants, electrification, employment, labor supply, etc.)	1	2	3
B. Housing and building (slum clearance, blight and deterioration, zoning, etc.)	1	2	3
C. Race and ethnic relations (school desegregation, housing segregation, racial violence, etc.)	1	2	3
D. Public improvements, services, and utilities (transportation, roads, streets, sewage, etc.) ...	1	2	3
E. Health (public & private hospitals, sanitation, etc.)	1	2	3
F. Culture (libraries, clubs, theaters, etc.)	1	2	3
G. Education (including school construction, curriculum problems, reorganizations, etc.)	1	2	3
H. Social improvement and welfare (child welfare, crime, delinquency, poverty, care for the aged, handicapped, etc.)	1	2	3
I. Air pollution (the regulation of industrial and private emissions)	1	2	3
J. Recruitment of capable public servants	1	2	3

3. (LET RESPONDENT KEEP CARD 1.) Would you now tell me whether
each of these subjects has provoked a great deal of controversy in
(city) during the years since 1960, has provoked a moderate amount
of controversy, or has provoked little or no controversy?

	A Great Deal of Controversy	A Moderate Amount of Controversy	Little or No Controversy
A. Industrial and economic development (new plants, electrification, tion, employment, labor supply, etc.)	1	2	3
B. Housing and building (slum clearance, blight and deterioration, zoning, etc.)	1	2	3
C. Race and ethnic relations (school desegregation, housing segregation, racial violence, etc.)	1	2	3
D. Public improvements, services, and utilities (transportation, roads, streets, sewage, etc.) ...	1	2	3
E. Health (public & private hospitals, sanitation, etc.)	1	2	3
F. Culture (libraries, clubs, theaters, etc.)	1	2	3
G. Education (including school construction, curriculum problems, reorganizations, etc.)	1	2	3
H. Social improvement and welfare (child welfare, crime, delinquency, poverty, care for the aged, handicapped, etc.)	1	2	3
I. Air pollution (the regulation of industrial and private emissions)	1	2	3
J. Recruitment of capable public servants	1	2	3

4. Is there any single person whose opposition would be almost impossible to
overcome or whose support would be essential if someone wanted to (run
for/be appointed to) the school board in (city)?

Yes.......(ASK A)........ 1
No ....(ASK B)........ 2

IF YES:
A. Who is that? _____

What is his position in the community? _____

IF NO:
B. What person comes closest to this description? _____

What is his position in the community? _____

5. Here is a list of groups and organizations. Please tell me for each whether their support is essential for the success of a candidate for the school board, whether their support is important but not essential, or whether their support is not important. (HAND RESPONDENT CARD 2.)

	Support Essential	Support Important, Not Essential	Support Not Important
A. Democratic Party	1	2	3
B. Republican Party	1	2	3
C. Chamber of Commerce	1	2	3
D. Church leaders	1	2	3
E. Newspapers	1	2	3
F. Bar association	1	2	3
G. Labor unions	1	2	3
H. Ethnic groups (IF NAMED AS ESSENTIAL OR IMPORTANT, ASK: Which ethnic groups?)	1	2	3
I. Neighborhood groups	1	2	3
J. Heads of local government agencies	1	2	3
K. City and county employees	1	2	3
L. Industrial leaders	1	2	3
M. Retail merchants	1	2	3
N. Bankers and executives of financial institutions	1	2	3
O. Other businessmen	1	2	3

6. Is there any single person whose opposition would be almost impossible to overcome or whose support would be essential if someone wanted to organize a campaign for a municipal bond referendum in (city   )?

Yes.......(ASK A)........ 1
No ....(ASK B)........ 2

IF YES:
A.   Who is that? _____

What is his position in the community? _____

IF NO:
B.   What person comes closest to this description? _____

What is his position in the community? _____

7. On this same list of groups and organizations, please tell me for each whether their support is essential for the success of a municipal bond referendum, whether their support is important but not essential, or whether their support is not important. (HAND RESPONDENT CARD 2.)

	Support Essential	Support Important, Not Essential	Support Not Important
A. Democratic Party	1	2	3
B. Republican Party	1	2	3
C. Chamber of Commerce	1	2	3
D. Church leaders	1	2	3
E. Newspapers	1	2	3
F. Bar association	1	2	3
G. Labor unions	1	2	3
H. Ethnic groups (IF NAMED AS ESSENTIAL OR IMPORTANT, ASK: Which ethnic groups?)	1	2	3
I. Neighborhood groups	1	2	3
J. Heads of local government agencies	1	2	3
K. City and county employees	1	2	3
L. Industrial leaders	1	2	3
M. Retail merchants	1	2	3
N. Bankers and executives of financial institutions	1	2	3
O. Other businessmen	1	2	3

8. Is there any single person whose opposition would be almost impossible to overcome or whose support would be essential if someone wanted to get the city to undertake an urban renewal project?

$$\text{Yes.......(ASK A)........ 1}$$
$$\text{No ....(ASK B)........ 2}$$

IF YES:

A. Who is that? _____

What is his position in the community? _____

IF NO:

B. What person comes closest to this description? _____

What is his position in the community? _____

9. On this same list of groups and organizations, please tell me for each whether their support is essential for the success of an urban renewal project, whether their support is important but not essential, or whether their support is not important. (HAND RESPONDENT CARD 2.)

	Support Essential	Support Important, Not Essential	Support Not Important
A. Democratic Party	1	2	3
B. Republican Party	1	2	3
C. Chamber of Commerce	1	2	3
D. Church leaders	1	2	3
E. Newspapers	1	2	3
F. Bar association	1	2	3
G. Labor unions	1	2	3
H. Ethnic groups (IF NAMED AS ESSENTIAL OR IMPORTANT, ASK: Which ethnic groups?)	1	2	3
I. Neighborhood groups	1	2	3
J. Heads of local government agencies	1	2	3
K. City and county employees	1	2	3
L. Industrial leaders	1	2	3
M. Retail merchants	1	2	3
N. Bankers and executives of financial institutions	1	2	3
O. Other businessmen	1	2	3

10. Is there any single person whose opposition would be almost impossible to overcome or whose support would be essential for a program for the control of air pollution in (city)?

Yes . . . . (ASK A) 1
No . . . . (ASK B) 2

IF YES:
A. Who is that? _____

What is his position in the community? _____

IF NO:
B. What person comes closest to this description? _____

What is his position in the community? _____

11. On this same list of groups and organizations, please tell me for each whether their support is essential for the success of a program for air pollution control, whether their support is important but not essential, or whether their support is not important. (HAND RESPONDENT CARD 2.)

	Support Essential	Support Important, Not Essential	Support Not Important
A. Democratic Party	1	2	3
B. Republican Party	1	2	3
C. Chamber of Commerce	1	2	3
D. Church leaders	1	2	3
E. Newspapers	1	2	3
F. Bar association	1	2	3
G. Labor unions	1	2	3
H. Ethnic groups (IF NAMED AS ESSENTIAL OR IMPORTANT, ASK: Which ethnic groups?)	1	2	3
I. Neighborhood groups	1	2	3
J. Heads of local government agencies	1	2	3
K. City and county employees	1	2	3
L. Industrial leaders	1	2	3
M. Retail merchants	1	2	3
N. Bankers and executives of financial institutions	1	2	3
O. Other businessmen	1	2	3

12. Is there any single person whose opposition would be almost impossible to overcome or whose support would be essential if someone wanted to run for mayor in (city)?

Yes.......(ASK A)........ 1
No ....(ASK B)........ 2

IF YES:

A. Who is that? _____

What is his position in the community? _____

IF NO:

B. What person comes closest to this description? _____

What is his position in the community? _____

13. On this same list of groups and organizations, please tell me for each whether their support is essential for a candidate for mayor, whether their support is important but not essential, whether their support is not important. (HAND RESPONDENT CARD 2.)

	Support Essential	Support Important, Not Essential	Support Not Important
A. Democratic Party	1	2	3
B. Republican Party	1	2	3
C. Chamber of Commerce	1	2	3
D. Church leaders	1	2	3
E. Newspapers	1	2	3
F. Bar association	1	2	3
G. Labor unions	1	2	3
H. Ethnic groups (IF NAMED AS ESSENTIAL OR IMPORTANT, ASK: Which ethnic groups?)	1	2	3
I. Neighborhood groups	1	2	3
J. Heads of local government agencies	1	2	3
K. City and county employees	1	2	3
L. Industrial leaders	1	2	3
M. Retail merchants	1	2	3
N. Bankers and executives of financial institutions	1	2	3
O. Other businessmen	1	2	3

14. Listed on this card are seven different things which most cities would like to do. (HAND RESPONDENT CARD 3.) However, no one city can do all of these things at the same time.

	A. From what you know, which *one* of these seven things does the *city council* consider most important?	B. Now, which *one* would you say the *city council* considers *second most important*?	C. Finally, which do they consider *third most important*?
(1) Seeing to it that this city becomes a very attractive place to live— with good residential areas and pleasant, convenient community facilities	1	2	3
(2) Seeing to it that this community has a good climate for business			

		A.	B.	C.
	which would encourage economic growth	1	2	3
(3)	Seeing to it that the city provides its poor and disadvantaged with a decent life—with adequate food, housing, and opportunity	1	2	3
(4)	Seeing to it that this is a city free from harmful strife between economic, religious, or neighborhood groups	1	2	3
(5)	Seeing to it that this city maintains its heritage and its traditional values	1	2	3
(6)	Seeing to it that the city has a government which is efficient, honest, and economical	1	2	3
(7)	Seeing to it that the city is a place where citizens play an active role in government	1	2	3

15. Now, with this same list of things, please tell me which the *community leaders* outside of government would

		A. Consider *most* *important*	B. Second *most* *Important*	C. Third *most* *Important*
(1)	Seeing to it that this city becomes a very attractive place to live—with good residential areas and pleasant, convenient community facilities	1	2	3
(2)	Seeing to it that this community has a good climate for business which would encourage economic growth	1	2	3
(3)	Seeing to it that the city provides its poor and disadvantaged with a decent life—with adequate food, housing, and opportunity	1	2	3
(4)	Seeing to it that this is a city free from harmful strife between economic, religious, or neighborhood groups	1	2	3
(5)	Seeing to it that this city maintains its heritage and its traditional values	1	2	3
(6)	Seeing to it that the city has a government which is efficient, honest, and economical	1	2	3
(7)	Seeing to it that the city is a place where citizens play an active role in government	1	2	3

16. When the city government in (city) is inaugurating a new project—
such as an urban renewal project, a new welfare program, a new capital
improvements program—is it the normal practice to hold a number of
public meetings on the proposal, to hold one or two public meetings on the
proposal, or doesn't the government usually hold public meetings on the
proposal?

A number of public meetings are usually held.... (ASK A)....... 1
One or two public meetings are usually held..... (ASK A)....... 2
Usually no public meetings are held............ (GO TO Q. 17).. 3

A. IF PUBLIC MEETINGS HELD: Do a large number of citizens
attend these meetings, or do almost no citizens attend these meetings?

A large number 1
Very few 2
Almost none 3

17. Are proposed projects of the city government very often altered because of
the testimony or suggestions made by citizens either in public meetings or
in other ways, or are proposed projects rarely altered, or are proposed projects never altered because of suggestions of citizens?

Often 1
Rarely 2
Never 3

18. To the best of your knowledge when the leaders of the Chamber of Commerce are making a decision about community affairs, to what group's
opinions do they give the greatest weight? (RECORD VERBATIM; THEN
CIRCLE APPROPRIATE CODE.)

Retail merchants 1
Industrial executives 2
Bankers and executives of financial
  institutions 3
Others (SPECIFY) 4

19. When the leaders of the Republican Party are making a decision about community affairs, to what group's opinions do they give the greatest weight?
(RECORD VERBATIM; THEN CIRCLE APPROPRIATE CODE.)

Local businessmen 1
Neighborhood groups 2
Ethnic groups (SPECIFY) 3
Labor unions 4
Heads of municipal agencies 5
Local newspapers 6
City and county employees 7
Negroes 8
Other (SPECIFY) 9

20. When the leaders of the Democratic Party are making a decision about community affairs, to what group's opinions do they give the greatest weight? (RECORD VERBATIM; THEN CIRCLE APPROPRIATE CODE.)

Local businessmen 1
Neighborhood groups 2
Ethnic groups (SPECIFY) 3
Labor unions 4
Heads of municipal agencies 5
Local newspapers 6
City and county employees 7
Negroes 8
Other (SPECIFY) 9

21. When the heads of municipal agencies are making policy decisions concerning community affairs, to what group's opinions do they give the greatest weight? (RECORD VERBATIM; THEN CIRCLE APPROPRIATE CODE.)

Local businessmen 1
Neighborhood groups 2
Ethnic groups (SPECIFY) 3
Labor unions 4
Heads of municipal agencies 5
Local newspapers 6
City and county employees 7
Negroes 8
Other (SPECIFY) 9

Today many American cities are facing new problems. Very often, these problems are so new that the public at large is not immediately aware of them. Some individual or group must bring these matters to the attention of civic leaders and the public.

22. Is there any specific person or group in this city who was first to bring the matter of *local* air pollution to the attention of the public?

No, the problem of air pollution has never been brought to the public's attention 1
No, the problem of air pollution has been brought to the public's attention, but not by any specific person or group 2
Yes ....(ASK A AND B)................... 3

IF YES:

A. What person or group was this? _____
(IF RESPONDENT NAMES AN INDIVIDUAL, ASK WHAT POSITION THAT INDIVIDUAL HOLDS IN THE COMMUNITY.)

B. When did they (__he/she__) first raise the subject of local air pollution? _____ (YEAR)

23. Have any of the people listed on this card (HAND RESPONDENT CARD 4) ever talked with you or any other officers of your organization about the problem of air pollution in (__city__)?

	Yes	No
City officials	1	2
Industrial executives	1	2
Retail merchants	1	2
Bankers and executives of other financial institutions	1	2
Other local businessmen	1	2
Labor union officials	1	2
Officers of local political party organizations (SPECIFY WHICH PARTY)	1	2
Other (SPECIFY)	1	2

24. It's often said that there are two sides to every issue. But on some matters, people may be divided into more than two sides. And in those few cases where everyone agrees about a subject, there is really only one side represented. How would you characterize the subject of air pollution, as it has been discussed in (__city__)? Has only one side been active, two sides, or more than two?

No sides—the subject has never come up ... (SKIP TO Q. 43).... 1
One side—everyone agrees .... (ASK Qs. 25–30).... 2
Two sides .... (ASK Qs. 25–36).... 3
More than two sides .... (ASK Qs. 25–42).... 4

25. Please tell me who are the leading persons and organizations:

IF TWO OR MORE SIDES:
On the side seeking the *most* extensive air pollution control?

IF ONLY ONE SIDE:
In the air pollution issue? (PROBE FOR EACH INDIVIDUAL'S POSI-
TION IN THE COMMUNITY.)

SUPPORTERS OF SIDE #1

_____

_____

_____

_____

_____

_____

_____

_____

_____

_____

26. What does this group propose doing?

27. Do they want federal, state, or local legislation or no legislation at all?
(CODE AS MANY AS APPLY.)

Federal	1
State	2
Local	3
None at all	4

28. Which sources of air pollution is this group most interested in regulating? (PROBE, UNLESS ALREADY MENTIONED: Would their proposal regulate factories, automobiles, home furnaces and incinerators?)

29. Why have they said they are in favor of what they propose? (PROBES: What else did they say about why the community should do this? Did they say anything about government intervention in the private sector?)

30. In addition to what they said, do you personally think there is any other reason why they took the position that they did?

IF ONLY ONE SIDE IN Q. 24, SKIP NOW TO Q. 43.

IF TWO OR MORE SIDES IN Q. 24, CONTINUE WITH Q. 31.

31. Please tell me now who are the leading persons and organizations: IF THERE ARE ONLY TWO SIDES: on the other side of the issue? IF THERE ARE MORE THAN TWO SIDES: on the side seeking the *next most* extensive air pollution control? (PROBE FOR EACH INDIVIDUAL'S POSITION IN THE COMMUNITY.)

SUPPORTERS OF SIDE #2

32. What did this group propose doing?

33. Did they want federal, state, or local legislation or no legislation at all? (CODE AS MANY AS APPLY.)

Federal 1
State 2
Local 3
None at all 4

34. Which sources of air pollution is this group most interested in regulating? (PROBE, UNLESS ALREADY MENTIONED: Would their proposal regulate factories, automobiles, home furnaces and incinerators?)

35. Why did they say they are in favor of this action? (PROBES: What else did they say about why the community should do this? Did they say anything about government intervention in the private sector?)

36. In addition to what they said, do you personally think there is any other reason why they took the position that they did?

IF ONLY TWO SIDES IN Q. 24, SKIP TO Q. 43.

IF MORE THAN TWO SIDES IN Q. 24, CONTINUE WITH Q. 37.

---

37. What about the side proposing the *least* extensive air pollution control? Who are the leading persons and organizations on this side?

(PROBE FOR EACH INDIVIDUAL'S POSITION IN THE COMMUNITY.)

SUPPORTERS OF SIDE #3

---

38. What did this group propose doing?

---

39. Did they want federal, state, or local legislation or no legislation at all? (CODE AS MANY AS APPLY.)

Federal 1
State 2
Local 3
None at all 4

40. What sources of air pollution was this group most interested in regulating? (PROBE, UNLESS ALREADY MENTIONED: Would their proposal regulate factories, automobiles, home furnaces and incinerators?)

---

41. Why did they say they were in favor of this action? (PROBES: What did they say about why the community should do this? Did they say anything about government intervention in the private sector?)

42. In addition to what they said, do you personally think there is any other reason why they took the position that they did?

43. Has the (__organization__) taken a position, either formally or informally, on the matter of local air pollution?

Yes.......(ASK A)........ 1

No ....(ASK B)........ 2

IF YES:

A. Does the (__organization__) agree with those who want the most extensive air pollution control program, the least extensive, or does it stand somewhere in between?

Most extensive 1

Least extensive 2

In between 3

IF NO:

B. Is this because the members are not interested in this subject, because they disagree among themselves about it, or for some other reason?

Members not interested 1

Disagreement among members ... 2

Other (SPECIFY) 3

44. Has the (<u>organization</u>) done any of the following in regard to air pollution?

		Yes	No
A.	Issued a public statement	1	0
B.	Helped to sponsor a study of the problem	2	0
C.	Gave members' or staff time for a study of the problem	3	0
D.	Gave members' or staff time for a campaign to initiate a program in this area	4	0
E.	Sponsored public meetings	5	0
F.	Printed literature on the subject	6	0
G.	Sponsored advertising on this subject in the local press	7	0
H.	Organized lectures or discussions on this subject at meetings of your organization	8	0
I.	Other activities (SPECIFY)	9	0

Now let's talk about the anti-poverty program.

46. We don't know if there are two sides to the issue of the poverty program in (<u>city</u>), or only one side, or more than two sides. How many sides are there?

No sides—subject has never come up . . . . . . (SKIP TO Q. 56) 1
One side—everyone agrees . . . . (ASK Qs. 47–49) 2
Two sides . . . . (ASK Qs. 47–52) 3
More than two sides . . . . (ASK Qs. 47–55) 4

47. IF TWO OR MORE SIDES:

First, who are the leading individuals and groups on the side which recommends the *most* extensive community action program?

IF ONLY ONE SIDE:

First, who are the leading individuals and groups in the issue of the poverty program?

SUPPORTERS OF SIDE #1

_____

_____

_____

_____

_____

48. What did these people propose in regard to a local poverty program? (PROBE: Are there some things they wanted that others did not?)

49. How influential would you say (___supporters of side #1___) (___has/have___) been in policy decisions?

Very influential 1
Somewhat influential 2
Slightly influential 3
Not influential 4

IF ONLY ONE SIDE IN Q. 46, SKIP TO Q. 56.

IF TWO OR MORE SIDES IN Q. 46, CONTINUE WITH Q. 50.

50. IF TWO SIDES:
Who were the leading groups and individuals on the other side of the issue?

IF MORE THAN TWO SIDES:
Who were the leading groups and individuals on the side proposing the *next most* extensive community action program?

SUPPORTERS OF SIDE #2

_____

_____

_____

_____

_____

51. What did these people propose in regard to a local poverty program? (PROBE: Are there some things they wanted that others did not?)

52. How influential would you say (supporters of side #2   ) (has/have   ) been in policy decisions?

    Very influential 1
    Somewhat influential 2
    Slightly influential 3
    Not influential 4

IF TWO SIDES IN Q. 46, SKIP TO Q. 56.

IF MORE THAN TWO SIDES IN Q. 46, CONTINUE WITH Q. 53.

53. Who were the leading groups and individuals on the side proposing the *least* extensive action?

SUPPORTERS OF SIDE #3

_____

_____

_____

_____

_____

54. What did these people propose in regard to a local poverty program? (PROBE: Are there some things they wanted that others did not?)

55. How influential would you say (supporters of side #3   ) (has/have   ) been in influencing policy decisions?

Very influential 1
Somewhat influential 2
Slightly influential 3
Not influential 4

56. Have any of the people listed on this card spoken to you or members of your organization about urban renewal in (city   )? (HAND RESPONDENT CARD 4.)

	Yes	No
City officials	1	2
Industrial executives	1	2
Retail merchants	1	2
Bankers and executives of other financial institutions	1	2
Other local businessmen	1	2
Labor union officials	1	2
Officers of local political party organizations (SPECIFY WHICH PARTY)	1	2
Other (SPECIFY)	1	2

57. Who *inside* the government is the most influential supporter of urban renewal?

58. Which individuals or groups *outside* of the city government are the most influential supporters of urban renewal in (city)? What is (his/ group's) position in the community? (PROBE: Who else is an important supporter? Anyone else?)

	Name	Position in community
1.		
2.		
3.		
4.		
5.		

ASK FOR EACH SUPPORTER NAMED IN Q. 58.

59. Is (he/that group) a supporter of a city-wide urban renewal program or is (his/group's) support primarily centered on one specific project?

Supporters	City-Wide Program	Specific Project (ASK A)	A. *If specific project*: What is the name of that project?
1.	1	2	
2.	1	2	
3.	1	2	
4.	1	2	
5.	1	2	
6.	1	2	

ASK FOR EACH SUPPORTER NAMED IN Q. 58.

60. What would you say has been (__his/group's__) major reason for supporting urban renewal?

Supporters	Major reason
1. _____	_____
2. _____	_____
3. _____	_____
4. _____	_____
5. _____	_____

ASK FOR EACH SUPPORTER NAMED IN Q. 58.

61. Why has (__he/group__) been important? That is, what resources or kinds of influence did they use?

Supporters	Resources or kinds of influence
1. _____	_____
2. _____	_____
3. _____	_____
4. _____	_____
5. _____	_____

62. Has there been opposition to urban renewal in (__city__)?

Yes ....(ASK Q. 63)........ 1
No ....(SKIP TO Q. 76).... 2

63. Has the opposition been directed at the program in general or at specific projects, or has it been directed at both?

Program in general ....(GO TO Q. 64)..... 1
Specific projects ....(SKIP TO Q. 68).... 2
Both ....(GO TO Q. 64)..... 3

64. Who have been the most influential persons and groups opposing the urban renewal program? (PROBE FOR PERSON'S POSITION IN COMMUNITY.)

Opponents	Position in community
1. _____	_____
2. _____	_____
3. _____	_____
4. _____	_____
5. _____	_____

65. What has been the main reason for the opposition of each of these opponents?

Opponents	Reasons
1. _____	_____
2. _____	_____
3. _____	_____
4. _____	_____
5. _____	_____

66. Have (opponents named in Q. 64) obtained all or most of their goals, have they obtained only a few of their goals, or have they obtained none of their goals?

Opponents	All or most	A few	None
1. _____	1	2	3
2. _____	1	2	3
3. _____	1	2	3
4. _____	1	2	3
5. _____	1	2	3

67. What resources or kinds of influence did these opponents use to obtain their objectives?

Opponents	Resources or kinds of influence
1. _____	_____
2. _____	_____
3. _____	_____
4. _____	_____
5. _____	_____

ASK Q. 68 IF "SPECIFIC PROJECTS" OR "BOTH" TO Q. 63; OTHER-WISE SKIP TO Q. 76.

68. Who have been the most influential persons and groups opposing specific projects? Please tell me for each which projects they opposed.

	Opponents	*Projects*
1.		
2.		
3.		
4.		
5.		

69. What has been the main reason for the opposition of each of these opponents?

	Opponents	*Reason*
1.		
2.		
3.		
4.		
5.		

70. Have (__opponents named in Q. 68__) obtained all or most of their goals, have they obtained only a few of their goals, or have they obtained none of their goals?

	Opponents	*All or most*	*A few*	*None*
1.		1	2	3
2.		1	2	3
3.		1	2	3
4.		1	2	3
5.		1	2	3

71. What resources or kinds of influence did these opponents use to obtain their objectives?

Opponents	Resources or kinds of influence
1. _____	_____
2. _____	_____
3. _____	_____
4. _____	_____
5. _____	_____

Now, let's talk about the opposition to (first project mentioned in Q. 68   ).

72. A.   First, was there opposition (READ ITEMS (1)–(7) AND CODE YES OR NO FOR EACH)

	Yes	No	Don't Know
(1) during preliminary planning?	1	0	X
(2) at the time of submission to the urban renewal board?	1	0	X
(3) at the time of submission to the city council?	1	0	X
(4) at the time of public hearings? ..	1	0	X
(5) at the time of submission to the federal government?	1	0	X
(6) at the time of selection of buildings to be demolished, rehabilitated, or conserved?	1	0	X
(7) at the time of resale of the land?	1	0	X

B.   To what aspects of the project was the opposition directed?

	Yes	No	Don't Know
(1) The choice of the site?	1	0	X
(2) The priority given to this site? ..	1	0	X
(3) The amount of demolition?	1	0	X
(4) The amount of relocation necessitated?	1	0	X
(5) The type of reuse of the land? ..	1	0	X
(6) The proposed redeveloper?	1	0	X
(7) Any other aspects to which there was opposition? (SPECIFY) ..	1	0	X

C.   Were the opponents to the project supporters of the general urban renewal program?

Yes 1
No 2

D. Were the opponents of the project supporters of other specific urban renewal projects?

$$\text{Yes} \ldots\ldots\ldots\ldots\ldots\ldots\ldots\ldots 1$$
$$\text{No} \ldots\ldots\ldots\ldots\ldots\ldots\ldots\ldots 2$$

ASK Q. 73 ABOUT 2ND PROJECT IN Q. 68; IF ONLY ONE PROJECT MENTIONED, SKIP TO Q. 76.

73. A. How about in (<u>second project mentioned in Q. 68</u>)—was there opposition (READ ITEMS (1)–(7) AND CODE YES OR NO FOR EACH)

	Yes	No	Don't Know
(1) during preliminary planning?	1	0	X
(2) at the time of submission to the urban renewal board?	1	0	X
(3) at the time of submission to the city council?	1	0	X
(4) at the time of public hearings? ..	1	0	X
(5) at the time of submission to the federal government?	1	0	X
(6) at the time of selection of buildings to be demolished, rehabilitated, or conserved?	1	0	X
(7) at the time of resale of the land?	1	0	X

B. To what aspects of the project was the opposition directed?

	Yes	No	Don't Know
(1) The choice of the site?	1	0	X
(2) The priority given to this site? ..	1	0	X
(3) The amount of demolition?	1	0	X
(4) The amount of relocation necessitated?	1	0	X
(5) The type of reuse of the land? ..	1	0	X
(6) The proposed redeveloper?	1	0	X
(7) Any other aspects to which there was opposition? (SPECIFY) ..	1	0	X

C. Were the opponents to the project supporters of the general urban renewal program?

$$\text{Yes} \ldots\ldots\ldots\ldots\ldots\ldots\ldots\ldots 1$$
$$\text{No} \ldots\ldots\ldots\ldots\ldots\ldots\ldots\ldots 2$$

D. Were the opponents of the project supporters of other specific urban renewal projects?

$$\text{Yes} \ldots\ldots\ldots\ldots\ldots\ldots\ldots\ldots 1$$
$$\text{No} \ldots\ldots\ldots\ldots\ldots\ldots\ldots\ldots 2$$

ASK Q. 74 ABOUT 3RD PROJECT IN Q. 68; IF ONLY TWO PROJECTS
MENTIONED, SKIP TO Q. 76.

74. A.   In (__third project mentioned in Q. 68__)—was there opposition
(READ ITEMS (1)–(7) AND CODE YES OR NO FOR EACH)

	Yes	No	Don't Know
(1) during preliminary planning?	1	0	X
(2) at the time of submission to the urban renewal board?	1	0	X
(3) at the time of submission to the city council?	1	0	X
(4) at the time of public hearings? ..	1	0	X
(5) at the time of submission to the federal government?	1	0	X
(6) at the time of selection of buildings to be demolished, rehabilitated, or conserved?	1	0	X
(7) at the time of resale of the land?	1	0	X

B.   To what aspects of the project was the opposition directed?

	Yes	No	Don't Know
(1) The choice of the site?	1	0	X
(2) The priority given to this site? ..	1	0	X
(3) The amount of demolition?	1	0	X
(4) The amount of relocation necessitated?	1	0	X
(5) The type of reuse of the land? ..	1	0	X
(6) The proposed redeveloper?	1	0	X
(7) Any other aspects to which there was opposition? (SPECIFY) ..	1	0	X

C.   Were the opponents to the project supporters of the general urban renewal program?

Yes 1
No 2

D.   Were the opponents of the project supporters of other specific urban renewal projects?

Yes 1
No 2

ASK Q. 75 ABOUT 4TH PROJECT IN Q. 68; IF ONLY THREE PROJECTS MENTIONED, SKIP TO Q. 76.

75. A. In (<u>fourth project mentioned in Q. 68</u>)—was there opposition

	Yes	No	Don't Know
(1) during preliminary planning?	1	0	X
(2) at the time of submission to the urban renewal board?	1	0	X
(3) at the time of submission to the city council?	1	0	X
(4) at the time of public hearings? ..	1	0	X
(5) at the time of submission to the federal government?	1	0	X
(6) at the time of selection of buildings to be demolished, rehabilitated, or conserved?	1	0	X
(7) at the time of resale of the land?	1	0	X

B. To what aspects of the project was the opposition directed?

	Yes	No	Don't Know
(1) The choice of the site?	1	0	X
(2) The priority given to this site? ..	1	0	X
(3) The amount of demolition?	1	0	X
(4) The amount of relocation necessitated?	1	0	X
(5) The type of reuse of the land? ..	1	0	X
(6) The proposed redeveloper?	1	0	X
(7) Any other aspects to which there was opposition? (SPECIFY) ..	1	0	X

C. Were the opponents to the project supporters of the general urban renewal program?

Yes 1

No 2

D. Were the opponents of the project supporters of other specific urban renewal projects?

Yes 1

No 2

IF MORE THAN FOUR PROJECTS MENTIONED IN Q. 68, ASK Q. 75
A–D ABOUT EACH OTHER PROJECT AND RECORD ON CONTINUA-
TION SHEET(S).

ASK EVERYONE

76. Has (organization) supported, opposed, or taken a neutral position
with regard to urban renewal?

Supported 1
Opposed 2
Neutral 3

77. Has (organization) done any of the following in regard to urban
renewal?

		Yes	No
A.	Issued a public statement	1	0
B.	Helped to sponsor a study of the problem	2	0
C.	Gave members' or staff time for a study of the problem	3	0
D.	Gave members' or staff time for a campaign to initiate a program in this area	4	0
E.	Sponsored public meetings	5	0
F.	Printed literature on the subject	6	0
G.	Sponsored advertising on this subject in the local press	7	0
H.	Organized lectures or discussions on this subject at meetings of your organization	8	0
I.	Other activities (SPECIFY)	9	0

78. What about Mayor (___name___)? Did your organization support him, oppose him, or take a neutral position in the last mayoral campaign?

Supported .....(ASK A).... 1
Opposed ......(ASK A).... 2
Took neutral position 3

A. IF SUPPORTED OR OPPOSED: Did your organization (READ ITEMS a–g AND CODE YES OR NO FOR EACH)

		Yes	No
a.	issue a public statement about the candidates?	1	0
b.	give members' or staff time for the campaign?	2	0
c.	sponsor public meetings concerning the campaign?	3	0
d.	print campaign literature?	4	0
e.	sponsor campaign advertising in the local press?	5	0
f.	sponsor lectures or discussions about the campaign at meetings of your own organization?	6	0
g.	engage in any other campaign activities? (SPECIFY)	7	0

Time Ended: _____

Interviewer's Name: _____

Date: _____

Note: This questionnaire was administered to the presidents of the Chamber of Commerce and the bar association, union officials, and newspaper editors. Separate questionnaires were drafted for local health commissioners, mayors, urban renewal directors, and political party chairmen. The questionnaire reproduced here contains most of the items that were selected from those others for use in the present study.

Bibliography

Agger, Robert E.; Goldrich, Daniel; and Swanson, Bert. *The Rulers and the Ruled*. New York: John Wiley, 1964.

American Iron and Steel Institute. *Directory of Iron and Steel Works in the United States and Canada*. 27th ed. New York: American Iron and Steel Institute, 1954.

Armour Research Institute. "Air Pollution Survey of Gary, Indiana." Chicago: By the Institute, 1958.

Bachrach, Peter, and Baratz, Morton. "The Two Faces of Power." *American Political Science Review* 56 (1962): 947–52.

Banfield, Edward C. *Big City Politics*. New York: Random House, 1965.

————. *Political Influence*. New York: Free Press of Glencoe, 1961.

————, and Wilson, James Q. *City Politics*. Cambridge, Mass.: Harvard University Press and M.I.T. Press, 1963.

————. "Public-Regardingness as a Value Premise in Voting Behavior." *American Political Science Review* 57 (1964): 876–87.

Benedict, Ruth. *Patterns of Culture*. Boston: Houghton-Mifflin, 1959.

Bernstein, Marver. *Regulating Business by Independent Commission*. Princeton, N.J.: Princeton University Press, 1955.

Blalock, Hubert M. *Social Statistics*. New York: McGraw-Hill, 1960.

Burdick, L. R., and Barkley, J. F. *Concentration of Sulfur Compounds in City Air*, U.S. Bureau of Mines Information Circular, no. 7066. Washington, D.C.: U.S. Government Printing Office, 1939.

Carr, Donald E. *The Breath of Life*. New York: W. W. Norton, 1965.

Chase, Robert L. "The Status of Engineering Knowledge for the Control of Air Pollution." *In Proceedings of the National Conference on Air Pollution*. Washington, D.C.: U.S. Public Health Service, 1963.

Coleman, James S. *Introduction to Mathematical Sociology*. New York: Free Press of Glencoe, 1964.

Dahl, Robert A. "The Concept of Power." *Behavioral Science* 2 (1957): 201–15.

————. "A Critique of the Ruling Elite Model." *American Political Science Review* 53 (1958): 463–69.

221

————. *Who Governs? Democracy and Power in an American City.* New Haven: Yale University Press, 1961.

Easton, David. *A Systems Analysis of Political Life.* New York: John Wiley, 1965.

Etzioni, Amitai. *A Comparative Analysis of Complex Organizations.* New York: Free Press of Glencoe, 1961.

Froman, Lewis A., Jr. "An Analysis of Public Policies in Cities." *Journal of Politics* 29 (1967):94–108.

Glaab, Charles N., and Brown, A. Theodore. *History of Urban America.* New York: Macmillan, 1967.

Goldberg, Arthur. *Econometric Theory.* New York: John Wiley, 1964.

Goldman, Marshall, ed. *Controlling Pollution.* Englewood Cliffs, N.J.: Prentice-Hall, 1967.

Greenburg, Leonard, et al. "Report of an Air Pollution Incident in New York City, November 1953." *Public Health Reports* 77 (1962):7–16.

Health Law Center, University of Pittsburgh. *Digest of Municipal Air Pollution Ordinances.* Washington, D.C.: U.S. Public Health Service, 1962.

Herber, Lewis. *Crisis in Our Cities.* Englewood Cliffs, N.J.: Prentice-Hall, 1965.

Hunter, Floyd. *Community Power Structure.* Garden City, N.Y.: Anchor Books, 1963.

Kaufman, Herbert and Jones, Victor. "The Mystery of Power." *Public Administration Review* 14 (1954):205–12.

Kaufman, Herbert, and Polsby, Nelson. "American Political Science and the Study of Urbanization." In *The Study of Urbanization,* edited by Philip Hauser and Leo Schnore. New York: John Wiley, 1965.

Lowi, Theodore. "American Business, Public Policy, Case-Studies and Political Theory." *World Politics* 16 (1964):677–715.

Long, Norton. "The Local Community as an Ecology of Games." *American Journal of Sociology* 64 (1958):251–61.

Martin, Roscoe. *Decisions in Syracuse.* Garden City, N.Y.: Anchor Books, 1965.

Olson, Mancur. *The Logic of Collective Action.* Cambridge, Mass.: Harvard University Press, 1965.

Ostrogorski, Moise. *Democracy and the Party System in the United States.* New York: Macmillan, 1921.

Ozolins, Guntis, and Rehmenn, C. "Air Pollutant Emission Inventory of Northwest Indiana." N.p: Northwest Indiana Air Resource Management Program, 1966.

————, and Smith, Raymond. *A Rapid Survey Technique for Estimating Community Air Pollution Emissions.* Cincinnati: U.S. Public Health Service, 1966.

Polsby, Nelson. *Community Power and Political Theory.* New Haven: Yale University Press, 1963.

Ridker, Ronald. *The Economic Costs of Air Pollution.* New York: Frederick A. Praeger, 1966.

Rossi, Peter, and Crain, Robert. "The NORC Permanent Community Sample." *Public Opinion Quarterly* 32 (1968):261–72.

Schattschneider, E. E. *The Semisovereign People.* New York: Holt, Rinehart, and Winston, 1960.

Schroeder, Gertrude. *The Growth of Major Steel Companies.* Baltimore: The Johns Hopkins Press, 1953.

Schuenemann, Jean I., et al. *Air Pollution Aspects of the Iron and Steel Industry.* Washington, D.C.: U.S. Public Health Service, 1963.

Steffens, Lincoln. *Autobiography.* New York: Harcourt, Brace, 1931.

Stern, Arthur, ed. *Air Pollution.* 2d ed.; 2 vols. New York: Academic Press, 1968.

Stouffer, Samuel, et al. *Measurement and Prediction.* Princeton, N.J.: Princeton University Press, 1950.

Sundquist, James L. *Politics and Policy: The Eisenhower, Kennedy, and Johnson Years.* Washington, D.C.: The Brookings Institution, 1968.

Tarbell, Ida. *The Life of Elbert H. Gary.* New York: D. Appleton, 1925.

U.S., Bureau of the Census. *Census of Populations: 1960. Detailed Characteristics, Indiana.*

U.S., Congress, House, Committee on Science and Astronautics, Subcommittee on Science, Research, and Development. *The Adequacy of Technology for Pollution Abatement.* 89th Cong., 1st sess., 1966.

U.S., Congress, Senate, Committee on Public Works, Subcommittee on Air and Water Pollution. *Air Pollution—1967.* 90th Cong., 1st sess., 1967.

U.S., Public Health Service. *Air Pollution Measurements of the National Air Sampling Network, 1957–1961.* Cincinnati: Robert A. Taft Sanitary Engineering Center, 1962.

———. *A Summary of National Air Sampling Network Data, 1957–1965.* Cincinnati: Robert A. Taft Sanitary Engineering Center, 1966.

Wallace, David. "Renaissancemenship." *American Institute of Planners Journal* 26 (1960): 157–76.

Wildavsky, Aaron. *Leadership in a Small Town.* Totowa, N.J.: Bedminster Press, 1964.

Williams, Oliver, and Adrian, Charles. *Four Cities.* Philadelphia: University of Pennsylvania Press, 1963.

Wilson, James Q. *Negro Politics.* New York: Free Press of Glencoe, 1960.

———, and Clark, Peter. "Incentive Systems: A Theory of Organizations." *Administrative Science Quarterly* 6 (1960): 129–66.

Wolfinger, Raymond. "A Plea for a Decent Burial," *American Sociological Review* 27 (1962): 841–47.

———. "Reputation and Reality in the Study of 'Community Power.'" *American Sociological Review* 25 (1960): 636–44.

Wolff, Robert Paul. *The Poverty of Liberalism.* Boston: Beacon Press, 1968.

Works Progress Administration Indiana Writers Project. *The Calumet Region Historical Guide.* East Chicago, Ind.: Garman Printing Company, 1939.

Wormuth, Francis J. "Matched-Dependent Behavioralism: The Cargo Cult in Political Science." *Western Political Quarterly* 20 (1967): 809–40.

Index

Adrian, Charles, 22n
Agger, Robert, 30n, 174–75
Air pollution: control techniques, 9–10, 51n; costs and benefits of, 85–86, 89–90, 118–20; health effects of, 7–8, 14; measurement of, 92–94; public attitudes about, 11–17, 58, 125–27; sources of, 7–8, 11, 39, 63, 65. *See also* Photochemical smog; Sulfur oxides; Suspended particulates
Air Pollution Control Advisory and Appeals Board (East Chicago), 46, 51, 54–55
Air Pollution Control Advisory Board (Gary), 74
Allegheny County, Pa., 71
Angelidis, Chris, 113; appointed chief of Gary Air Pollution Division, 73; drafts air pollution ordinance for Gary, 69–72; releases results of air sampling survey, 74; seeks stronger pollution ordinance, 75
Anti-poverty programs. *See* Poverty and welfare
Applegate, George, 51, 79; and introduction of East Chicago pollution ordinance, 52–53; leads Chamber of Commerce delegation in East Chicago pollution negotiations, 46–48; supports pollution regulation within Chamber of Commerce, 48–49
Armour Research Institute, 66, 68–69, 78, 159; asked to draft pollution ordinance for Gary, 67; conduct Gary air pollution study, 61–62; criticized, 64–65; recommendations of, to City of Gary, 63–64

Bachrach, Peter, 21, 23
Banfield, Edward C., 134n, 136, 154, 174
Baratz, Morton, 21, 23
Benedict, Ruth, 22n

Bernstein, Marver, 70n
Bias: in community political agendas, 158, 173, 175–76, 178, 183; mobilization of, 22–23, 183; of pluralism, 155; of political party organizations, 150
Birmingham, Ala., 60
Blough, Roger, 60–61
Board of Public Works and Safety: East Chicago, 43–44, 52; Gary, 58
Business and industrial development, 165–66, 169–72

California, 9
Campbell, Oliver, 48–49
Chacharis, George, 56, 67–69, 76–78, 142–43
Chambers of Commerce: East Chicago, 46–54, 79, 83; Gary, 67, 72, 76–77, 83; in local ecology of organizations, 147–50; positiontaking activities of, 89, 91, 100, 103, 118, 123; respondents in NORC survey, 31, 87, 95–97, 113, 163
Chicago, Ill., 11, 50, 64, 69
City council, 90, 97; East Chicago, 44–45, 52–54; Gary, 36, 56–57, 62, 66, 72–74
Clark, Peter, 149, 156–157
Clean Air Act: of 1963; 10, 75; of 1967, 183
Cohen, Loyd, 43–44, 57, 63, 77, 79, 141–42; background of, 41–42; drafts air pollution ordinance for East Chicago, 45–46; negotiates with Chamber of Commerce, 46–51; presents pollution ordinance to city council, 52–53
Coleman, James S., 102n
Collective benefits, 137–41, 156, 166–68, 176
Costs of pollution control, 51n, 85–86, 89–90, 118–20

225

THE JOHNS HOPKINS PRESS

Designed by Laurie Jewell

Composed in Times Roman text with News Gothic Condensed display
by Monotype Composition Company

Printed on 60-lb. Perkins and Squier R
by Universal Lithographers, Inc.

Bound in Columbia Riverside Linen RL-3439
by L. H. Jenkins, Inc.